Psychotherapy
with
Children

Psychotherapy with Children

RICHARD A. GARDNER, M.D.

Clinical Professor of Child Psychiatry
Columbia University, College of Physicians and Surgeons

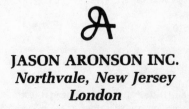

JASON ARONSON INC.
Northvale, New Jersey
London

First softcover edition 1993

Copyright © 1993 by Richard A. Gardner

10 9 8 7 6 5 4 3 2 1

Library of Congress Cataloging-in-Publication Data

Gardner, Richard A.
    Psychotherapy with children / by Richard A. Gardner.
      p. cm.
    Includes bibliographical references and index.
    ISBN 1-56821-030-2 (pbk.)
    1. Child psychotherapy. I. Title.
    [DNLM: 1. Psychotherapy—in infancy & childhood.
    2. Psychotherapy—methods. WS 350.2 G228p 1993]
    RJ504.G346 1993
    618.92'8914—dc20
    DNLM/DLC
    for Library of Congress   93-708

Manufactured in the United States of America. Jason Aronson Inc. offers books and
cassettes. For information and catalog write to Jason Aronson Inc., 230 Livingston
Street, Northvale, New Jersey 07647.

To Patricia Ann

You and this book
both represent
a culmination and
a commencement

Other Books by Richard A. Gardner

The Boys and Girls Book About Divorce
Therapeutic Communication with Children:
    The Mutual Storytelling Technique
Dr. Gardner's Stories About the Real World, Volume I
Dr. Gardner's Stories About the Real World, Volume II
Dr. Gardner's Fairy Tales for Today's Children
Understanding Children: A Parents Guide to Child Rearing
MBD: The Family Book About Minimal Brain Dysfunction
Psychotherapeutic Approaches to the Resistant Child
Psychotherapy with Children of Divorce
Dr. Gardner's Modern Fairy Tales
The Parents Book About Divorce
The Boys and Girls Book About One-Parent Families
The Objective Diagnosis of Minimal Brain Dysfunction
Dorothy and the Lizard of Oz
Dr. Gardner's Fables for Our Times
The Boys and Girls Book About Stepfamilies
Family Evaluation in Child Custody Litigation
Separation Anxiety Disorder: Psychodynamics and Psychotherapy
Child Custody Litigation: A Guide for Parents
    and Mental Health Professionals
The Psychotherapeutic Techniques of Richard A. Gardner
Hyperactivity, The So-Called Attention-Deficit Disorder,
    and The Group of MBD Syndromes
The Parental Alienation Syndrome and the Differentiation
    Between Fabricated and Genuine Child Sex Abuse
Psychotherapy with Adolescents
Family Evaluation in Child Custody Mediation, Arbitration,
    and Litigation
The Girls and Boys Book About Good and Bad Behavior
Sex Abuse Hysteria: Salem Witch Trials Revisited
The Parents Book About Divorce - Second Edition
The Psychotherapeutic Techniques of Richard A. Garnder - Revised
The Parental Alienation Syndrome: A Guide
    for Mental Health and Legal Professionals
Self-Esteem Problems of Children: Psychodynamics
    and Psychotherapy
Conduct Disorders of Children: Psychodynamics and Psychotherapy
True and False Accusations of Child Sex Abuse

Contents

Acknowledgments

I deeply appreciate the dedication of my secretaries Linda Gould, Carol Gibbon, Donna La Tourette, and Susan Monti to the typing of this manuscript in its various forms. I am grateful to Barbara Christenberry for her diligence in editing the manuscript. She provided useful suggestions and, at the same time, exhibited respect for my wishes regarding style and format. I am grateful to Colette Conboy for her valuable input into the production of the first edition of this book, from edited manuscript to final volume. I appreciate the efforts of Robert Tebbenhoff of Lind Graphics for his important contributions to the revised edition.

My greatest debt, however, is to those children and families who have taught me so much over the years about the development and alleviation of psychopathology. What I have learned from their sorrows and grief will, I hope, contribute to the prevention and alleviation of such unfortunate experiences by others.

Introduction

In this volume I describe both the theoretical background of my psychotherapeutic approaches to children and many of the technical procedures that I have found useful. I begin by tracing historically the development of child psychotherapeutic techniques in the twentieth century, with particular focus on those contributions that have played an important role in my own thinking. Next, I present what I consider to be the central elements in the psychotherapeutic process. I have attempted here to condense into one chapter the basic factors that I consider to be operative in such treatment.

The therapist–patient relationship is often spoken of glibly as the foundation of treatment but it has not, I believe, been studied to the depth that is warranted. Here I attempt to delineate specifically those factors in this relationship that are crucial to the development of a foundation for the psychotherapeutic process. Without such a solid relationship it is not likely that the treatment will be successful. Furthermore, if the therapist does not have a good relationship with the child's parents, it is likely that the treatment will also be compromised. Accordingly, I pay specific attention to the involvement of the parents in the child's treatment and describe specifically the ways in which their assistance can be optimally utilized.

It has been a great source of gratification to me that *The Talking, Feeling, and Doing Game* has become standard equipment in child psychotherapy. However, I am surprised that there are very few references to it in the child psychotherapeutic literature, the widespread use of the game notwithstanding. Here I present a detailed description of the game's utilization with clinical vignettes in which I provide the kinds of responses I have found useful for a wide variety of clinical situations.

Although psychoanalytically trained, and although I was on the faculty of the William A. White Psychoanalytic Institute for many years, I have progressively moved away from the traditional psychoanalytic approach, both theoretically and therapeutically. However, my treatment approach is very much psychoanalytically oriented in that I still hold that unconscious processes play an important role in the development of psychogenic psychopathology. The ways in which both the patient's and the therapist's insights into these underlying processes can bring about therapeutic change are described in detailed.

The last chapter discusses the utilization of the home video cassette recorder in the psychotherapeutic process. I have been treating children now for 35 years and have been witness to a wide variety of psychotherapeutic interventions. Some of these have been incorporated into the mainstream of treatment and others have fallen into disuse. I consider the home video cassette recorder, however, to be the greatest contribution to psychotherapy, both for children and adults, since Sigmund Freud's seminal work. It is my hope that the reader, after reading the last chapter of this book, will agree with what may have initially appeared to be a surprising statement.

In short, this book is a compendium of the basic principles of my psychotherapeutic approaches. I believe that it contains many "golden nuggets" derived from 35 years of dedication to the treatment of children. Although some of the ideas presented here may be somewhat different from the traditional, I believe that therapists who try these techniques will find them useful in the treatment of their patients.

ONE

Historical Considerations Regarding Child Psychotherapeutic Techniques

*There is but one way left to save a classic; to give up revering him
and use him for our own salvation--that is, to lay aside his
classicism, to bring him close to us, to make him contemporary, to
set his pulse going again with an injection of blood from our own
veins, whose ingredients are our passions . . . and our problems.*

Ortega y Gasset on Goethe

CHILD PSYCHOANALYSIS

To the best of my knowledge, the first article ever published on the psychotherapeutic treatment of a child was Sigmund Freud's case of Little Hans, published in 1909. Hans was a five year old who suffered with a fear of horses. His father, Max Graf, was a Viennese music publisher with an interest in a variety of cultural matters, including psychoanalysis. He was one of a group of friends and colleagues who met with Freud once a week to discuss Freud's analytic work. When Freud heard about Hans' fear, he concluded that the boy was suffering with a phobia, a psychoneurotic symptom, that should be amenable to psychoanalytic therapy. It would have been consistent with Freud's previous approach to such problems to have suggested that Max Graf bring his son to Freud's office and to have Hans lie down on the couch and free associate in the hope that the insights so gained would be useful for Hans in curing his phobia. However, Freud did no such thing. Rather than treat the child himself, he decided to have the father serve as the therapist and Freud would be the supervisor. The reason for this decision is described in the very first paragraph of this article (page 114):

> No one else, in my opinion, could possibly have prevailed upon the child to make any such avowels; the special knowledge by means of which he was able to interpret the remarks made by his five-year-old son was indispensable, and without it, the technical difficulties in the way of conducting a psychoanalysis on so young a child would have been insuperable.

In short, Freud did not believe that Hans would be comfortable enough with him to provide the kinds of personal information that would be necessary for a successful psychoanalysis, and so he chose the father to be the therapist. One might question here why Freud did not choose the mother. Was this a manifestation of male chauvinism on his part? In Freud's defense, we do know that the mother had been a patient of his. Perhaps this was a reason why he chose the father. We know, as well, that the father had been schooled in psychoanalytic theory, and perhaps this was the reason. In any case, Freud did not treat the child himself and the approach was straight psychoanalytic. The theory behind Hans' treatment was that "cure" (a word Freud used freely, a word that I do not use in regard to any form of psychotherapy) of Hans' neurosis would be brought about via the process of Hans' gaining conscious awareness into the unconscious processes that were contributing to the development of his symptom. The fundamental dictum of psychoanalytic treatment was applied to Hans: "Where there is unconscious, there shall conscious be." At no point was there any mention of play therapy. Actually, this concept was outside of Freud's scheme of things. Hans did enjoy an alleviation of his symptoms. Freud believed that this was the result of Hans' gaining insight into the unconscious processes that underlay his neurosis. Elsewhere (1972b) I have described what I consider to have been more important factors that brought about the alleviation (I do not use the word "cure" here) of Hans' symptoms.

If Freud's report is accurate, Hans' was an "easy case." The child appears to have willingly involved himself in the psychoanalytic process. Most child therapists would agree that the vast majority of children are not so receptive to psychotherapy, whether it be psychoanalytic or any other kind of psychiatric treatment. Children are not coming to us voluntarily, stating that they wish to delve into the unconscious processes that they suspect are at the roots of their psychoneurotic problems in the hope that the insights so gained will bring about an alleviation (or "cure") of their symptomatology.

Most children are referred against their will, have little motivation to change themselves, and do not appreciate how their therapeutic experiences will fit into their life patterns. Commonly, the only things children want from the therapist is that he or she be instrumental in getting their parents, teachers, and others who are dissatisfied with their behavior "off their backs." Even those children who have some insight into the fact that they do have problems, and may exhibit some motivation to change things, will often still prefer to play with friends, watch television, or just hang around doing nothing. Children are basically hedonistic and avoid unpleasant thoughts and feelings, the toleration of which is vital for meaningful therapy. Children basically prefer to live in the present. They do not take a long range view of things in which they are willing to give up present pleasures (or suffer present discomforts) for future gains or rewards. Rather than introspect, children tend to act out. Rather than view themselves as contributors to their difficulties, they prefer to externalize and consider their problems as caused by forces in the environment. Rather than see themselves as initiating their difficulties, they frequently see themselves as innocent victims. And this view only lessens even further the likelihood of the child's being motivated for therapy, especially one that relies on their gaining insight into their unconscious processes. If child therapy is to succeed with children who are less motivated for treatment than little Hans—and this would include about 99 percent of all child patients—then other techniques have to be devised to engage them. I discuss here, roughly in chronological order, the various methods that have been devised to engage children meaningfully in psychotherapy.

PSYCHOANALYTIC PLAY THERAPY

L. Kanner (1957) credits H. von Hug-Hellmuth with having published in 1913 the first article describing the introduction of play into psychoanalysis. Her 1921 article appears to be the first in the English language on the use of play techniques in child psychoanalytic treatment. Hug-Hellmuth ascribed meaning to just about every act and verbalization of the child, and tended to interpret the child's behavior along strictly classical Freudian lines. Although one might disagree with her specific interpretations, her observation that the child's play fantasies and activities can be a valuable source of information about his or her psychodynamics was a formidable contribution to the field.

Although S. Freud (1908), as early as 1908, commented briefly on one psychological aspect of play (The "opposite of play is not serious occupation, but reality"), it was von Hug-Hellmuth's work that stimulated an interest in play as a tool in child therapy—an interest that persists to the present. In the 1920s M. Klein and A. Freud began using play in child psychoanalysis. M. Klein (1932) considered the fantasies that the child wove around his or her play to be the equivalent of the adult patient's free associations and the resistances revealed in such verbalization to be susceptible to analysis. She directly confronted children as young as one to two years of age with what she regarded to be the psychodynamic meaning of their play and considered children capable of understanding her interpretations and utilizing therapeutically the insights so gained. M. Klein's critics are generally dubious about the ability of such young children to comprehend the formulations she presented them and consider many of her interpretations to express the content of her own mind rather than the child's (L. Kanner, 1940).

A. Freud (1946, 1965) was generally more cautious than Klein in applying adult psychoanalytic technique to children. She recognized play as a valuable source of information about the child's psychodynamics (although she did not consider play verbalization to be the exact equivalent of adult free association) and as a useful tool in helping the child overcome resistance to treatment. She utilized play in the early phase of therapy to facilitate the child's forming a close and trusting relationship with the analyst; in later phases, she attempted to involve the child in analyzing the play verbalizations (including resistance fantasies). However, her approach to such analysis was always more cautious than Klein's. In general, she approached children through their defenses and tried to get them to derive insights on their own rather than presenting them with the Kleinian kinds of direct interpretations.

Although M. Klein and A. Freud differed in regard to the interpretations they would give to children's play fantasies, they both worked very much within the classical Freudian framework. Specifically, they both believed that a primary goal of therapy was to help the child gain conscious awareness of the unconscious processes that were at the foundation of his or her symptoms. They subscribed to the dictum: "Where there is unconscious, there shall conscious be." They believed that such insight was central to the therapeutic process and that without it, any clinical improvement was not as likely to be as enduring as that which was obtained by this method—an assumption that I take issue with. As will be described so many times over in this book, I believe that more important factors are involved in the therapeutic process and, furthermore, that insight is one of the *least* effective ways of bringing about therapeutic change in children (and even in many adults). M. Klein's and A. Freud's work is based on the assumption that children are cognitively capable of gaining and utilizing psychoanalytic insights at very young ages. I disagree with this hypothesis and have Piaget's support for my position. It is not until children reach the age of 10 or 11, that is, the level of cognitive development that Piaget referred to as "formal operations," that children are cognitively capable of separating an object and the symbol that denotes it, and then moving back and forth between the two. And such capacity is central to the ability to engage in meaningful psychoanalytic treatment. Although some highly intelligent children can do this earlier, most cannot. A. Freud and M. Klein appeared to have been oblivious to this obvious developmental fact. I suspect that they may have reported on their most obvious successes with highly intelligent children or (and this was especially the case for M. Klein) described more their own projections than that which went on in the minds of their child patients.

M. Klein's and A. Freud's studies stimulated an intensive interest in the psychology of children's play that persists to the present. In 1933 Waelder described the value of play as a medium for the child's wish fulfillments, parental emulation, gratification of regressive needs, and dealing with traumatic events (through desensitization and identification with the traumatizer, for example, the dentist).

COMMUNICATION AT THE SYMBOLIC LEVEL

Recognizing that the child's self-created fantasies are a valuable source of information about the child's psychodynamics has resulted in therapists' giving the highest priority to the child's expressing such material in the session. Therapists found, however, that most child patients resisted revealing themselves in this way, often from an awareness (at some level) that even the symbolic representations may reveal material they do not wish divulged. Many of the techniques to be described subsequently were designed to overcome such resistance. To varying degrees, they have also attempted to solve the problem of how to make therapeutic use of the rich information that children's fantasies so often provide us. They are all essentially attempts to deal with the problem of how to utilize the child's play fantasies as a vehicle for bringing about therapeutic change.

The Play Interview

One of the earliest modifications of psychoanalytic doll-play therapy was described by J. Conn, who referred to his approach as the "Play Interview" (1939, 1941a, 1941b, 1948, 1954). Conn considered the fantasies that children wove around their doll play to be highly valuable sources of information about their basic problems. He defined these primarily, however, as direct reality problems. He believed that the child's gaining insight into these here-and-now issues was more important than inquiries into the "classical" psychoanalytic conflicts of the past. His therapeutic approach focused on children's gaining a more objective view of themselves, appreciating their own role in bringing about their difficulties, and acquiring more adaptive ways of handling life's conflicts. He frequently urged children to suppress everyday anxieties and to desensitize themselves to them while entering the anxiety-provoking situation. He took an active role in the play, asked many questions, and often set up specific situations that would channel the child's attention into specific areas that Conn considered to be important. Whereas classical psychoanalysts at that time considered catharsis to be an important therapeutic modality, Conn did not have a high opinion of the value of catharsis in the treatment of most psychological disorders, whether such release was obtained from doll play or in other ways. He worked actively with parents in the attempt to change environmental contributions to the child's difficulties.

Active Play Therapy

During the same period J. Solomon, a student of Conn, described a somewhat similar therapeutic approach which he referred to as "Active Play Therapy" (1938, 1940, 1951, 1955). He considered his more structured and active therapeutic approach to be indicated when the child exhibited resistance to verbalizing in association with free play. He believed that doll-play catharsis could be salutary especially, for hostile release. He viewed his approach as a modality through which the therapist could reduce guilt, provide therapeutic suggestions, and encourage desensitization through repetition. Although he too emphasized the importance of focusing on present problems, he considered attention to the past to have a definite, albeit less important, role to play in therapy. As he saw it, the child did not necessarily need to gain insight in order to achieve therapeutic change. He observed that what the therapist transmitted through the doll play had therapeutic value even when it was directed only to the dolls and not ostensibly to the child him- or herself. In fact, keeping the discussion at the third person (or animal) level was, in his view, one of the most efficacious ways to diminish children's resistance to self-revelation. For more receptive children, he advised helping them relate the doll fantasies to themselves; however, he warned against encouraging such inquiry too rapidly as it might cause the child to become so anxious that he or she would resist completely any further work through doll-play fantasy.

I consider Solomon's work to represent a landmark contribution in the field of child psychotherapy. His belief that it was not necessary for the patient to gain insight to bring about therapeutic change and that one could provide therapeutic communications at the symbolic level represents a breakthrough. For example, if the child, who is not particularly receptive to analyzing his or her self-created stories (the usual case), tells a story about a cat who bites a dog, the therapist, instead of trying to help the child analyze the story, might respond with such questions as, "Why did the cat bite the dog?" and "Is there a better way the cat could have handled that problem with the dog, other than biting the dog?" He recognized that children were most comfortable communicating at the symbolic level and was comfortable himself communicating with them at the same level. I consider my mutual storytelling technique to be a direct derivative of Solomon's work. I consider myself to be sitting on his shoulders.

DOLL PLAY

Figurines representing various family members have traditionally been among the mainstays of the child therapist's playroom. Many consider such dolls to be among the most valuable items in the child therapist's armamentarium—facilitating as they do the production of fantasies that concern the individuals most involved in the child's difficulties. However, there is an intrinsic contaminating aspect to them, a contaminant that exists in all ready-made objects used as foci for the production of the child's fantasies. Because they have a specific form, they are likely to suggest particular fantasies, thereby altering the purer fantasy that might have been elicited from a less recognizable object or from one that the child him- or herself had created (Woltmann, 1964a). A preferable "doll" would be one that is more nondescript—a lump of clay on the top of a pencil, for example. To carry this principle further, the ideal "doll" would be no doll at all—because then there would be no contamination of the natural fantasies. The worst kind of doll for therapeutic use is an elaborate, and often expensive, one which presents multiple stimuli that not only restrict fantasies but may be focused upon by the child in the service of resistance. In spite of their potential for fantasy contamination, such dolls are still useful for the child who is too inhibited to verbalize without them. In addition, it is likely that the pressure of impulses to express themselves in fantasies related to the child's unconscious complexes is far greater than the power of the external facilitating stimulus to alter significantly the elicited fantasies.

The therapist does well not only to listen to the stories that the child creates around the dolls, but to observe the child's movements as well. The child's various nonverbal activities and the ways in which he or she physically structures the doll play can provide additional information of considerable value. Such structuring, however, may be used in the service of resistance. Most therapists have had the experience of a child's spending significant time placing various family members in even rows and then repeatedly becoming dissatisfied with each new arrangement. Or the child may endlessly rearrange the furniture in the dollhouse, never seeming able to get to the story. Accordingly, it seems wiser not to have furniture displayed on the therapist's toy shelves. One may, however, keep certain items in a closet such as a bed and a toilet which, in special circumstances, can be introduced into the play. Similarly, dolls such as soldiers, cowboys, and Indians tend to elicit stereotyped, age-appropriate play ("war," fighting, etc.) that is not particularly revealing. The reason for this is that the normal fantasies so produced are difficult to differentiate from the pathological. Such figurines usually elicit hostile fantasies in normal children as well as those who have hostile acting-out problems. Accordingly, such dolls are best left in the closet and only brought out if the therapist wishes to use them for specific therapeutic purposes. More will be said about doll therapy throughout the course of this chapter.

ALLEN'S "RELATIONSHIP THERAPY"

F.H. Allen considered certain transactions in the therapist-patient relationship to be the crucial elements in successful treatment. He referred to his approach as "Relationship Therapy" (1942). Allen considered the experiences of the present, especially those that occurred in the therapeutic situation, to be the most important focus for therapeutic attention. Accordingly, he did not concern himself with helping the child gain insight into past events. He assumed that the child would repeat past pathological behavior in the session, and worked with the present repetition. He considered this to be the most efficacious way of alleviating the child's symptoms because then "living and understanding became one." Allen believed the child's problems to stem primarily from environmental repressive forces, the reduction of which he considered to be salutary. Providing the child "freedom" was a paramount element in Allen's approach: ". . . the therapeutic value of talking lies less in the content and more in the freedom to talk." In his view, the child has the innate capacity to discover healthy values and capabilities;

the therapist's task is to provide the kind of accepting environment that would allow for their expression. However, Allen still understood that the therapist had to place reasonable controls on the child. The child was aware that these limitations would protect him or her from the untoward consequences of total abandonment to free expression. Given such controls, children would then be more comfortable in expressing themselves. Allen suggested that the therapist concentrate more on what the child is attempting to accomplish with verbalizations in the therapeutic relationship than on the verbal content per se. For example, the child may be talking about his or her difficulties not so much in the attempt to resolve them, but in the hope that the therapist will magically cure his or her problems. Allen appears to be less concerned than many other therapists with the problem of dealing with resistances. What were often considered to be obstructions to treatment by others were viewed by Allen as healthy expression and self-assertion. For Allen, these were manifestations of the child's trying to overthrow the restrictive environmental influences that were the primary source of his or her pathology.

Although Allen referred to his treatment as "Relationship Therapy," there is little in his work suggesting that he gave proper appreciation to the importance of the therapist-patient relationship as the foundation on which I believe effective treatment is built. Accordingly, I believe the name he gave to his treatment approach is misleading. It is more a cathartic type of therapy and is based on the belief that there lies within all children an inner knowledge of what is best for them and one need only provide them with freedom of expression and disinhibition and the healthy forces will express themselves. I am not in agreement with this view. I cannot agree that we are born with some inner knowledge as to what is healthy or unhealthy for us, with the exception of certain biological survival reactions such as fight and flight. Also, Allen's focus on the freedom to talk as opposed to focusing on the content of what is being said is an unfortunate emphasis. I believe that *both* are important and therapists who do not give proper attention to verbal content are depriving themselves of vital information. I suspect also that Allen's approach contributed to the perpetuation of antisocial acting out, in that he tended to interpret such expressions in the interview as healthy attempts to overthrow social repression, rather than as possible displacement of pathological anger onto the therapist.

ROGERS' "NONDIRECTIVE"
OR "CLIENT-CENTERED THERAPY"

C. Rogers referred to his approach as "Nondirective or Client-centered Therapy" (1951, 1967). To Rogers, the term "patient" implied inferior status, whereas "client" connoted responsibility. I am in disagreement with Rogers on this point. The word "patient" does not have any intrinsic connotation of inferiority. Some words may, but the word "patient" is not one of them. If a person who works with a therapist has feelings of inferiority because the word *patient* is used to refer to him or her, it is generally a manifestation of some problem on the patient's part. One could argue that the word "client" has an intrinsic derogatory connotation. Many nonmedical therapists, however, welcome the word "client" because it protects them from potential litigation. If they were to refer to an individual as a patient, then the therapist might be brought up on charges of practicing medicine without a license. However, if one does not use the word patient, then a nonphysician therapist may protect him- or herself from such an allegation. Rogers' referring to his treatment as "client-centered" has the implication that other therapists are not focusing enough attention on their patients. There is a definite note of superiority here. It is reminiscent of the advertising campaign of some politicians who claim that they are supportive of the needs of widows and orphans—with the implication that their opponents are just the opposite.

Rogers considers there to be a "self-actualizing" drive present in all human beings from birth. He believes that there exists within all of us some knowledge of what is healthy and useful for us and what is not. He considers that there is some potpourri of thoughts and feelings in which there is some knowledge, at birth, about what would be in our best interests. Repression by social forces of these impulses produces various types of discontent—one type of which is psychopathology. Again, I am in disagreement with Rogers on this point. I do not believe that we are born with some pool of knowledge of what is in our best interests. Rather, we have to learn these things from our culture and society, and each individual's milieu differs with regard to the input in this area. I have found it of interest, even to the point of its being humorous, that many of the patients who undergo Rogerian therapy, when they are self-actualized, look very much like many other people who have been similarly self-actualized. In the 1960s and 1970s, it was common for these people to decide to move to a commune in Vermont, weave baskets, grow natural foods, and remove themselves from society in general. In their so-called nonconformity they were slavishly conformative in imitation of others who self-actualized themselves in compliance with an identical personality pattern.

The purpose of the treatment is to foster full expression of one's self-actualizing impulses. This is said to be most efficaciously accomplished when therapists exhibit certain important attitudes in their relationships with their clients. They must have an attitude of what Rogers called "unconditional positive regard" for the client, that is, they should be completely free of judgments, both positive and negative. It is only in such a permissive attitude that the patient will be willing to drop resistances to self-expression and self-actualization. Again, I am in disagreement with Rogers on this point. I cannot imagine any human being taking an attitude of unconditional positive regard on an ongoing basis. Inevitably, in any human relationship, there must be some times when one of the parties is going to do something that will irritate the other. And the therapeutic relationship is no exception. For a therapist to maintain a position of "unconditional" regard requires duplicity. It requires the therapist to withhold critical thoughts and feelings about the patient that must be experienced from time to time. Strictly refraining from the expression of such reactions deprives the patient of important therapeutic input and is therefore a disservice to the patient.

A number of years ago, the *Listerine* mouthwash company ran an advertisement about a young woman who had bad breath and her best friends didn't tell her. The primary caption was: "Your Best Friends Won't Tell You." Accordingly, she was lonely and dateless. After she started using *Listerine*, the phone didn't stop ringing. I believe that the therapist should be better than a best friend. The therapist should tell patients things that a best friend might hesitate telling. However, crucial here is that the therapist's motivation be benevolent, rather than malevolent. A friend criticizes benevolently. One's own mother does not give one "unconditional positive regard." Therapists who claim to be providing their patients with this attitude are deceiving themselves (if they believe that they are) or their patients (if they know that they aren't). In either case it is a fabrication and an unhealthy situation for the patient. In addition, Rogers recommends that the therapist not pass judgments. He apparently is a subscriber to the advice that one should not judge one's patients. I find this impossible to imagine. We are continually judging other people in our human relationships. We are always making decisions as to whether or not the other person's thoughts, feelings, or actions are good, bad, right, or wrong. We must do so if we are to interact properly and decide in what way we are going to involve ourselves with others. Therapists should not only be comfortable making therapeutic judgments but should be willing to share them at the proper time with their patients. One has to differentiate between therapeutic judgments transmitted benevolently and those that are transmitted malevolently. When the former is the case, then one has an extremely useful therapeutic situation; when the latter is true, it is likely that the treatment will be detrimental.

Rogers suggests that the therapist assume a completely passive and nondirective role. He refers to his technique as "nondirective therapy." It is only in such an atmosphere that the patient will be willing to drop resistances to self-expression and self-actualization. Rogers considers individuals, even children, to have both the innate capacity and the strength to devise the proper steps toward mature behavior, especially when placed in this unguided and nondirective milieu. The therapist attempts to help the patient by reflecting back the latter's verbalizations and feelings in such a way that self-awareness is accomplished. This often involves repeating the last segment of the patient's statement. However, therapists were also instructed to intuitively make guesses as to what the patient might be feeling and express these emotions as well, for example, "That must have made you feel very sad." The highly skilled therapist should be able to intuitively ascertain what the patient's unconscious processes are and help bring these into self-awareness. The overwhelming majority of therapists, I believe, do not possess such insights and intuition. Accordingly, in practice, the therapy often degenerates into the therapist's providing parrot-like mimicry of the last fragments of the patient's comment and merely reflects back the obvious thoughts and feelings the patient is expressing.

In line with Rogers' view that the child has the ability to assume responsibility for his or her own actions, and that what the child does is generally in the child's best interests, the concept of resistance takes a different form. Traditional therapists would view the child's obstructionistic attitude toward treatment to be a manifestation of pathological processes. Rogers would more likely view such behavior as a manifestation of the child's desire to actualize him- or herself. Traditional resistances then are viewed as healthy expressions of the child's inner needs and they no longer appear to be an obstruction to the therapeutic process. The child is then viewed to be freer to grow in directions natural to him or her. Because of the significant overlap between symptoms and resistances (the same psychodynamic mechanisms are often used in both), I suspect that Rogerian therapists often promulgated psychopathology with the nondirective approach. V.M. Axline (1947, 1964) is probably the most well known therapist to have applied Rogerian techniques to the treatment of children.

RELEASE THERAPY

D.M. Levy held that catharsis in certain situations could be therapeutic and referred to his techniques for promoting emotional expression in these situations as "Release Therapy" (1939, 1940). Levy described three types of release therapy. In the first, simple release, a child is allowed free expression of inhibited impulses (usually regressive or hostile): spilling, throwing, aggressive outbursts, and so forth. This form of treatment is indicated for children whose parents will not or cannot allow such release. In the second type, the child is encouraged to express inhibited feelings which are derived from standard situations such as sibling rivalry and curiosity about nudity. For such children the doll material and the therapist's remarks are so structured that comments in these specific areas are likely to be evoked from the child. The third type is designed for children who are reacting pathologically to a specific trauma and whose untoward behavior relates to their having suppressed or repressed recollection of the event. In the treatment of such conditions, the dolls are set up to resemble the situation in which the trauma occurred; the therapist's comments are then designed to elicit responses related to the event. Generally, the technique works best for children who are relatively healthy prior to the traumatic event and for whom the symptoms are of short duration. One danger of Levy's method is that the children may be led prematurely to deal with issues with which they are not ready to cope. Great anxiety will then be produced and they may become even more resistant to therapeutic work. However, for the situation for which the third type of release therapy is in fact indicated (admittedly a small segment of the children who are brought for therapy), the technique may prove useful.

FANTASIES CREATED
AROUND DRAWINGS

In the 1920s and 1930s, therapists primarily used dolls as the objects on which children projected their fantasies. In the 1940s therapists began experimenting with other children's play equipment in the hope that they would prove useful in therapy. The child's self-created drawing then became a therapeutic standby. Actually, it is superior to doll play in that the child's picture is self-created and does not have any significant external contamination such as is the case with doll play. The doll has an obvious size, shape, sex, and is often clothed. All of these items provide potentially contaminating stimuli. The only restriction that the self-created drawing has is that it has a border and generally confines the child with regard to what can be placed therein. However, even then, the therapist can generally advise the child to tell a story that goes beyond the borders of the page and to introduce whatever else the child wishes. The picture as well as the stories created around it can be a rich source of psychodynamic information. The self-created picture generally portrays external projections of various aspects of the child's personality.

In order to facilitate the child's drawing such pictures, the therapist does well to create an atmosphere that is likely to produce the freest and most uncontaminated pictures and accompanying fantasies. I have found a useful opening for this purpose to be: "Here's a piece of drawing paper and some crayons. I'd like you to draw a picture, a made-up picture." To a child who shows some initial reluctance, I might say, "I'd like to see how good you are at drawing pictures." I introduce a slightly competitive element ("See how good you are") in order to enhance the child's motivation. I have no problem with benevolently motivated competition. It is the malevolent kind that we have to avoid. This point is an important one. Those who would attempt to remove competition entirely because of the destructive type would deprive us of an important motivational enhancement. For the child who is more resistant and says that he or she can't draw well, I will generally impress upon the child that this is not an art contest. The child may reveal resistances by drawing a design. I might then encourage the child to draw something "more interesting," something that would be enjoyable to talk about. I might replace the paper with another blank one and say that "designs don't count."

After the child has completed the picture I will then ask the child to tell me something about the picture, especially a story. I request first a description because it is easier to do and may not be as anxiety provoking as telling a self-created story. To the child who exhibits some hesitation telling a story, I might respond, "Every picture has a story. What's the story about this one? I want to see how good you are at making up stories." A common resistance maneuver is for the child to tell a story that is mundane and basically nonrevealing. An example of such a story would be one that itemizes the events of the day—when the child got up in the morning, what was eaten for breakfast, what occurred in school with regard to the various subjects studied, and what happened after school. In such cases, I will generally tell the child that that was kind of an uninteresting or boring story and encourage him or her to tell one that is more interesting or exciting.

When a child has difficulty telling a story, I may draw cartoon-style balloons over the heads of each of the figures and ask the child to write in the balloon what the figures are saying. Of course, generally only key words will fit and a certain amount of erasing may be necessary. Using a blackboard and chalk facilitates this procedure because of the ease with which the messages can be erased. I have found this approach particularly useful for children with neurologically based learning disabilities or linguistic problems. They may have difficulty verbalizing and may do better writing down their thoughts. This technique enables them to do so, and they then provide meaningful psychodynamic material. Furthermore, because of auditory receptive linguistic problems, many of these children have trouble retaining what they hear, but have less difficulty retaining what they read.

L. Bender (1952) was one of the first to describe in detail the ways in which children's self-created fantasies around drawings could provide useful psychodynamic material. However, her interpretations were generally along strict classical psychoanalytic lines. She tended to interpret especially the sexual and aggressive impulses revealed therein. She also gave emphasis to the motor release aspect of stories and drawings, as well as the psychological significance of the configurational elements.

D.W. Winnicott (1968, 1971) devised a projective drawing technique that he called the "Squiggles Game." The therapist scribbles something formless with pencil on a blank sheet of paper. The child is asked to add lines in order to convert the "squiggle" into some recognizable form. The child then draws his or her own squiggle and the therapist transforms it into something distinguishable. Back and forth the game goes. Each drawing serves as a point of departure for a therapeutic interchange. Generally, Winnicott tried to guide the conversation in a direction in which the child was helped to gain insight (usually along classical psychoanalytic lines) into what the squiggles and the associated verbalizations revealed. The game was designed primarily for situations when only a short-term therapeutic process was possible; however, it can prove useful as a tool in long-term therapy as well. It is certainly a technique with which the child therapist should be familiar. However, it is likely that many of the dramatic cures which Winnicott attributed to the Squiggles Game (often accomplished in one or two interviews) were less related to the interpretations Winnicott provided than they were to the effect of certain aspects of Winnicott's personality and of the situation in which the consultations occurred. When reading Winnicott's material I am often dubious about how much his interpretations actually "sink in." Often obtruse psychoanalytic interpretations are presented to the child in rapid order. I doubt whether much was comprehended by the child under such circumstances. Also, Winnicott did not seem to appreciate the importance of the child's trying to derive his or her own insights into the meaning of the story; rather Winnicott typically spoon fed his interpretations to the child. Because I am dubious about the validity of many of these interpretations, I am less impressed with Winnicott's work than many. Having seen Winnicott personally a few years before he died, I suspect that other factors were operative in the improvements that he described, factors related to his personality. In Chapter Four I will discuss this factor in Winnicott's treatment in greater detail.

R.C. Burns and S.H. Kaufman (1970) have developed a technique which they call "Kinetic Family Drawings." When utilizing this method, the child is asked to draw a picture of the various members of the family—with each person *doing* something. It is not simply a test in which the child is asked to draw a family. Of importance here is the fact that the child is asked to have the family member *do* something. They claim that this technique provides more information than the less directive approaches. My experience with the instrument has been that the drawings so produced do not provide as much useful information as those created around more freely drawn pictures. I found that the child's stories tend to be more stereotyped and mundane.

J.N. Buck (1948) and E.F. Hammer (1960) used the "House-Tree-Person Technique." The child is asked to draw these three entities and to tell stories about what has been drawn. An attempt is made to score objectively some of the items, but I am not impressed with the utilization of these drawings for that purpose. However, as a focus for self-created stories, they can be useful. Others who have described the use of children's drawings as a vehicle for projective material in therapy are P. Elkisch (1960), M.L. Rambert (1964), and R. Kellogg and S. O'Dell (1967).

DIRECT INTERPRETATION OF THE DRAWING

In the previous section I have described the use of the child's self-created drawing as a focus on which the child is asked to project a story. The story is then used as a source of understanding of the child's underlying psychodynamics and as a point of departure for various types of psychotherapeutic interchange. However, one can also use the drawing per se as a source of information about underlying psychodynamics. Of course, one can do both. In each situation there is a certain amount of speculation. K. Machover (1949, 1951, 1960) was one of the early investigators in this area. She appears to have been an acute interpreter of such drawings and has provided a wealth of information about how to interpret them. Her most well-known work was with the Draw-a-Person Test in which a child is simply asked to draw a person without any specific statements regarding the age, sex, or any other aspects of the person to be drawn. Then the child is asked to draw a person of opposite sex to the one depicted in the first picture. The body parts and coverings are separately analyzed: hair, eyes, ears, nostrils, mouth, shirt, dress, jewelry, etc. The interpretations are not based on any standardized data, but rather Machover's own personal clinical experiences and speculations. Eyes glancing sideways are said to suggest suspiciousness or avoidance mechanisms. Eyes closed suggests denial. Areas blackened are those about which there may be anxiety. The interpretations appear reasonable. My main objection to her work is the speculation involved and the paucity of confirmatory clinical data. One does not have to confine oneself to the drawings per se. One can use the drawings in the context of the clinical interview as well as in a setting in which associated fantasies, discussion, and stories are obtained. The conclusions that one then derives are more likely to be valid. For this instrument to be useful the child must be free enough to draw more than stick figures, because such figures are not likely to provide as much information as those pictures that depict richer material.

A child begins to draw recognizable human figures between the ages of three and four. Most often the earliest figures include a head with some facial characteristics and the extremities, typically emanating from the face. The head and the body may be depicted as one circle or oval. With increasing age the child's drawing of the human figure becomes more complex and accurate. F. Goodenough (1926) was the first to provide a scoring system to assess the child's developmental and intellectual level from the sophistication of the drawings of the human figure. D.B. Harris, in 1963, updated and refined Goodenough's scoring system. It cannot be denied that children's drawings become more complex, sophisticated, and accurate as they grow older. However, the Goodenough and Harris scales do not differentiate between the drawing that is immature because of intellectual impairment and the one that is below the chronological age level because of psychological immaturity. This is one of this technique's greatest defects, a deficiency not often appreciated by some examiners.

FINGER PAINTS, CLAY, BLOCKS, AND WATER

Finger Paints

Finger painting is generally pleasurable to young children. Such paintings, like drawings, can serve as a source of information about underlying psychodynamics—both with regard to the picture per se and the fantasies woven around it. Finger painting can provide regressive gratifications because of the smearing and messing outlets that they provide. Some therapists believe that this is a valuable aspect of finger painting because such regression is necessary before the child can then progress to higher levels of developmental functioning. The theory goes that one must allow the child to experience past gratifications that he or she may have been deprived of at that particular stage of development. Having then gratified these desires, the child is presumably in a better position to mature. I am dubious about this theory. I am more of the persuasian that what is past is past and that, although one may learn from history, one cannot go back in time and change it. This utilization of finger painting is based on the theory that one can. Accordingly, I generally do not encourage regression in my therapeutic work. There are, however, times when a child may regress in the face of some particular psychological trauma. Regression then provides a certain amount of solace, but I do not encourage it on an ongoing basis. Rather, after permitting a reasonable degree of regression, I will encourage a child to proceed along the developmental track to higher levels of functioning.

Finger painting can also be useful for inhibited children from homes where such free expression is neither encouraged nor tolerated. The pictures created with crayons are less easily changed; those produced with finger paints can be altered significantly before the final picture has dried. Accordingly, they allow for a richer elaboration of fantasies. The process of drawing the picture provides the child with tactile, kinesthetic, and visual gratifications that may have some therapeutic value. Lastly, drawing such a picture can provide the child with creative gratifications. Because less skill is necessary than drawing with crayons, the younger less accomplished child is more likely to gravitate toward finger painting (P.J. Napoli, 1951). I, personally, have never used finger paints in my therapeutic work with children. This relates in part to the inevitable mess that I would not be comfortable with. Furthermore, I view them as being more *play* than *therapy*, with significant nontherapeutic time spent in the physical activity.

Clay

One of the advantages of using clay as a focus for self-created stories is its malleability. Whereas a drawing is a relatively fixed stimulus for such fantasies, clay can be altered. Drawings have two dimensions whereas clay obviously has three. The medium almost asks the child to do things with it. It thereby expands the possibilities for the child's projected fantasies (A.G. Woltmann, 1964a). Of course, less technical skill is required to work with clay than to draw. It is appealing therefore to younger children, especially those who are less skilled.

Because clay almost invites the child to pound it, it is viewed by many therapists as a useful vehicle for the expression and release of tensions and hostility (M.R. Haworth and A.I. Rabin, 1960). I do not have much respect for therapeutic techniques that provide for such gratifications. All too often the therapist views such hostile release as a therapeutic end in itself. That is, the therapist believes a primary goal in therapy is to provide a vehicle for the release of pent-up hostility. Such therapists often lose sight of the fact that a more judicious goal of therapy, a goal that is more likely to help the person deal with real-life situations, is to help patients (regardless of age) to deal with their anger at the earliest moment and to direct it toward the source of frustration and irritation. The purpose of anger is to help increase the patient's efficiency in removing a noxious stimulus, the stimulus that is bringing about the anger in the first place. So removed, there will be little anger to express. Therefore, this use of clay, although a common one, is in my opinion misguided.

Clay resembles feces and therefore allows certain children regressive manifestations. Children can get messy with it and can smear with it in a manner that is approved of rather than forbidden. Therapists who believe that this can be therapeutically useful are likely to introduce clay into the child's play. I personally am not too enthusiastic about this use of clay, nor, as mentioned, am I enthusiastic about encouraging patients to regress.

Classical Freudian analysts are often quick to see sexual symbols in the objects that a child makes with clay. If a child rolls a piece of clay, it is difficult to imagine something coming out that doesn't resemble a snake. Many therapists of this persuasian reflexly assume that the child has then formed a penis with the clay. Under such circumstances, just about all children will receive the same interpretation, not a very therapeutically convincing thing for a therapist to do. Or the child is likely to roll the clay into a ball. The same therapists may automatically assume that the child is now creating a breast or testicle. Again, such "rubber stamp" interpretations are not very convincing to me. These therapists would do well to consider the possibility that there is absolutely no symbolic significance at all to many play activities and that the clay modality lends itself extremely well to the creation of objects of these shapes.

It is only with additional self-created fantasies that one is in a position to determine whether or not the therapist's own fantasies about the meaning of the clay figures are valid.

My experience has been that one of the important drawbacks of clay as a therapeutic vehicle is its pliability and lack of cohesiveness. Frequently a figure's arms and legs fall off, especially when it is moved. The child then spends an inordinate amount of time trying to get the extremities to stick to the body of the figurine. This wastes valuable therapeutic time. Because I am a somewhat obsessive and orderly person, and am not comfortable with the child's dirtying up my office with clay, I keep it in the closet and only bring it out for special purposes. I may not be the optimum therapist for children who come from homes which are extremely uptight. However, most of the children I see have problems because they are too loose, disorganized, and just the opposite of obsessive. Accordingly, I believe that for the vast majority of children, my personality type is preferable. All therapists should recognize the areas in which they can be helpful and those in which they cannot and should refer patients with pathology in certain areas to other therapists. We cannot be all things to all people. If our personality styles are such that we cannot be of help to certain patients, it is only ethical to refer them elsewhere.

Blocks

Many therapists have blocks in their play rooms. Proponents of their use describe them as providing valuable outlets for suppressed and repressed hostility. The child can throw them, drop them as "bombs," and so on. I am dubious about the therapeutic value of such hostile play. In fact, it may even encourage such acting out in that the therapist is catalyzing expression of hostility. Furthermore, anger, like other emotions has a way of "getting out of bounds." This unbridled expression of angry feelings may bring about a situation in which the expression of feelings becomes an end in itself and a vicious cycle spirals upward. This phenomenon has not been given the attention it deserves by therapists. For example, a murderer stabs a person in the heart. Most would agree that one or two such stabs will suffice to kill the individual. However, occasionally a murderer may stab the dead person 10 or 15 times in association with the homicidal act. Clearly, one or two stabs is enough to kill the individual. The additional stabs do not seem to serve any useful purpose. But they do serve a purpose. They allow for the release of the anger that is generated by the earlier anger. The anger then seems to build up in its own right, beyond the original purpose of its formation. Teachers know this phenomenon well. Children in classes can get out of control. They know they must try to interrupt the process early or everyone else goes wild. Therapists should not be encouraging their patients to "go wild."

Children enjoy building houses, castles, and other edifices which give them a sense of achievement and power. Such structures can be used to satisfy regressive fantasies by the children's building cozy retreats in which they can withdraw in womb-like fashion. E.H. Erikson (1950) has emphasized the importance of the configurational aspects of the structures that the child builds with blocks. He considers these to be of diagnostic value as well as useful points of departure for therapeutic interchanges.

Water Play

Water play has not been as popular as some of the aforementioned therapeutic modalities. In part, this probably relates to the fact that most therapists don't enjoy the mess of puddles of water all over their offices. Proponents of its use (Hartley et al., 1964) consider it to be the most flexible play medium that therapists can use—the most fluid of the various therapeutic modalities used in the playroom. Some child psychoanalysts claim that water stimulates play that involves urination, just as clay stimulates play that involves bowel movements. I am dubious about the symbolization here, but even if such interpretations are valid, I would often have a hard time translating such play into useful therapy. The use of water and clay for these purposes is based on the theory that symbolically playing with one's urine and feces can be therapeutically useful in that it provides gratifications that may not have been provided at earlier developmental levels. I have already expressed my opinion of such utilization of play materials, namely, that the past is dead, one cannot relive it, and doing so serves little if any therapeutic purpose.

Water is also used as a medium for the release of pent-up hostile feelings. By spitting, splashing, throwing, and spilling water, one releases anger. As mentioned, I am dubious about the use of catharsis as a therapeutic modality. A child who comes from a restrained and restrictive home may find playing with water a useful release from which he or she can gain a sense of freedom. I think swimming would provide more of a sense of freedom than the therapist's office, and it is far less costly and impractical.

Further Comments on Finger Painting, Clay, Blocks, and Water Play

When utilizing clay, finger paints, water, and blocks (and to a lesser degree, other play materials), the therapist does well to differentiate *psychotherapy* from that which is *psychotherapeutic*. Psychotherapy is a process that requires the talents and skills of a person trained in the treatment of psychological disturbances. However, a child can have many experiences that are psychotherapeutic—without the participation of a psychotherapist. Most healthy pleasurable activities are ego-enhancing and thereby contribute to the alleviation of psychological disturbance. The gratifications that flow from creative activity are in general psychologically beneficial. Physical activities can reduce tension and serve to release pent-up aggression. Sexual encounters can reduce tension, give pleasure, and facilitate benevolent human interchanges—all of which can be psychologically salutary. Because individuals can gain psychotherapeutic benefit alone or from interactions with others who are not trained therapists, it behooves the therapist to provide patients with something *beyond* what can be obtained elsewhere.

Clay, finger paints, water, and blocks along with other traditional toys used in therapy create the possibility that play therapy with them may be more *play* than *therapy*. Mention has been made of their value in providing the child with a greater sense of freedom and in reducing inhibitions. Obviously, such an experience is not valuable for all child patients; there are many children who need just the opposite. Their main problems relate to the fact that they are too uninhibited. Providing them with a therapeutic approach that encourages release and free expression may be antitherapeutic and merely frighten them or entrench their pathology. The aforementioned modalities have been described as providing the child with opportunities for regressive satisfactions: with return-to-the-womb gratifications and opportunities for symbolic play with urine and feces. Some hold that such regressive gratifications can be therapeutic, especially for the child who has been deprived of them; however, there is danger in providing too much such satisfaction and thereby entrenching regressive symptomatology. Finally, the value of these modalities in releasing hostility is often a naive approach to the treatment of hostility problems. I like to use the analogy here of anger as a kettle of boiling water with the flames under it symbolizing the anger generating frustrations and noxious stimuli. The person who needs anger release is viewed as someone who has a cork or plug in the spout of the kettle. Therapists of such a patient might consider their job to be that of pulling the cork out of the spout of the boiling kettle. This, in my opinion, is an oversimplification of the therapist's role. The therapist must not only help the patient pull the cork out but help the patient connect a tube from the spout to the underlying flames in order to extinguish the fires that are causing the water to boil in the first place. The therapist's role is to help the patient him- or herself pull the cork out and then connect a pipe from the spout to the flames that are generating the anger. If he or she is successful in this regard, the flames will be extinguished and there will be no anger generated— at least with regard to that particular issue.

PUPPETS AND MARIONETTES

Puppets and marionettes, like dolls, are used to stimulate fantasies (A.G. Woltmann, 1951, 1964b). My own experience with puppets is such that I rarely use them in therapeutic work. When children are given two puppets, one on each hand, it is likely that they will bang their heads together or engage them in some kind of aggressive play. The equipment almost asks for such utilization. The therapist then is not in a good position to know whether significant pent-up hostility is being expressed by such play or whether the puppet is serving as a vehicle for the expression of normal playful activity. Although one may have a large number of puppets, the human being has only two hands. Accordingly, the medium has an intrinsic restricting element in that one can only utilize two figures at a time.

Marionettes are occasionally used in child therapy. I have limited experience with them, mainly because I discarded them years ago. A significant amount of time was spent on untangling the strings, obviously a waste of therapeutic time. The fact that only one figure can be used at a time is also a serious detriment. L.

Bender (1952) and A.G. Woltmann (1972) tried a therapeutic technique in which hospitalized children were presented with puppet shows that were designed to elicit material of psychological significance. Puppets and marionettes were utilized in these theatrical performances and the issues presented in the plays were used as points of departure for analytically oriented group discussions. My main criticism of this technique is that the stories, although selected to cover a wide variety of life situations, were intrinsically restricting of the child's fantasies and so had a contaminating potential in the psychotherapeutic process. I have much greater commitment to the encouragement of free and self-created fantasies. The Bender and Woltmann stories are just the opposite.

DRAMATIZATION

Most children love plays and will welcome the opportunity to act in them. Children spontaneously play act their fantasies, the traditional game of "house" being one of the more common examples. In such games, the child entrenches adult identifications, reflects relationships and experiences, gratifies wishes, releases unacceptable impulses, and attempts to work through various problems and experiences (R.E. Hartley, L.K. Frank, and R.M. Goldenson, 1952). Play acting a theme of psychological significance provides the child with a far richer experience than merely talking about it and possibly emoting over it. With dramatization, various other sensory elements are brought into the experience: kinesthetic, tactile, an enhancement of the visual, and occasionally the olfactory and gustatory. This multisensory stimulation provides greater input than a single sensory modality and increases the likelihood that the experience will be remembered and incorporate itself into the child's psychic structure. Encouraging children to play act their fantasies enables the therapist to gain a deeper appreciation of their social interactional processes; it may help children as well to see more clearly how they relate to others. Through play acting, children can desensitize themselves to an anxiety-provoking situation, one that is either experienced or anticipated.

I. Marcus (1966) found children's donning costumes to be a useful device in helping some children overcome their resistances to revealing their fantasies. Wearing a costume appears to encourage children to "act" and hence reveal themselves. Marcus has found a box of hats to be similarly useful. He found that passive children tend to become more active and less defensive when wearing the costume. The material so elicited is used for psychoanalytic inquiry. The child has the opportunity to choose from a variety of costumes and an assortment of hats. One drawback to this technique is that it provides intrinsic contaminants to the child's productions in that the hats and costumes serve as foci for the fantasies that might otherwise be more freely self-created. However, a contaminated fantasy is generally more valuable than no fantasy at all (because the child often introduces idiosyncratic material), and for some children a costume or hat may enable them to provide material that would not otherwise have been obtained.

R.B. Haas and J.L. Moreno (1951) have utilized what they call the "Projection Action Test." They describe both diagnostic and therapeutic utilization of this instrument. When using this technique, children are encouraged to involve themselves in a series of structured dramatic situations from which projective material is likely to emerge. For example, a child may be asked to imagine him- or herself on a stage with an imaginary person. A series of questions is then asked about who the person is and what the child is doing with that person. The material so derived then becomes a focus for therapeutic discussion. In *Storytelling in Psychotherapy with Children* (Jason Aronson, 1993) I discuss the mutual storytelling technique, a therapeutic device in which self-created stories are elicited from the child followed by the examiner's creating stories of his or her own that are specifically tailored to the psychological needs of the child. I also discuss the dramatization of these stories as an enhancement of the original technique.

Dance can also be a useful aspect of therapeutic dramatizations. L. Bender (1952) considered dance to be an excellent way to lower children's inhibitions. She considered it therapeutic in other ways: it provides pleasure (which in itself is often therapeutic), it can be ego-enhancing (as the child gains confidence in it), it reduces tension, and it serves to sublimate sexual desires. Hartley et al. (1952) emphasized the therapeutic role of dance in lessening tensions, providing primitive pleasure (especially kinesthetic), inducing spontaneity, and as a release for hostility. I am less enthusiastic about the hostility release element here, but I cannot deny that it serves the other purposes.

"PARAVERBAL THERAPY"

E. Heimlich (1965, 1972, 1973) uses a technique which she refers to as "paraverbal therapy." As a therapeutic modality she attempts to unite the therapeutic aspects of music (listening, singing, playing instruments, mime, dance, and finger painting). In her techniques, she sings with the child a song that is likely to touch upon issues relevant to his or her pathology. Her purpose is not only to provide strong and dramatic carthartic release but to use the issues in the song as points of departure for therapeutic discussions. There is no question that music, properly utilized, can be an extremely useful therapeutic modality. The most resistant and withdrawn children are likely to be engaged in musical activities, both verbal and along with musical instruments. It touches something primitive in all of us. If one adds words to music, there is a greater likelihood that the words will be heard—they seem to float on top of the music into the brain. Messages transmitted verbally are less likely to be incorporated into the psychic structure than those which utilize the musical vehicle of transmission. Heimlich adds to these mime, dance, and other elements of physical movement, all of which attempt to enhance the efficacy of the therapeutic communications. The method is especially useful for children who have proven resistant to other modes of treatment, but it should not be viewed simply for them. It can also be utilized for more cooperative children.

TRADITIONAL COMPETITIVE BOARD GAMES

Many child therapists have available traditional board games for utilization in therapy with children. I am very dubious about the basic therapeutic value of most of these instruments. I am not claiming that they have no therapeutic benefit at all; only that they are of limited therapeutic value and that most of the other instruments described in this chapter are much more efficient. One cannot deny that, while playing a traditional competitive board game with a child, many aspects of the child's personality will be revealed without the child's appreciating what is happening. A child's reactions to winning and losing, how competitive a child is, if a child is prone to cheat, if a child plays aggressively or passively, and if the child shows forethought and planning may be revealed in the course of playing the game (Gardner, 1969a, 1986a). Games may also be fun and therefore therapeutic in their own right in that pleasure is generally therapeutic. These benefits notwithstanding, the disadvantages of the utilization of these games generally far outweighs their advantages. The time during which useful information is being gained about the child often represents an extremely small fraction of the therapeutic session. The rest of the time is just spent playing a game. When most of the other instruments described in this chapter are utilized, there is often a higher frequency of meaningful material being provided.

For many therapists the utilization of traditional competitive board games is essentially a "cop out." They require little therapeutic talent or skill, and the therapist can rationalize that useful therapy is being accomplished when, in actuality, all the therapist is doing is whiling away the time with the child by playing games. Obviously, more uncooperative and inhibited children are likely to be engaged by such instruments. The hope of some therapists is that after some period spent on this relatively low-key activity, the child will be groomed for deeper, more introspective treatment. The danger of such an approach is that after many months, and even years, this goal may never be reached (the usual situation). Other more predictably successful resistance-reducing approaches (mentioned throughout this book), might have been utilized with a better chance of a positive therapeutic outcome. Play therapy should be much more *therapy* than play. The use of these games is often much more *play* than therapy.

CONCLUDING COMMENTS

Most of the therapeutic instruments described in this chapter are designed to elicit fantasies from children. Such utilization is based on the theory that self-created fantasies may be a rich source of psychodynamic information about the processes that underly the child's symptomatology. The therapist must appreciate, however, that eliciting this material too quickly, especially in the very guarded, fragile, and borderline child, may frighten the child and thereby induce resistances to self-revelation that would not have occurred if the therapist had proceeded more cautiously. Therefore, therapists do well to hold off encouraging such inhibited children to reveal themselves until later in treatment, after a trusting relationship has been established.

Most of the techniques described in this chapter are basically those that I was familiarized with during the course of my residency during the late 1950s. I have discussed what I consider to be the advantages and drawbacks to most of them. As mentioned in Chapter One, my educational background was such that I was strongly encouraged to attempt to provide improvements of work of which I was critical. The rest of this book, in a sense, can be viewed as an attempt to rectify the deficiencies and drawbacks of the techniques described in this chapter. In addition, it represents an attempt to enrich and expand upon those therapeutic modalities that I consider worthy of utilization and perpetuation.

TWO

Central Elements in the Psychotherapeutic Process

A good man is one who knows what he feels, says what he means, and means what he says.

Hasidic saying

A teacher affects eternity; he can never tell where his influence stops.

Henry Brooks Adams

The theoretical principles presented here regarding the origin of symptoms and the central elements in the psychotherapeutic process are applicable to children, adolescents, and adults. Although the general principles presented here apply to all three age categories, there are differences in the therapeutic application of these principles regarding the degree to which the therapist relies on the patient to make active contributions to the treatment. The younger the child, the more it behooves the therapist to actively elicit, encourage, and even suggest the ways in which the child should respond to particular life situations that are causing difficulties. The older the patient the more the therapist should encourage (and at times require) the patient to contribute him- or herself to the solutions to these life problems. But even with the most mature and healthy patient, a certain amount of suggestion and introduction of behavioral solutions are warranted.

THE ORIGIN OF SYMPTOMS

I view symptoms to represent maladaptive and inappropriate ways of dealing with the problems of life with which we are all confronted. The patient's selections of solutions to these problems have originally been devised because they appeared to be the most judicious. What we refer to as psychodynamics are basically the pathways and processes by which these problems produce symptoms. Symptoms then can be viewed as the "tip of the iceberg"—the most superficial manifestations of the disease process. At the base of the iceberg are the fundamental problems of life for which the symptom represents an injudicious solution. Between the base and the tip of the iceberg are the processes by which the symptomatic solution is created. These processes are called psychodynamics.

The iceberg analogy holds because most of the etiological processes that are operative in the symptoms' formation are not apparent to conscious awareness; it is as if they were submerged. (In the case of the iceberg, six-sevenths is under water.) What is above the surface is well viewed to be the conscious material (what is readily observable), and what is below the surface is well considered to be subconscious (not immediately in conscious awareness, but readily available to such scrutiny) and unconscious (not readily available to conscious awareness, but potentially so via such procedures as psychoanalytic therapy, especially dream psychoanalysis).

As an example of the above let us take Bob's situation. Bob is eight years old and in the third grade. His teacher has informed the class that there will be a big test the next day. Bob is quite upset about this because he was looking forward to watching his favorite television program. The problem then for Bob is whether he should watch his program or study for the test. If he indulges himself and watches the TV program he may get a low grade on the next day's examination. A good grade might only be obtained by his depriving himself of the television program. Bob is being confronted here with one of the common dilemmas of just about all schoolchildren. Bob is facing one of the fundamental problems of life which, like all such problems, lends itself well to the utilization of maladaptive solutions.

Bob decides to watch the program in the hope that he will be lucky enough to know the answers to the questions his teacher selects to give on the test (already we sense trouble, that is, a maladaptive solution). On the next day, as luck would have it, Bob finds that he doesn't know the answers to most of the questions. In order to protect himself from the embarrassments and discomfort of getting a poor grade, he decides to copy from the paper of the little girl sitting next to him. Such behavior is called *cheating*, a symptom. Like all symptoms, it is an inappropriate adaptation and may result in more trouble and discomfort for Bob than that which he would have suffered had he studied for the test and deprived himself of the gratifications of watching his favorite television program.

Now let us consider the possible outcomes of Bob's symptomatic resolution of this conflict. One outcome is that the teacher will catch him cheating, scold him, give him a failing grade, and possibly report the event to his parents. He may then suffer further disapprobation at home. Perhaps the teacher won't catch him but his classmates observe what he is doing. He may suffer from them a certain amount of criticism and alienation. Or, the girl from whom he is cheating may get angry at him, cover her paper, and then may reject him subsequently as a "cheater." Perhaps none of these occur and he appears to be "successful." However, when the grades come back, and Bob sees that he has gotten a high one, if he has anything approaching healthy superego development, he is likely to feel less proud of his high grade than he would have had he come by it honestly. In his heart he knows that it was not deserved and so he cannot enjoy the gratification he otherwise would have had he achieved his high grade by honest effort.

All of these outcomes are examples of the principle that the selection of the symptomatic solution generally results in the individual's suffering with more difficulties than he or she would have if the more judicious and healthy solution had been utilized. In this case it would have been Bob's deciding to forego the pleasures of television and appreciating that such deprivation would ultimately be less painful than the discomforts and embarrassments associated with the consequences of his cheating.

However, the possibility still remains that Bob could have cheated and *not* suffered any of the above difficulties. Let us suppose there was no negative feedback from any of the aforementioned individuals (that is, "he got away with it") and his superego development was so limited that he suffered no guilt or remorse over his behavior—behavior that would generally be considered unacceptable in the classroom. But even then there would be the untoward effect of his not having gained the optimum benefit from his educational process. His failure to study would have deprived him of the information learned by those who had studied. Although this outcome might not have caused Bob any immediate discomfort, in the long run, especially if this pattern were repeated, Bob's education would suffer. Thus, the aforementioned principle still holds.

Another example: A boy does not have friends because of personality problems. However, he learns that he need not suffer loneliness very long if he provides peers with candy, toys, and other presents. His utilization of *bribery* (the name of the symptom) is seemingly successful in that he now finds himself more popular. He enjoys thereby an alleviation of the painful feelings of loneliness. However, his pleasure is compromised by the inner knowledge that his friends are being bought and that they would not be there if he did not have the wherewithal to pay them off. In addition, his position is a precarious one because he does not have a steady supply of bribes to insure that he will not once again be lonely. And this unstable feeling also compromises his pleasure. At some level he probably senses that his "friends" do not basically respect him, and this cannot but lower his feelings of self-worth. Last, if and when he does run out of bribes (the usual case), he cannot but feel "used." Bribing, the psychopathological symptom, was devised in an attempt to deal with the common human problem of loneliness. Ostensibly, it served its purpose of providing friends; however, it was an injudicious selection. As is usually the case when psychopathological symptoms are used to resolve a problem, the individual usually ends up being worse off than he or she was before.

Jim is afraid to join *Little League*. He fantasizes public humiliation if he strikes out at bat or if he drops a ball in the course of the game's action. Jim is a well-coordinated boy, and there is no reason to believe that he would humiliate himself to a significant degree. He chooses to take the safe course and doesn't try out for *Little League* and thereby protects himself from his anticipated humiliations. The solution that Jim has chosen does "work" in that he doesn't suffer the tensions he would have experienced had he joined. However, he suffers even worse repercussions as a result of his withdrawal. He becomes somewhat lonely in that when his friends are playing baseball, he has little to do. But more important, he has deprived himself of the ego-enhancing gratifications that he would have gained as the result of his participation. He has deprived himself of the joys of playing well in an area in which he has every reason to believe he would have been competent.

There is an extremely important principle demonstrated here that pervades many aspects of living. Most new things are anxiety provoking. The healthy person tolerates such fear with the knowledge that it is usually transient and that the benefits to be derived outweigh the loss of joy and ego-enhancement to be suffered from failure to act. The philosophy is epitomized in the aphorism: *Nothing ventured, nothing gained.* All individuals can choose the safe course and avoid risk and anxiety. In the extreme, the individual psychologically digs a hole in the ground, hides therein, thereby protecting him- or herself from the vast majority of life's rejections, disappointments, indignities, and traumas. However, a heavy price is paid for such "safety." One leads an extremely boring existence, and one is deprived of the ego-enhancement that comes from accomplishment. Again, the psychopathological solution to this problem causes the individual more difficulty than he or she would have suffered had the healthier course been pursued.

Here is another example common to childhood. While playing alone with a ball, Jane accidentally breaks a neighbor's window. To the best of her knowledge, no one has observed the incident. A conflict is immediately set up. On the one hand, she would like to run away as fast as she can and thereby avoid any responsibility or repercussions for the damage. On the other hand, part of her appreciates that such flight would be "wrong" and that she would not respect herself for doing so. Furthermore, she might be observed and then would suffer punishment for having "run from the scene of the crime." Jane decides to take her chances and run as fast as she can. She gets home and breathes a sigh of relief. To the best of her knowledge she was unobserved, and she feels that she has "gotten away with it." However, there is some lingering guilt and fear that she might have been seen and that word of her misdeed will ultimately get to her parents. So even at this stage the pathological course is not without its negative repercussions. She is enjoying the pleasure of not having to own up to her responsibility for her transgression, but her pleasure is compromised by her guilt and fear of disclosure. Of course, if her superego development has been impaired, she will not suffer this guilt and she truly will have "gotten away with it." Last, if she were observed, and the incident is reported to her parents, then she is likely to suffer repercussions for her flight.

Had she gone to the neighbor and reported the incident, she would probably have been respected and even praised for her honesty, even though the neighbor might have been angry as well. If she offered to pay for the window, she would have to suffer the privations attendant to such payment. However, this negative element would have been offset by the ego-enhancement that comes with the knowledge that one is doing the "right" thing. In addition, she might have been praised by others for her honesty, and this could further enhance feelings of self-worth. She would have avoided the guilt and fear of detection that she might have suffered following the commission of her "crime." The ancient aphorism *honesty is the best policy* is not trite. There is great wisdom in it. The honest course usually (though certainly not always) is the best course because its advantages usually outweigh its disadvantages. People who utilize psychopathological mechanisms for resolving disputes may not be aware of this ancient truth.

Now, some examples from adult life. A man is very dissatisfied with his boss. He dreads going to work most days because of the indignities he suffers in his office. He is a somewhat timid person who fears expressing resentment. He feels that if he were to assert himself with his employer he might lose his job. In addition, even if he were not to lose his job, he is afraid of his boss's anger. These fears contribute significantly to his failure to assert himself and to discuss in a civilized manner the problems he has with his employer. Most often (but not always) such failure to assert oneself is pathological. It is a heavy price to pay for job security and protection from the possible resentment of the person to whom a complaint is directed.

A healthier course for this man would be to assert himself and make reasonable attempts to resolve the conflict with his boss. If he is successful in this regard, he will have accomplished his goal of a better work relationship with his boss. In addition, he will have reduced, if not eliminated, his loathing of work as well as the self-loathing that comes with repression and suppression of pent-up resentment. He will enjoy the sense of well-being that comes with successful resolution of a problem. However, such assertion could conceivably result in his being fired. This repercussion will have to be taken into consideration before he decides to assert himself. Having made the decision to act, he must bear this risk. He might even have to suffer the discomforts of trying to find another job, and he might not even be able to find one. He has to consider the discomforts and loss of self-worth that come with unemployment and being a public charge. Although these are certainly formidable negative repercussions of self-assertion, the man would at least be free from the self-loathing and the painful effects of not expressing his resentments.

Another example from adult life. A teller in a bank makes an error. Although some discrepancy will ultimately be detected in the accounting process, the person who caused the error may not readily be identified. The teller knows that if she reveals the error, there might be some criticism and reprimand. However, her position is such that it is extremely unlikely that she would lose her job. Moreover, if she says nothing, there may be no repercussions because the process of detecting the person who made the error is so cumbersome that the company accountants may not wish to go to the trouble. Or, another person might be falsely implicated. She decides to say nothing. During the ensuing days she hears talk about the repercussions of her mistake and the resentment felt by her superiors toward the individual (still unknown) who could have been so careless. Although "innocent," she suffers with the fear of disclosure and some guilt. Had she admitted the error, there would have been some criticism, but no job loss and no ongoing fear of disclosure. The pathological way seemed easier at first but ended up being the more difficult course.

I do not claim that the examples given above explore in great depth all the ramifications of a psychological act. They focus on the symptom as a manifestation of the individual's attempt to find the solution to a common, if not universal, life problem. They demonstrate how the pathological solution causes the individual more trouble than the healthy one. The examples have not focused on complex psychodynamic factors that play a role in determining whether the individual chooses the healthy or pathological adaptation to the conflict. Nor have I elucidated the psychodynamic pattern by which the fundamental conflict brings about the symptomatic solution.

THERAPY AS A WAY
OF OPENING UP NEW OPTIONS

Therapy involves helping people learn better ways of dealing with these inevitable conflicts and problems. Therapy must open up new options—options that may not have been considered by the patient previously, options that may not have been part of his or her repertoire. The utilization of these more adaptive solutions *over time* lessens the likelihood that the patient will have to resort to the maladaptive, symptomatic solutions. In Bob's case (the boy who cheated on the test), the therapist might have tried to help him appreciate in advance how short-sighted was his decision to indulge himself in television viewing without giving serious consideration to the potential consequences of his utilizing the cheating solution. In the course of such a discussion, the therapist might have asked Bob if he could think of any other solution to his dilemma. If Bob's family owned a video cassette recorder, then the option of making a videotape of the program and studying at the same time could have been discussed. Then, he could watch the program on the weekend and so both television watching and studying would have been accomplished. Or, if Bob himself doesn't own a video cassette recorder, he could be asked if he had a friend who might be prevailed upon to tape the program for him. The videotape recorder resolution, then, becomes a new option—an option that may not have previously been considered by Bob. Once utilized, this solution might become an automatic consideration for Bob when confronted in the future with this conflict. Although this new option originated in treatment, it can now become a part of Bob's repertoire of options.

In each of the other examples, the therapist could have helped the patient consider healthier options. The boy who used bribes "to gain friendships" could have been helped to appreciate the precariousness of his situation and the lowered feeling of self-worth that comes from being so utilized. Jim, the boy who was afraid to join *Little League*, could have been helped to appreciate the wisdom of "nothing ventured, nothing gained"—that those who do not venture forth will often lead very lonely and unrewarding lives. Jane, the girl who accidentally broke a neighbor's window, could have been helped to appreciate that it was ultimately to her benefit to take the initially painful but more courageous course of admitting her guilt. And the man who was dissatisfied with his boss could be helped to appreciate that the security and ego-enhancement potentially derived from healthy and civilized self-assertion are much more likely to outweigh the risks and disadvantages associated with passive submission. The teller in the bank could have been helped to appreciate the wisdom of the "honesty is the best policy" aphorism.

COMMENTS ON
TIME-LIMITED THERAPY

The reader may recall that in the above discussion on therapy as a way of opening up new options, the words *over time* are italicized. My purpose here is to emphasize the point that meaningful therapeutic changes are not likely to take place quickly. Although there are rare occasions when a brief encounter with the therapist can bring about long-term therapeutic results, such situations are unusual. Therapy first requires the establishment of a meaningful therapist-patient relationship (to be discussed in detail in Chapter Four). In the context of such a relationship, therapeutic messages are received by the patient with receptivity and therapeutic experiences take place that, when repeated over time, bring about personality change. Freud feared that psychoanalysis would degenerate in the United States because of the lack of patience that Americans had for solutions that might require a long-term investment of time and energy. He feared that the method would be bastardized by a wide variety of quick and seemingly attractive short cures. And he was right. Short-term methods of treatment have sprung up everywhere and promise better, more rapid, and less expensive results than long-term psychoanalytic therapy or psychoanalysis. I consider this to be a deplorable development. It is not that I do not have criticisms of psychoanalytic treatment (many have been and will continue to be presented in this book); it is only that I am critical of quick methods of treatment, especially those that promise results in a prescribed period of time, even before the patient's problems are known.

Short-term and brief psychotherapies are very much in vogue. Often a specific time limit is imposed upon the patient from the outset. Ten to fifteen sessions is a common figure. The selection of such a number demonstrates complete ignorance of what I consider to be a crucial requirement of meaningful psychotherapy. One cannot possibly know how long it will take to develop the kind of relationship in which meaningful therapy is most likely to be productive. Furthermore, the imposed time limits are likely to compromise significantly the nature of the work accomplished in each of the sessions. If the patient is watching the clock, is pressured into working quickly, and is trying to figure out a solution to a particular problem within time limitations, it is likely that the solutions so derived will be injudiciously selected.

If a boy were to call up a girl and ask her to go out with him for ten dates and then break up, he would be considered strange. If a man asked a woman to marry him for twelve days, weeks, months, or even years—and then to divorce—he would probably be considered by the woman to be insane. Yet the same kind of arrangement is frequently made between therapists and patients, and there are many who do not consider this absurd. It is not that I do not do brief psychotherapy. I do it all the time, but I only do it in situations where happily it takes place. It occurs in situations where I cannot know beforehand how long the treatment will take, and in some cases it does indeed turn out to be brief. But I have never promised it would be brief at the outset because I could not know the degree to which the parties would cooperate, whether or not a relationship would be established, whether there would be receptivity to what I had to say, and what things would come up in the course of the treatment.

Psychotherapy in which a patient is told at the outset that a specific number of sessions is all that will be required is basically a "rip off" by clinical administrators on a gullible public. It is one way of rationalizing giving a little therapy to a lot of people rather than a lot of therapy to a select few. If one is going to do this, then one should at least be honest and let people know that they are getting a watered-down form of treatment. Time-limited therapy is mainly for the poor, who often have little choice. People who are in better financial positions most often get as much treatment as they need. And those rich people who do opt for brief psychotherapy are often the naive and gullible ones, those who, despite their financial positions, are still simple-minded enough to be attracted to this absurd form of treatment.

THE THERAPIST-PATIENT RELATIONSHIP

If patients are to experience an alleviation (the reader should note that I did not use the word *cure* here) of the presenting symptomatology, it is highly desirable that both the therapist and the patient possess certain qualities. The importance of the therapist-patient relationship in therapy is often spoken of. However, the specific personality qualities that are important for each to possess and the ways in which these bring about symptomatic alleviation and therapeutic change are not often elaborated upon. The main reason for this, I believe, is that these issues have not been studied to the degree that is warranted. I present here a few of the important elements that I consider necessary to be present in each party if therapy is to be meaningful. Only basic principles will be presented here. In Chapter Four I will discuss these principles in greater detail, especially as they apply to child psychotherapy.

Genuine Respect vs. Idealization and/or Idolization of the Therapist

The patient should be reasonably respectful of the therapist because of *actual* qualities that the therapist has that engender such respect. Idealization (viewing the therapist as perfect) and idolizing (viewing as God-like, worthy of worship) of the therapist is antitherapeutic in that it creates unfavorable comparisons with the therapist that are ego-debasing to the patient and makes it unlikely that the patient will relate realistically to other human beings who will inevitably reveal their deficits. The classical analytic model, especially, is likely to result in such distortions of the therapist. One might argue that the kind of "blank screen" created by the analyst sitting behind the couch will provide him or her with the "purest" kinds of free associations, associations that are less likely to be contaminated by input from the analyst. However, whatever benefits there are to be derived from this approach (and I do not deny that they exist), there is a heavy price to be paid for them—a price that far outweighs the benefits. As stated, one of the prices is that the patient, having been studiously deprived of vital information about the therapist, is likely to view him or her as being perfect or close to it. This is intrinsically ego-debasing because it produces unfavorable comparisons between the patient and the therapist. Feelings of low self-worth are intrinsically associated with most (if not all) forms of psychogenic psychopathology. Idealizing and idolizing the therapist only adds to this disparity. Furthermore, this unreal atmosphere interferes with the patient's relating to others in the world who will inevitably reveal their deficits and who will not provide the patient with the same kind of accepting and tolerant environment that the therapist provides.

We live in a world where certain conspiracies of silence are prevalent. When speaking with someone in a social situation it is generally considered inappropriate to criticize directly the individual's spouse or analyst. A woman, for example, may meet someone at a cocktail party who tells her that she is in treatment with Dr. X. The listener may know that Dr. X's general reputation at the hospital is that everyone of his five wives despised him. In addition, two of them might have been personal friends of hers so she knows first-hand that this is the case. Yet, she may not reveal any of this information to Dr. X's patient, lest she "rock the boat" and/or compromise the treatment. I believe that it would be far better for the listener to present the information that she knows even at the risk of its being somewhat distorted. The information would certainly serve as "grist for the mill" during the next session. As a result of the patient's confronting her therapist with this information, there could be one of two outcomes. The patient might decide to leave the therapist, from the recognition that his personality deficiencies are so grave that it is not likely he can be of help to her. Or, she might decide to stay in treatment because of the appreciation that Dr. X still has enough on the positive side to warrant his remaining an effective therapist. In either case she is less likely to view him as a perfect person, and this cannot but be therapeutic.

Receptivity to the Therapist's Messages

The patient should be receptive to the therapist's comments, but not to the point of gullibility. If there has been no idealization or idolizing of the therapist, then there is less likely to be gullibility. If there is a good relationship and genuine respect, that is, respect based on genuine qualities that the therapist possesses and exhibits (as opposed to fantasized ones), then there is a greater likelihood that there will be healthy receptivity. Respect must be earned, and healthy respect is not likely to be earned in a fantasized relationship. Healthy respect is based on knowledge of both a person's assets and liabilities. When there is healthy respect, the balance tips in favor of those qualities that engender respect in others. In such situations people recognize another's liabilities but consider them small in comparison to assets. It is only by judicious revelation of deficiencies (to be discussed in detail in various parts of this book) that such genuine respect is likely to evolve.

Identification with and Emulation of the Therapist

There should be a reasonable desire to emulate qualities in the therapist that would serve the person well in life. (This may be conscious or unconscious.) As a result of such emulation, there will be some identification with the therapist's traits and values. I do not believe that there is any psychotherapeutic interchange that does not involve some attempt on the therapist's part to transmit his or her own values to the patient. It is hoped that the values and qualities so taken on will be in the patient's best interests.

There are many who take issue with what I have just said about identification with the therapist's traits and values. Many have been taught in their training that one should strictly avoid doing or saying anything, either implicitly or explicitly, that involves the communication of, let alone imposition of, the therapist's values on the patient. I believe that this is well-meaning but injudicious advice. I cannot imagine a psychotherapeutic interchange that does not involve, at some level, the process of transmission of the therapist's values to the patient. Even in silence such imposition is taking place. Implicit in the therapist's silence is the message: "What you're saying is all right with me. I don't think it warrants any comment on my part. I don't have any books that say it is unhealthy, inappropriate, unreasonable, or otherwise maladaptive."

When we use the word "values" we refer to that which we consider to be good and bad, right and wrong. The therapist is continually making such judgments. At times, however, the term sick and healthy may be utilized. But even here, values are intrinsically present in that what we refer to as psychopathological is basically an opinion regarding whether or not the behavior is good or bad, right or wrong. And this is very much determined by the "eye of the beholder." A mother brings a seven-year-old boy to the psychotherapist with the complaint that, although of superior intelligence, the child shows little academic motivation or curiosity. The therapist, after detailed inquiry into the family life, decides that the child has psychological problems that stem from family difficulties. The therapist recommends a therapeutic approach in which the child is treated individually along with active work with the family. The goal here is to reduce those family tensions and pressures that are contributing to the child's difficulties. The goal, as well, is to help the child himself deal with these family stresses in such a way that academic performance returns to the expected level.

By the therapist's agreeing to treat this patient, he or she is implicitly subscribing to the value judgment that education is a "good" thing and that those who do not avail themselves of their educational opportunities are doing a "bad" thing. One could argue that this is only the therapist's personal opinion. One could say (as many in our society do) that all one needs to do in life is to learn how to sign an X on one's welfare check. Under these circumstances, one will receive (in cash, goods, and services) almost as much as the average working man or woman (especially woman) or perhaps 10 to 15% less. By agreeing to treat this child and help this child reach his academic potential, the therapist is implicitly subscribing to the parents' value judgment that education is a "good" thing. I personally happen to share this value, but I am very clear that it is a value nevertheless.

Another example: A 35-year-old man enters treatment with complaints of depression and excessive drinking. He fears that he may become an alcoholic. In the course of the history taking, the therapist learns that the man's father died when he was in grade school and that he is an only child. Although 35, he still lives with his mother. He does not consider this to be a problem, rather he states that he and his mother have agreed that both would be unreceptive to any therapeutic approach that might ultimately result in his leaving home. It may be the therapist's opinion (supported by many books in his library) that this man has an "unresolved Oedipus complex" and that he is far too old to be living with his mother. Consistent with this opinion, one of the aims of therapy should be to help this man "resolve his Oedipus complex," move out of the house, meet a woman, get married, and have children— like other normal, healthy human beings. Although I am in agreement with this goal (even though I might not agree that the man's problems relate to the so-called "Oedipus complex") I recognize that my position on this subject is still a value judgment. An anthropologist might say that there is an island in the South Pacific where people do this routinely. (There is always an island in the South Pacific where one can justify practically any conclusion regarding human behavior!) Again, my point here is that the therapist cannot take a position on a therapeutic issue without an implicit attempt to impose his or her own values on the patient. In short we must be honest about the fact that we are "brainwashing" our patients. We must also accept the fact that in the context of such brainwashing, many patients have been done terrible disservices and much grief has been caused by such impositions.

Accordingly, therapy is a very "risky business." This problem of value imposition is further compounded by the fact that whether or not one sees something as good or bad is highly individualized and strongly determined by what the therapist brings to the situation, that is, his or her own anticipations, hopes, and even neurotic distortions. The point is well made by the anecdote of the rabbi who dies and finds himself in the hereafter, but he doesn't know whether he's in heaven or hell. He's not experiencing very much pain, so he decides he's probably not in hell. But he's not enjoying very much pleasure either, so he concludes that he's probably not in heaven. As he's groping about, trying to determine where he is, he suddenly sees coming out of the distant clouds none other than Rabbi Isaac Cohen (his mentor from the Talmudic Academy, dead now these 30 years). Rabbi Cohen, he well recalls, was one of the most religious and pious men he ever knew. In his 87 years in life he never broke one rule, so pious was he. Happily, he runs toward his old mentor. He then notices that standing next to the old, stooped man's side is a beautiful, young, voluptuous woman—obviously the old rabbi's companion. The two rabbis embrace, tears running down their cheeks, happy to see one another after all these years.

At this point, the younger rabbi states: "Rabbi Cohen, it's so good to see you here. I've been roaming about, lost. I didn't know whether I was in heaven or hell. But it's obvious that if *you* are here, this must be heaven! A more religious and pious man never lived. It's obvious, also, that this beautiful, young voluptuous woman is God's reward to you for all the good works you've done on earth!"

To which the old rabbi replies: "I'm sorry to have to tell you, rabbi, two things. First, this is not heaven, this is *hell*. And second, this beautiful, gorgeous, voluptuous woman is *not* God's reward to me. I am her punishment!"

The anecdote demonstrates my point that the aspirations and hopes that one brings to a situation are going to be an important determinant of how one interprets it. Shakespeare's Hamlet put it well: "There's nothing either good or bad, but thinking makes it so." The point is demonstrated again in a wonderful scene from the Woody Allen movie, *Annie Hall*. In a split-screen vignette, Woody Allen is on one side complaining to his psychoanalyst, and Diane Keaton is on the other side, complaining to her analyst. Woody is complaining bitterly about Diane's lack of sexual receptivity to him. He complains about how "up tight" she is and how painful is his ongoing state of sexual frustration. The deprivation is driving him crazy and he's practically tearing his hair out so distraught is he over his sexual privation. When the analyst asks him how often he is having sexual relations, he replies, "Imagine, only two or three times a week."

At the same time, Diane Keaton is complaining that Woody is continually bothering her with his sexual advances, from the moment he gets up in the morning, throughout the course of the day, until the moment he goes to sleep at night. He rarely gives her any peace. In the course of her complaining she refers to him as an animal. After further complaints about Woody's insatiable lust, her analyst asks Diane how frequently she is having sexual relations. To which she replies, "Imagine, two to three times a week, the beast." The vignette demonstrates well my point regarding the role of "the eye of the beholder" in determining whether something is good or bad, right or wrong. Therapists are no exception. Our value judgments are colored by our own experiences, anticipations, and aspirations. And these inevitably will be transmitted to our patients. Let us hope that we don't do too much damage.

Most have heard at some time or other anecdotes about people who are looking for "the secret of life"—the one great wisdom under which is encompassed all the meaning of life's experiences. The jokes and/or stories often involve seeking the secret from some guru, often seated in some mountain cave in India or high in the Himalayas. Finally after a long circuitous route, during which time the individual may be exposed to many dangers, the wise man is finally confronted with the question: "What is the secret (or meaning) of life?" Well, I have the answer here for the reader. (Remember, it was I who told it to you.) The secret of life is this: *Life is a Rorschach test!* Yes, that's it. Life is a Rorschach test. Under this dictum one can subsume all the experiences in life. In every experience there is the reality and there is the interpretation that we make of it, depending upon our own psychic structure. There is the Rorschach inkblot, and there is the patient's projection which gives meaning to the inkblot. There is the external reality, and there is the interpretation we give to it. There is the glass of water, and there is our interpretation as to whether it is half empty or half full, or whatever other meaning we want to give to it. The reality then is not simply an external entity. Rather, it is a *combination* of an external entity and the meaning and interpretation that our internal psychic structure gives to it. Then the two together determine our thoughts, feelings, and actions. Let us hope that our projections and our interpretations of what is good and bad for our patients will serve them well.

Trying to Help Patients vs. Helping Patients

The therapist should have a genuine desire to help the patient. There should be a reasonable degree of sympathy (an intellectual process) and empathy (an emotional resonance) with the patient. Therapists should have a reasonable capacity to identify with their patients, that is, put themselves in their patients' positions to view situations from their vantage point. The therapist's goal should be that of *trying* to help the patient, but he or she should not feel that the failure to do so represents a failure in him- or herself. I have emphasized the word *trying* because many therapists consider it their goal to "cure" patients or to bring about significant improvements. Many such therapists suffer with what I call *The Statue of Liberty syndrome*. This name is derived from a poem, written by Emma Lazarus, a poem that was placed at the base of the statue when it arrived in this country in 1886. It says:

> Give me your tired, your poor,
> Your huddled masses yearning to breathe free,
> The wretched refuse of your teeming shore,
> Send these, the homeless,
>   the tempest-tossed to me.
> I lift my lamp beside the golden door.

These lines are certainly inspiring. With the exception of those who are American Indians and those who trace their heritage to pre-Columbian days in South America, all of us are either immigrants ourselves or are the descendants of immigrants, either recent or remote. This principle, however, is extended by many mental health professionals to:

> Give me your chronic hebephrenic schizophrenics,
> Your alcoholics, your drug addicts, your criminals,
> Your psychopaths, your prostitutes,
> And all your other rejects from society.
> I will give them sympathy, empathy, and understanding.
> With analytically oriented psychotherapy,
> I will help them gain insight into the underlying psychological
>   processes that cause their disorders.
> And with such treatment I will raise them to new heights of
>   mental health.

Those therapists who exhibit manifestations of *The Statue of Liberty syndrome*, whether they realize it or not, are placing terrible demands upon themselves. They are doomed to suffer frustration because their claims are impossible to achieve. The pathology that we deal with (even the less severe types) is generally generations in the making, and it is therefore grandiose on the part of anyone to believe that he or she can help more than a small fraction of those who come our way.

We generally interview parents of our child patients, and often get information about grandparents. But we rarely get information about earlier generations. Yet, it is naive to assume that the influences of these ancestors have not played a role in our patients' pathology. Furthermore, we are often impotent to change the formidable social and cultural factors that are likely to have played a role in the development of our patients' psychopathology. Accordingly, therapists do well to have very modest goals in regard to the treatment of their patients. We should be comfortable with small changes. To believe that we can do more is to impose upon ourselves goals that may be extremely frustrating for us. The therapist's goal should be that of *trying*. The therapist should be able to say, after a failure, that he or she has worked to the best of his or her ability. That is all that we can ask of ourselves and that is all that our patients should be asking of us.

Those who are afflicted with *The Statue of Liberty syndrome* are welcomed by various individuals in our society. Jails are overcrowded and judges are happy to learn about people who claim that they will bring about the prevention of criminal recidivism. School principals are happy to "get off the hook" by telling complaining parents that a troublemaking child is "in therapy." Even worse is the principal who tells parents that if their child does not go into therapy he or she will be discharged from the school. (This is an extremely misguided statement and compromises significantly the likelihood of the child's being helped by treatment.) Last, therapists who try too hard are likely to defeat their own purposes because the pressures placed on the patient are apt to lessen the likelihood that treatment will be effective.

I have discussed here, somewhat briefly, some of the elements that I consider central to the meaningful therapist-patient relationship. In Chapter Three I will elaborate upon these and discuss in detail other factors I consider to be important.

THERAPY—AN EDUCATIONAL EXPERIENCE

In the context of a good therapist-patient relationship, the therapist helps the patient learn better how to deal with the fundamental problems and conflicts of life with which we all are confronted and must deal in the course of our existence. After a detailed study of the factors operative in bringing about change in psychoanalysis (one form of psychotherapy), H. Strupp (1975) concluded that the most important elements in bringing about therapeutic change were the "lessons in constructive living" that the patient learned. I am in full agreement with Strupp on this point. The more judiciously and intelligently a person deals with the problems of life, the less likely it is that the individual will resort to pathological modes of adaptation. Therapy, more than anything else, should enhance one's capacity to deal with life's challenges. Therapy, more than anything else, involves helping people learn how to deal with these inevitable problems. The younger the patient, the more guidance, advice and instruction the therapist should be willing to provide, and the older the patient, the more the therapist should facilitate the patient's finding his or her own solutions to these problems. However, even with the most mature adults, some guidance and instruction is warranted *after* the patient has made every reasonable attempt to re-solve the problem him- or herself. Accordingly, the therapeutic process is very similar to the educational.

The Therapist as Teacher

This similarity between the educational and therapeutic processes goes further. An important determinant of whether a student will learn from the teacher relates to whether the student will identify with the teacher. Teachers who are bored with teaching or unmotivated and watch the clock throughout the day are not likely to teach their students very much. In contrast, teachers who are enthusiastic, who genuinely enjoy learning and teaching what they themselves have learned, are much more likely to impart knowledge to their students. The former teach little, the latter are likely to create an atmosphere in which their students are swept up in the learning process. An important factor in this process is that of identification with the teacher. Children in the classrooms of the enthusiastic teacher want to "join in on the fun," and they thereby imitate the teacher in order to derive similar enjoyments. We learn best from those we admire and respect, and we are going to learn little from those who produce little desire for identification and emulation. Worse yet is the teacher who is feared. She not only teaches her students little, if anything, but may contribute to a generalized distaste and revulsion of the educational process and the development of psychopathology as well.

The Levels of Therapeutic Learning

Intellectual and Emotional Learning   The therapeutic learning process occurs at many levels. I believe that the *least* efficacious is the intellectual. An intellectual insight acquired by the patient is, however, more useful than one provided by the therapist. Classical analytic treatment focuses heavily on the intellectual. It is based on the theory that the primary way of bringing about clinical change is to help the patient gain conscious insight into the unconscious processes that are bringing about the psychopathology: "Where there is unconscious, there shall conscious be." As will be discussed in detail throughout this book, I believe that this focus on intellectualization robs both the therapist and the patient of more predictably therapeutic experiences. When emotions are associated with intellectual learning, there is a greater likelihood of change. Classical analysts appreciate this and recognize that an emotional loading adds clout to an intellectual insight and is more likely to be remembered.

The Metaphor Metaphorical communications are especially potent. Aristotle recognized this long ago and considered the metaphor to be the richest and most valuable form of verbal communication (Poetics, 1459a):

> The greatest thing by far is to be a master of the metaphor; it is the one thing that cannot be learned from others; and it is also a sign of genius, since a good metaphor implies an intuitive perception of the similarity in the dissimilar.

A metaphor is basically a figure of speech in which two entities, which have no intrinsic relationship with one another, are equated. An example of a metaphor would be: "He is a rock!" There is no intrinsic relationship between a rock and a particular man. However, when one equates them, one provides a statement that is richer than the two separate entities that are being equated. The whole here is indeed greater than the sum of its parts. "She is a flower" is another example of a metaphor. Probably the greatest creator of metaphors in the English language was William Shakespeare. One of my favorites is from *Macbeth*. One could say that life is transient and that before you know it, it's over. However, one could also say, as does Macbeth (v, 5):

> Out, out brief candle!
> Life's but a walking shadow, a poor player
> That struts and frets his hour upon the stage
> And then is heard no more: it is a tale
> Told by an idiot full of sound and fury,
> Signifying nothing.

The same message, but obviously Shakespeare's way of putting it makes the initial statement weak and sterile. I do not believe that the creation of metaphors can be taught. The ability to see linkages where others do not and to make the proper selections so that rich metaphors are formed is a talent that I believe to be inborn. Of course, we therapists do not have the creative capacity of William Shakespeare, and our ability to form metaphors is far more limited. However, to the degree that we can utilize them in our work, to that degree we will enhance the efficacy of our therapeutic communications.

Metaphors become even more enriched when incorporated into the context of allegories, anecdotes, and other narrative forms. This is not only true of children who traditionally enjoy stories, but of adults as well in that they will often learn better from a well-selected anecdote or the relating of an experience by the therapist. M. Erickson (J. Haley, 1973) was especially appreciative of the value of the metaphor in therapy. My main criticism of his work, however, is that the metaphors he would often present to his patients appeared to be "pulled out of the sky" and were not, I suspect, as carefully tailored to the needs of the patient as he professed. I say this because the information upon which he would often select his metaphor was often miniscule and, accordingly, his metaphorical presentations often had a high degree of speculation.

Conceptualizations and Abstractions vs. Concrete Examples
Conceptualizations and abstractions are far less potent vehicles for clarifying issues than specific concrete examples, especially examples that relate to the patient's immediate experiences. Many therapeutic interchanges are quite sterile and therapeutically unproductive because the therapist and the patient are speaking at abstract levels. It is much harder to pay attention to an abstraction, which cannot be visualized, than a concrete example, which can. One of the reasons why philosophy textbooks are so boring to students is that they dwell to a significant degree on abstractions. In contrast, the traditional detective story is very specific and concrete regarding the details it provides and is therefore much more likely to maintain the reader's interest. If a patient, for example, talks about being depressed, the patient is speaking at a conceptual level. The therapist does well, in response, to ask the patient what he or she is specifically depressed about, what in concrete terms are the exact thoughts and feelings that the patient is experiencing and, even more important, to focus on the specific situations that have brought about the depressed feelings. The best way to alleviate the psychogenic components in the depression is to focus in detail on the specific concrete events that have contributed to it.

The Experience The most potent mechanism for modifying behavior is the experience. The old proverb, "A picture is worth a thousand words," is well known. I would add to this, however, that "An experience is worth a million pictures." To the degree that the therapist can provide experiences, to that degree will he or she be able to bring about clinical change. This hierarchy of the efficacy of the various forms of learning is well epitomized by the following comparisons. Let us take, for example, the experience of reading a play. Reading the play is purely a visual experience, both at the level of reading the written page and the visual imagery that is engendered by such reading. It is primarily an intellectual experience, although some emotions may certainly be engendered. Let us compare this with attending a theatre and observing the play being acted. It is likely that the individual will be more affected by the play because an auditory modality of input has now been added to the visual experience associated with reading the play. If one becomes an actor in the play, then one is even more likely to remember its messages. The reason for this is that one is now adding physical action to the visual and auditory modalities of input. With each additional modality, there is a greater likelihood that the story will have an impact. However, the emotions being exhibited in the play are feigned. No matter how convincing the actor is, the emotions are still turned on and off in accordance with the dictates of the script. The actor is still play acting. Compare this with emotions that are caused by an actual experience. Here, the reactions are engendered by reality and are even more likely to be recalled in the future.

Therapy, more than anything else, should be an experience. It is an experience that is one slice of life. It is a living experience in which one has an ongoing encounter with a person who is more honest than any other individual with whom one may be involved in one's lifetime. Our best friends may hesitate to criticize us, lest they hurt our feelings. Therapists criticize benevolently with the purpose of helping remove those behavioral manifestations that alienate others and that interfere with our dealing most effectively with the problems in life with which we are all confronted.

Although the therapist's specific knowledge and experience may increase the likelihood that an involvement with him or her will be therapeutic, such encounters were taking place long before Sigmund Freud was born. Let us take, for example, a young woman, in her late twenties, who comes to therapy because she is not yet married and is concerned that she may never meet a man with whom she will have a satisfactory marital relationship. Let us assume that the therapist is a man in his late fifties, approximately the age of her father. Let us assume further that she reports early in treatment that her father was particularly cruel and rejecting and that she learns in therapy that her anticipation of similar rejection from young men is playing a role in her avoidance and rejection of them. In the course of her treatment she discusses with the therapist her male relationships, and this insight helps her avoid a repetition of her childhood experiences. The therapist is sympathetic, understanding, sensitive, and kind. At no point does he treat her in a way similar to her father. Let us assume that her treatment was successful and she ultimately marries a man with whom she has a stable and rewarding relationship.

I believe that the *insights* this woman gained in her therapy were far less important in bringing about the therapeutic change than the *experience* she had with the benevolent and sympathetic therapist. Without necessarily having any conscious insight into the process, the experience with the therapist enabled her to reduce and possibly even remove her generalization that all men would treat her similarly. Similarly, the therapist's discouraging her from involving herself in the same pathological pattern with other young men increased the likelihood that she would have *experiences* with men who were more kindly disposed to her. In short, then, I believe that the major elements in bringing about change in this woman had less to do with intellectual insights and more to do with the quality of the therapist and the men that she subsequently encountered. Had the therapist been aloof, cool, and unsympathetic, she probably would not have changed—all her insights notwithstanding. I would speculate further that this experience was had by a multiplicity of women long before Sigmund Freud's birth. With similar upbringing they too had difficulties in their relationships with young men. However, if they had the good fortune to form a relationship with an older man (an uncle, teacher, or mentor, etc.), then this might have modified their views of men and lessened the likelihood that they would carry the generalization over into their courting patterns. All this may have occurred without conscious awareness and was certainly much more likely to have taken place outside of conscious awareness in the days prior to psychoanalysis. In short, it was the experience that was the best teacher, not the insight.

CONCLUDING COMMENTS

The material presented in this chapter represents a statement of my views regarding the basic factors that contribute to the development of psychogenic symptoms and the fundamental elements operative in the psychotherapeutic process. This "blind man" sees the elephant this way in the mid-1990s. It was not the way I saw things in the mid-1950s, 1960s, 1970s, and 1980s. I have learned things over the years, and I suspect some modifications of my present position by the year 2000. My purpose here has been to present a relatively short statement of my views on these issues. Throughout the course of this book, however, I will be elaborating on all of these points with many clinical examples. Throughout this book, as well, I will be making reference to these principles because they are the basic foundation of just about everything that is described herein.

There is an old Hasidic saying: "A good man is one who knows what he feels, says what he means, and means what he says." The statement could very well serve as a central therapeutic goal. Although less applicable to children's than to adult's therapy, it epitomizes the kinds of qualities that therapy attempts to engender in patients. We want our patients to know what their feelings are and to be able to use them judiciously. We want them to be forthright and express themselves honestly. And we want them to be viewed as credible human beings who have the courage to follow through with their convictions. Therapists who possess these qualities themselves are more likely to engender them in their patients. Passive therapists, those who hide behind "blank screens," those who are fearful of appropriately revealing themselves, and those who are vague and/or indecisive, are not likely to be of much assistance in helping their patients reach these goals.

THREE

The Therapist–Patient Relationship

There is no psychotherapy without a genuine relationship. For a relationship to be genuine it must be human. Therapy without humanity is a farce, a caricature, an act, a waste of time for both—even though one party may derive some financial gain from the charade.

R. A. Gardner

THE THERAPIST'S PERSONALITY

The therapist's personality, probably more than any other factor, is the ultimate determinant as to whether therapy will be successful. The personality qualities that contribute to one therapist's being successful with children and another's failing are vital to understand and yet we know little about them. To the best of my knowledge, there is a paucity of articles in the psychiatric and psychological literature describing in depth this crucial entity—especially with regard to the factors that bring about a good therapist-patient relationship and how it can be achieved. Yet we continue to neglect what may very well be the most important focus for our investigations. Many believe that the reason why therapists of different persuasions can report successes is not that the techniques utilized are so valuable or that one technique is better than another, but that subtle personality characteristics of the therapist have been the crucial elements in bringing about the described improvements. Thus, we are ill-equipped to evaluate and compare the efficacy of various therapeutic techniques if we remain ignorant of the personality characteristics of the therapists who have been using them.

Language Limitations

In this chapter I will attempt to delineate some of the personality qualities that contribute to a good therapist-patient relationship. I recognize that in attempting to do so I am handicapped not only by our ignorance of the processes but by the limitations of our language, which does not have specific words for many of the characteristics I will attempt to delineate. Our English language, the richest on earth, with almost five hundred thousand words, is still inadequate to define certain phenomena accurately. For example, my dictionary defines *déjà vu* as "the illusion of having previously experienced something actually being experienced for the first time." It informs me, as well, that in French *déjà vu* means "already seen." Most of us have had, at some time or other, a *déjà vu* experience. And we know how insufficient that definition is. There are other qualities in the experience that make the words *already seen* banal to the point of being misleading. The dictionary says nothing of the *uncanniness* of the experience, the altered state of consciousness, the futile quest for the time and place of the alleged original experience, and the frustration in not being able to pinpoint it. Even my description of these other elements in the phenomenon does not convey accurately what it is actually like to a person who never had the experience. It does not enable him or her *really* to know what I am talking about. My term *uncanny* is in itself too vague, too inaccurate, to convey truly the feelings.

Our language is replete with words that only purport to describe the phenomena they are labeling. When people use such words, we get fooled into thinking that they are talking about the same thing. Take the word *orgasm*, for example. In interviewing a woman suspected of frigidity, a therapist generally does not rely on a yes or no answer to the question of whether she has ever achieved orgasm. He goes by the *quality* of her response—by whether the affirmative answer communicates: "I know exactly what you're talking about." If she says, "I think so," or "Maybe," then the therapist knows that she hasn't. There are many other examples of such words: *beautiful, schizophrenia, cool, rapport, irony,* and *love.*

I recognize that the qualities that I will attempt to describe are not those that a therapist can easily acquire. With some, the recognition of their absence may be a step toward their acquisition. Others may have to accept their deficiencies. However, this need not mean that they must necessarily discontinue doing child therapy. No therapist can possibly have *all* the qualities that one should ideally possess to be an effective child therapist. However, therapists who possess few of these qualities are not likely to work successfully with children.

Liking Children

The first, and possibly most important quality, is that of genuinely liking children. I cannot imagine someone's involving him- or herself meaningfully and effectively in the field of child therapy without basically liking children. I am not suggesting that he or she needs to like children *all the time*; in fact, I would be distrustful of anyone who claimed that he or she did. (Children inevitably cause us periods of resentment and exasperation.) Rather, I am only suggesting that a significant percentage of therapeutic experiences with them should be benevolent and moderately enjoyable.

Projection of Oneself Into the Child's Position

Therapists must have the capacity to project themselves into the child's situation, to see the world through the child's eyes—and probably to feel the way the child feels. We know little of this phenomenon. Why is it easy for some and for others impossible? Piaget's panoramas (in which the child is asked to determine which card shows the view that the little model man in the center of the panorama sees as his position is changed) could give us information about this quality. Some would easily be able to see the view of the model, and others would have trouble. But this is only part of the phenomenon. It describes only a *visual-mechanical* aspect of the projective process; the *human elements* are far more complex. We use such terms as *sympathy* and *empathy* in our feeble attempt to describe this quality, but we still have much to learn about it—its mechanics, its psychodynamics, and the factors that play a role in its development. Does an accurate memory of one's own childhood play a role in this capacity? I think so, but as far as I know this has not been tested. And, indeed, it might be hard to evaluate accurately. *Egocentrism* (another one of those umbrella terms) may inhibit this quality. But we still have to define how. Therapists who lack this capacity to a significant degree are ill-equipped to help their patients. If they cannot view the world through their patients' eyes (not necessarily agree with their patients, however), then they are handicapped in helping them.

Treatment of the Projected Self

This phenomenon has broad implications for many aspects of treatment, for both the patient and the therapist, and has not been given the attention it deserves. For example, adults in individual therapy, who tend to see all others as harboring or exhibiting certain alienating qualities, are usually denying these same characteristics in themselves by projecting them on to others. Similarly, those who do group therapy frequently observe patient A suggest an interpretation of patient B's behavior that is totally irrelevant to B, but a clear statement of A's difficulties. This defense is well known to therapists and we most often have little difficulty detecting it. It is when we ourselves utilize the mechanism that we are less likely to be aware of it. I believe that all of us use it to varying degrees. When properly utilized, it can enhance the efficacy of our work; improperly used, it can seriously interfere with it.

Practically every therapist has been asked at some time or other, "How can you listen to that stuff all day long?" If the question is benevolently asked (and it often isn't) and if the therapist is inclined to respond seriously (and he is not often so inclined), one of the answers, if he or she is to be completely honest, is: "In treating my patients, I treat vicariously my projected self, and this is an important determinant of my interest." Although many factors certainly contribute to one's choice of psychotherapy as a profession, one that is central for most, if not all, is the desire to cure one's own pathology. Rarely is personal analysis, or other forms of therapy which the therapist may experience, enough to accomplish this goal. We are still at too primitive a level in our knowledge to use comfortably the word *cure*; at best, we usually strive toward significant alleviation of our own and our patients' difficulties. And whether previously treated or not, the therapist, I believe, continually attempts to lessen his or her own psychological problems through psychotherapeutic endeavors (whatever other purposes they serve). Without this factor operative, I do not think the therapist would maintain for long interest in the psychological minutiae that patients in treatment can often endlessly discuss. In fact, if one could indeed *cure* a prospective therapist of all neurotic problems (whatever that really means), then I question whether he or she would continue on as a therapist—so vital do I believe this mechanism to be as a motivating factor for those who do psychotherapy. There are certainly other motivating factors operative—and many of these are far less self-serving—but it is a vital one that is not given the attention it deserves. The child therapist is, in all likelihood, treating vicariously childhood problems that have yet to be resolved.

If therapists are using patients to treat themselves vicariously, may this not be detrimental to the patient? Doesn't this interfere with the patient's therapy? Does not this tendency result in the therapist's seeing things in the patient that do not exist? The questions are rhetorical. They describe real dangers in the therapeutic situation—dangers that we have not studied enough to enable us to avoid them effectively. Yet, if what I have said is true—that a certain amount of this need is necessary if the therapist is to be meaningfully interested in the patient—what is the solution to this problem? It lies, I believe, in determining that level at which the salutary use of the therapist's treatment of the projected self ends and the pathological begins. How can we learn then to make this important distinction between the helpful and detrimental use of this mechanism? It is not within the scope of this book to discuss in detail possible methods that we might utilize to make this important distinction. Elsewhere (1973c) I have proposed some techniques by which we might be able to differentiate between healthy and pathological treatment of the projected self.

Memory of One's Own Childhood

The ability to remember one's own childhood experiences deserves further emphasis. There are people who will say with all honesty that they cannot remember a thing about their lives before the age of eight, or ten, or even twelve. The person who is so repressed regarding memories of his or her childhood experiences is not likely to be an effective child therapist. Therapists have to recall how it was when they were the same age their child patient is at the time of treatment, if they are to appreciate optimally the child's situation. Child therapists have to be able to put themselves in the positions of their patients if they are to be successful. They need to be able to project themselves back in time. In addition, child therapists must be able to involve themselves in both processes, both present and past projections. Their task, therefore, is much more difficult than that of the adult therapist.

Charles Dickens, in his *The Personal History of David Copperfield* (1850), stated this phenomenon well:

> This may be fancy, though I think the memory of most of us can go farther back into such times than many of us suppose; just as I believe the power of observation in numbers of very young children to be quite wonderful for its closeness and accuracy. Indeed, I think that most grown men who are remarkable in this respect, may with greater propriety be said not to have lost the faculty, than to have acquired it; the rather, as I generally observe such men to retain a certain freshness, and gentleness, and capacity of being pleased, which are also an inheritance they have preserved from their childhood.

Excitation

I introduce discussion of the next quality anecdotally. When I was a freshman medical student, an instructor once commented to a small group of us, "You fellows are still in the 'gee whiz' phase of medicine." To which I replied, "I hope I never get out of that phase." (I would like to think I haven't.) Many gifted child therapists carry this quality with them throughout life. One such person was the late British child psychiatrist D.W. Winnicott, who exhibited many of the qualities I describe in this chapter. I had the good fortune to hear him speak on a few occasions a number of years ago and served on a panel of his discussions. To say he was enthusiastic and interested in what he was doing when he was with child patients is an undertstatment. There was a certain "wow" quality (I cannot describe it any better, but that's close to it) to him which he shared with his child patients. This was not loudly stated; he did not seem the kind of man who would loudly say, "Wow!" Rather it came through in the tonal qualities of his voice. There were intonations of excitement and of slight breathlessness—all subtle, but nevertheless there. These qualities, of course, are exhibited by all but the most sick children, and Donald Winnicott retained them to the end of his life. They must have contributed to his patients' thinking, at some level, "He's one of us, even though he's a grown-up. He gets excited about the same kinds of things we get excited about."

How this quality contributes to therapeutic change is speculative. But I shall speculate. With such a person children cannot but feel better about themselves. Here is an adult who enjoys being with them—and this cannot but raise the child's self-esteem. Because most, if not all, psychogenic symptoms are formed, at least in part, to adapt to or bolster a low self-esteem, this esteem-enhancing experience with Dr. Winnicott was salutary.

The Inner Warmth Response

The next quality of Donald Winnicott's that I wish to describe is also best introduced anecdotally—this with an incident that occurred during my residency training. I was seeing a little boy of four who had what I can best describe as an *infectious personality* (another one of those vague terms). When I would walk down the hall with him from the waiting room to my office, adults who passed us would look at him and smile. There was a *cuteness* (another one of those words) about him which engendered a heartwarming feeling in adults. I cannot say exactly what it was about the child that produced this response. I know it had something to do with his smile, his seriousness, and his little-man-trying-to-act-big quality as he strutted down the hall. Once, in the midst of a session with him, a schizophrenic woman mistakenly came to my office earlier than the appointed time. She opened the door, saw that I was still with the boy, and with a stony facial expression closed the door. I was struck by the fact that she did not smile. Although rivalrous feelings with another patient and disappointment that she could not see me exactly when she wanted may have contributed to her reaction, I believe that she was incapable of the "inner warmth" response that other adults almost invariably had to this child. (I even thought half-seriously that with this episode I might have come upon a good test for schizophrenia.)

Donald Winnicott had this "warm inner glow" response. Those who have had it know exactly what I am talking about. Those who have not may never appreciate what I am saying. We use the term *heartwarming* to describe the phenomenon. It does feel as if it comes from the chest, but this may be socially induced. We are taught that love comes from the heart, yet to the best of our knowledge the brain and often the genitalia seem to have something to do with it as well. There must be physiological correlates to the experience that can be measured: changes in blood pressure, cardiac rate, and biochemical reactions. These have yet to be identified. When with a person who enjoys such a response to him or her, the child cannot but feel: "He(she) likes me. I am likable. I give him (her) pleasure. I am worthwhile." And such responses contribute to the child's improvement.

Childlike Personality Characteristics

M.M.R. Khan (1972) describes Dr. Winnicott as having had: "A childlike clownish spontaneity (that) imbued his movements." All of us retain some childlike, even childish (the pejorative term), qualities. Some of these are probably necessary to preserve our sanity. When someone retains, as an adult, too many childhood characteristics, we call him or her "immature," "fixated at infantile levels of development," or "regressed." Where does one draw the line? Where does the normal, healthy degree end and the pathologic being? D.W. Winnicott had, without question, more than the average degree of childlike qualities. Since they were obviously so constructively used, one cannot label them pathological. Effective child therapists have, in my opinion, more such childhood residua than their adult counterparts, and these can serve them well in their work. These residua enable therapists to play unself-consciously (or less self-consciously) on the floor with their patients. They contribute to the pleasure of their work. They are a dangerous asset, these childhood residua, in that therapists may go too far in this regard when they do play therapy and accomplish more *play* than *therapy*. Where one ends and the other begins is still a relatively unexplored area. My hope is that the readers of this book—whose play therapy has been more play than therapy—will shift the balance and conduct a play therapy that is more *therapy* than *play*.

"On the Same Wavelength"

An analogy from the physical sciences may be of help in describing my next point. When a vibrating tuning fork is placed next to a nonvibrating fork of the same intrinsic frequency of vibration, the second will begin to vibrate along with the first. We know that there are people with whom we "vibrate," and there are others with whom we do not. We say, "I can't really talk to her; he understands me," or "There are times when we don't even have to say certain things; we just know what one another is thinking," or "We think alike; we're on the same track." Many young people today even use the term *vibrate* to describe this phenomenon. D.W. Winnicott vibrated with children. He was on the same wavelength as most of them. And this, I am sure, contributed to his therapeutic efficacy. But what is this phenomenon? We know so little about it. Why do we experience it with some people and not with others? Does some form of extrasensory perception have something to do with it? It is another important element in the therapeutic process that is yet to be understood. Certainly, we are more likely to be on the same wavelength with people who resemble significant figures in our early upbringing, especially our parents. I am sure that sexual attraction plays a role in many adults. Similar educational experiences are also probably operative in that our cognitive processes are very much affected by our educational experiences.

A Strong Parental Instinct

Then there are the so-called *instincts*. We speak in psychiatry and psychoanalysis about maternal instincts, but far less about paternal instincts. Dr. Winnicott, most would agree, exhibited toward his patients what appeared to be a strong paternal instinct. M.M.R. Khan (1972), refers to him as "a caring and concerned mother." What is this instinct? Why do some exhibit it more than others? Is this merely biological variation? Or can environmental factors significantly influence its expression? And how does this play a role in the child therapist's work with patients? The term *parental instinct* is only a rubric, subsumed under which are a host of qualities and personality characteristics. Feeding, protecting, touching, cleaning, loving, guiding, and enjoying are only some of these elements. Khan refers to D.W. Winnicott's generosity to his regressed patients and at times his exaggerated need in this regard. He refers to Mrs. Winnicott's reference to her husband's "illusions of munificence."

How therapeutic was Winnicott's tendency to give? When was it excessive? And by what criteria? Therapists have to be giving to some degree if they are to help their patients. But how far should they go? Where do we draw the line? There is still much we have to learn in this area. The reader interested in further comments of mine regarding qualities in D.W. Winnicott that I consider operative in his therapeutic successes should refer to my article on him (1972c) and my review of two of his books(1973d). And the reader who is interested in reading about the work of Edgar Baldock, another man whom I consider to possess qualities similar to Winnicott's, may wish to refer to his article on the therapeutic relationship (1974).

Frustration Tolerance

There are certain frustrations that child therapists must be willing to tolerate that their adult counterparts need not contend with. One such potential problem is the child's parents. They often feel threatened by the therapeutic process. Having a child in therapy may be considered proof of the parents' failure, and many defenses may be utilized to avoid coming to terms with this notion. Many parents come not because they have seen the problems themselves (they have often been denied for months to years), but because some outside agency (most often the school) has suggested psychiatric consultation. Such parents often hope to hear the child is completely normal and that the referrer was in error. Once the child is in therapy, their ambivalence may manifest itself through forgotten appointments, lateness, cancellations with meager excuses, withholding payment of bills, failure to follow through with recommendations, hostility toward the therapist, and other gambits that are consciously or unconsciously designed to undermine the treatment. Sudden withdrawal of the child from treatment is common.

At any particular time the child therapist has to keep three people involved: a child who would prefer to be playing with friends; a mother whose life is hectic enough caring for the house and other children without having to bring the patient to the therapist; and a father who could find much better ways to spend his money. If, at any point, any one of these three develops significant psychological resistances, the others are dragged down and the project fails. I often feel like I'm juggling three greasy balls and that when one of them drops, the whole act is over. Some therapists get fed up and gradually confine themselves to adult work. When in residency, one of the definitions we had of a child psychiatrist was: "someone who used to do child psychiatry." The humor stemmed from the recognition that many of our supervisors were no longer doing child therapy, merely supervising it. The general consensus was that people got tired of doing such therapy after the age of 40 or so. I passed that landmark uneventfully (with regard to my enthusiasm for child therapy) and also passed the age 50 landmark. As I write this, I am 54 and starting to get tired. Perhaps it's my age, perhaps the frustrations of the field are finally getting to me. At the same time, my interest still appears to be quite high.

However, the frustrations may be more than counterbalanced by certain gratifications that the adult therapist may not so frequently enjoy. The satisfactions of therapeutic success are more easy to come by in child work than in adult therapy. The child's problems are generally of shorter duration than the adult's and may be less deeply imbedded in his or her psychic structure. In addition, more change can be effected in the child's environment. The deleterious influences to which the child is exposed can be altered more readily—parental attitudes modified; misconceptions rectified; management advice provided; and schools, clubs, and camps recommended. Adults who come for treatment are usually deeply entrenched in their life situations. They may be locked into a bad marriage from which it is difficult to remove themselves because of children and the financial privations attendant to a divorce. And their work situation may be similarly rigid in that quitting a job or changing one's field may not be a viable option for them.

Flexibility and Creativity

Child psychiatrists must be capable of utilizing a wider variety of therapeutic techniques than those used by adult therapists and must be flexible enough to alter these at a moment's notice. They are often requested to make specific recommendations for immediate action. The child therapist may be required to take action on the spur of the moment—much more frequently than the adult therapist. The parents who ask what to do about a child's fire setting cannot be told that no immediate or specific suggestions can be given and that the child must work this through in the therapeutic sessions. The therapist must be able to say: "On the basis of what I know thus far, I suggest we try this. If it doesn't work out, there are other options. As I learn more, I hope to be in a better position to advise you." They must be comfortable providing tentative advice.

The child therapist who has had adult psychoanalytic training may be faced with a conflict. The analytic training emphasizes the importance of a very passive role, whereas in child work such passivity can be antitherapeutic and even, at times, dangerous. Accordingly, such a therapist must be able to switch readily between the two orientations. At times the two types of training may tend to contaminate one another. The analytic training may result in the therapist's being too passive in his or her work with children; and the child therapy training causes the therapist to be too active in his or her work with adults. I would not, however, recommend that the child therapist avoid psychoanalytic training in order to avoid these problems. The enrichment that psychoanalytic training can provide the child therapist far outweighs its disadvantages.

Child therapy and adult therapy differ in regard to the predictability of the process. Although there is a universe of possible communications between the adult patient and the psychiatrist, in adult treatment the participants talk to one another and there is little action. This is not the case in child therapy, where there are many more possibilities. There is much greater unpredictability, as the child is less likely to "follow the rules"of treatment. Child therapists, then, must be ever on their toes and, in addition, generally need to be much more flexible and even creative than their adult counterparts. (This is not to say that such qualities are not desirable in the adult therapist, but they are much more continually demanded of the child therapist by the patient.)

Most adult therapists find group therapy to be a useful experience for their patients. In such groups, interactions that could not be observed in individual sessions become observable to the therapist. Much more firsthand information becomes available to the therapist. Child therapists cannot generally avail themselves of this therapeutic modality. Children do not generally sit quietly in a circle and talk about their problems, especially with an orientation toward gaining insight. Rather, such discussions are predictably interrupted by horseplay, joking, and the children's general rest-lessness. *The Talking, Feeling, and Doing Game* (1973a) (described in detail in Chapter Five) provides the kind of structure that may facilitate the therapist's doing group therapy with children. Some of the difficulties of group therapy with children are somewhat obviated with this tool.

Similarly, family therapy generally entails much more conversation between the adults and teenagers than with younger children. The latter appear to have low frustration for such meetings, may easily become restless, and are not generally interested in prolonged discussions centering on why people do the things they do. Although such family discussions can certainly be useful for children with psychiatric problems, the therapeutic benefit comes not so much from the child's direct involvement with the treatment as from the changes in the adults that such meetings bring about. In short, because group therapy and family therapy are of less value to children (especially younger ones), the child therapist cannot often use these techniques with children and must utilize a variety of other modalities.

The Therapist as Parent

The question is sometimes raised as to whether it is necesary for child therapists to have had children of their own. It is certainly possible to be an effective and accomplished child psychotherapist without having had such experiences, but I believe that the lack may compromise one's therapeutic abilities. The child, when seen in an office setting, is in an artificial situation. The childless therapist has not had the experience of living and growing with children in their natural setting; fathering and mothering; worrying and scolding; changing diapers; seeing them through physical illness; handling their fights with siblings and peers; and of involving themselves in the thousands of other activities that enrich one's knowledge and appreciation of children. Childless therapists, no doubt, gain many of these experiences vicariously through their patients. They may, indeed, be able to involve themselves with their patients to a greater degree than therapists who have children of their own. These considerations notwithstanding, I believe that having one's own children enhances one's efficacy as a child therapist.

Boredom

If the therapist lacks enthusiasm and interest in his or her work, the patient will sense these feelings and will respond similarly. I cannot imagine effective therapy being done in such an atmosphere. I am not suggesting that the therapist should *never* be bored during the session (I myself get bored at times); we can't possibly be on a "high" all the time. Rather, I am suggesting that when therapists occasionally find themselves bored, they should try to look into the reasons why and attempt to rectify the situation—both for their own sakes and that of the patient. Therapists do well to avoid involving themselves in therapeutic activities that they basically do not like. To do so inevitably produces resentment which will be picked up by the child. A child cannot, in my opinion, possibly gain anything therapeutic at a time when the therapist is in such a state of mind. Some of the games and therapeutic activities I will be describing in this book have served to reduce such antitherapeutic reactions in me, and my hope is that they will serve the reader similarly.

I wish to emphasize that we cannot be all things to all people; that the personality characteristics we possess will inevitably attract some and alienate others. There have been many patients with whom, in spite of my best efforts, I have been unable to relate to in a way that I would consider therapeutically beneficial. My practice in such cases has been to inform the child and parents my belief that things are not proceeding well, and I suggest that we all together try to find out what the difficulties are and try to rectify them. At times we have been able to improve things, and at other times referral to another therapist or discontinuation of treatment has been necessary.

Comfort with Therapeutic Failure

Last, it is important that therapists be comfortable with therapeutic failure. Therapists who think that it behooves them to alleviate the difficulties of all (or most of) those who come to them, will suffer significant frustration and a deep sense of failure. Children often present with a total life of exposure (even though only three to four years old) to the detrimental influences that have contributed to their difficulties. Their parents generally have been living with their own problems for many years as well. But things do not stop there.

Not only may the pathological processes have been transmitted down numerous generations, but social and cultural processes have usually contributed as well. It is therefore grandiose of therapists to consider themselves capable of rectifying all these pathological influences, and they are assuming unrealistic obligations if they consider it their responsibility to do so. The best attitude therapists can take is that they will commit themselves to the therapeutic process and try their best to do what they can. If they can say to themselves, with regard to the unsuccessful case, that they have tried their best and possibly learned a few things that will serve them in good stead in the future, they should be able to accept therapeutic failure without undue guilt and self-recrimination. I have spoken previously (Chapter Two) about *The Statue of Liberty syndrome*. Therapists should ask themselves whether they are exhibiting manifestations of this disorder. If they are, they do well to cure themselves as soon as possible; otherwise, they are doomed to lead very frustrating lives.

FACTORS IN THE THERAPIST-PATIENT RELATIONSHIP CONDUCIVE TO BRINGING ABOUT THERAPEUTIC CHANGE

Introduction

Possessing certain qualities requisite to doing effective work with children is of little value if these qualities are not utilized in building a good relationship with the child. A good therapist-patient relationship is crucial to successful therapy. It is the focal point around which the various therapeutic experiences occur, and I cannot imagine therapy's being successful if the relationship is not a good one.

A meaningful relationship with other human beings is vital to survival. Provide a newborn infant with food, clothing, and shelter, but deprive it of the tender loving care of a mother (or her substitute) and the child will lose its appetite, become unresponsive to the environment, and may actually waste away and die. Others similarly deprived may survive infancy but may develop such severe withdrawal from others that they become effectively nonfunctioning individuals, living in their own mental worlds, and gaining whatever little gratification they can from their fantasies. The deprivation need not be overt (such as physical abandonment) but can result from psychological rejection in the form of parental withdrawal, hostility, uninvolvement, or other kinds of detrimental interaction with the child. In short, it is only through meaningful and gratifying involvement with others that we develop into human beings; without such exposure we may survive, but we cannot then be called truly human.

Meaningful relationships with others are the stuff of life. More than anything else they enrich us; without them we become shells—mere imitations of living individuals. From the moment we are born until the time of our death we need others—necessary times for solitude notwithstanding. The child in treatment has generally suffered some difficulties in the ability to form and gain gratifications from involvement with others. It is hoped that therapy will help the child accomplish this. But I cannot imagine its being successful if a meaningful relationship hasn't been accomplished between the therapist and the patient.

Time Alone Together

I can conceive of an experiment in which all patients coming to a mental health clinic were divided into three groups which were matched for age, sex, socioeconomic status, and diagnosis. Children in the first group would receive the full course of treatment indicated for their particular problems. Children in the second group would come to the clinic with a parent at a frequency that would be indicated for the treatment of their problems. However, instead of receiving therapy, the parent and child would merely sign in and then immediately return home. No therapy would be given. Those in the third group would not come to the clinic at all and receive no therapy at home either. Then, at the end of a prescribed period (such as two years), all three groups of children would be reevaluated with particular emphasis on whether there had been any improvement in the presenting problems. I believe that those children in the first group would exhibit the most improvement; those in the second group some improvement as well (but less than those in the first group), and those in the third group, least of all. I suspect that the second group would *not* be half way between the other two in regard to the degree of improvement, but closer to the first group than the third. In addition, if one studied the second group in detail to determine if there was any relationship between the distance traveled to the clinic and the amount of clinical improvement, I believe a positive correlation would be found. In other words, the longer the child had to travel to get to the clinic the greater would be the improvement. Furthermore, I would guess that the same would hold true for those in the first group as well.

We have not given proper attention to the therapeutic effects of the parent's (usually the mother's) time alone with the child as they travel to and from the therapist. Often, it may be the only time the child and mother may be able to be alone together. At home, the child must vie with siblings for mother's time and attention; when traveling to the therapist, she is a captive audience. Often the mother may bring books and games along in order to entertain the child. Sometimes they may talk together in depth, and such discussions can be extremely therapeutic. Most children's symptoms are, in part, the result of some degree of deprivation of parental affection. Spending time alone with a parent while engaged in pleasurable activities is the most specific therapy for such deprivation. Similarly, enjoyable time spent by the child with the therapist can also be therapeutic. Accordingly, even if all the child does is play games (and unfortunately this is all that does happen in some children's therapy), he or she can derive some therapeutic benefit. (This is one of the reasons, I believe, why practitioners of a wide variety of therapeutic techniques claim that their methods produce clinical improvement.) It is to be hoped that the play therapy will involve more therapy than that which can be derived from play. It is the purpose of this book to provide the therapist with some methods of enhancing this likelihood.

The Therapist's Affection
for the Patient

The therapist's affection for the child can serve to compensate for some of the privations the patient may have experienced in relationships with others. However, there are significant limitations in the degree to which the therapist can do this. After all, although the parents may exhibit formidable deficiencies, they most often are providing the child with food, clothing, shelter, protection, and guidance. Even though they may have serious psychological problems, they are in all likelihood more bonded with the child than the therapist and probably will always be. The child who has been severely deprived, so much so that there are and there never will be any bonds established with any human being, is not likely to benefit from the therapist's affection. It is the child who has suffered *some* (but not formidable) deprivation in this area who will be most likely to profit from the therapist's affection. Such affection can be ego-enhancing to the child and therefore therapeutic. In a way, it is easier for the therapist to provide the child with unadulterated affection than the parents and others may be able to give. The therapeutic situation is so structured that therapists need not have to do much of the "dirty work" entailed in raising children. Therapists don't have to change diapers, get dawdling children dressed in the morning, bring them to emergency rooms in the middle of the night, worry about them when they are not home on time, and so on. They, like the grandparents, can enjoy children in the most relaxed and nondemanding situations—when few demands and restrictions are placed on any of the parties—and so there is less chance that there will be conflicts, power struggles, and other difficulties.

I am not suggesting that the therapist should like the child all the time. It is unrealistic to expect anyone to like anyone else more than a significant percentage of the time. Children will do things at times that will irritate their therapists, bore them, and alienate them in a variety of ways. It is hoped that the therapist will use these negative reactions in constructive and therapeutic ways. I do not agree with those who hold that therapists should have "unconditional positive regard" for their patients. Those who claim that they do are either lying or just not in touch with the inevitable frustrations and irritations we experience in our relationships with all human beings—patients included. Patients who are told that the therapist "accepts" them (a condescending remark if there ever was one) regardless of what they do or say, will distrust the therapist (and justifiably so). They will recognize the duplicity inherent in such an attitude and this must be antitherapeutic. Accordingly, the optimum experience children can have in regard to their therapist's affection is that they view the therapist as someone who likes them most of the time and that when they do things that alienate the therapist, the latter will use his or her negative reactions in the service of helping them.

Intimately associated with the affection the therapist has for the child is the feeling of pleasure that the therapist may experience with the child. The child's appreciation, at some level, that he or she is capable of providing another individual with pleasure on a continual (but not necessarily uninterrupted) basis is gratifying and ego-enhancing. And this is yet another element in the therapist-patient relationship that can be therapeutic.

Taking the Child's Side
in His or Her Conflict with the Parents

There are therapists who believe that taking the child's side against parents or other authority figures is a good way of engaging the child in treatment and entrenching the therapeutic relationship. One of the earliest and most well-known proponents of this approach was August Aichhorn, a Viennese schoolmaster who tried to apply Freudian psychoanalytic techniques to the treatment of delinquent boys. In his classic *Wayward Youth* (1925) he described the difficulties that arose in such boys' treatment because they were very defiant of authority and tended to see him as another authority against whom to rebel. He found however, that if he looked at the world from their vantage point and identified with them in their antisocial attitudes, he could form a relationship with them. In words, but not in act, he expressed sympathy for their antisocial behavior. He would become a psychological ally in order to win their confidence. Once such a relationship was established he would gradually shift his position and attempt to bring about a stronger superego in the youngsters. His hope was that their desire to maintain their relationship with him would motivate them to follow along with him as he encouraged and became a model for pro-social behavior.

There is an obvious duplicity involved in such an approach, and I myself would not be comfortable utilizing it. I think that most youngsters would sense the therapist's artificiality and would thereby lose respect for him or her—and this could not but be antitherapeutic. Most therapists today would not utilize this approach.

There are therapists, however, who consider themselves to be the protectors of their child patients against the indignities they suffer at the hands of their parents. Such a position has a divisive effect on the family. It puts the child in between the therapist and the parents in a tug-of-war—and thus is antitherapeutic. To a lesser degree there are therapists who feel that they should try to take their child patients' positions whenever possible and tend to side with them in order to engage them in treatment and entrench the therapeutic relationship. I think this is an error. Children, at some level, will appreciate that the therapist's reflex support of their positions is not provided with full conviction and this will compromise the relationship. They will sense the therapist's dishonesty here.

I believe that the ideal therapeutic situation is one in which children come to view their therapists as impartial, as criticizing them benevolently when such criticism is warranted, and equally ready to criticize the parents when the therapist considers them to be in error. In the context of such impartiality, the therapist can still serve to protect child patients from irrational and inappropriate attitudes and reactions they may be exposed to. In such situations children may feel quite helpless; having someone whom the parents respect (and the ways in which this can be brought about will be discussed in Chapter Four) and who can bring about a reduction and even elimination of parental detrimental exposures can be most salutary for the child. It reduces tension and anxiety, takes a heavy burden off the child, and removes environmental influences that may be significantly contributory to the child's symptoms.

Ideally, the therapist's position should be one of providing information and advice to both parents and children. It is hoped that the parents will be receptive to the therapist's recommendations. If not, therapists should listen with receptivity to the parents' disagreements. If modification is justified, the therapist should be comfortable doing so. If the therapist remains unconvinced that his or her suggestion should be altered, the following statement should be made: "Well, this is what I think would be in the best interests of your child. Perhaps one of us may change his or her opinion in the future."

Therapists should not be viewed by the child as the manipulator of the parents but as someone who provides advice and information for them. Children should not view the therapist as someone who controls the parents, but rather as someone who provides advice and information and leaves it up to the parents to decide whether or not they wish to accept the therapist's opinions and implement his or her recommendations. If the therapist is seen as the manipulator of the parents and if the child sees the parents as being unduly dependent on the therapist, as people who hang on the therapist's every word and put them into action, the parent-child relationship is likely to be compromised. In addition, such a situation may produce in the child some discomfort with the therapist because he or she is jeopardizing the respect that the child has for the parents.

Ideally, both parents and the child should come to view the therapist as truly impartial, as attempting to be as objective as possible and as not favoring anyone. They should come to view the therapist as someone who sides with healthy behavior—regardless of who exhibits it—and benevolently criticizes unhealthy behavior—regardless of who manifests it. Generally, the criticisms tend to balance out and no one tends to feel that the therapist is prejudiced against him or her. In such an atmosphere, both the child and parents will generally come to respect the therapist. In contrast, when therapists attempt to favor the child, they will alienate the parents and lose the respect of the child, who senses the duplicity—a situation that is definitely antitherapeutic.

Child Talk

There are those (both therapists and nontherapists) who tend to use "baby talk" with children in the obvious attempt to ingratiate themselves to them. Although infants may like this sort of thing, the average child of five to six and above gets turned off by it. Children want to believe that they are more mature than they actually are; therefore, communicating with them with babyish intonations and language is alienating.

Generally, therapists should speak to a child patient as they would to an adult—with the important exception that they avoid using words that they suspect the child will not understand. Such an approach can in itself be therapeutic. Speaking to the child in this manner helps enhance self-esteem (enhancing self-esteem is one of the universal antidotes to most, if not all, forms of psychogenic pathology). It makes the child feel bigger and more mature. Avoiding the use of words children will not understand protects them from the ego-debasing experience of being talked to with words they cannot comprehend. Such exposure may result in the child's thinking: "How stupid I am. I can't understand what he(she) is saying."

To avoid using words that children cannot understand and to speak at their level, I have found certain words and expressions particularly useful. They are terms that the child is generally familiar with and they not only enhance communication but improve the therapist-patient relationship. When referring to the child's psychological difficulties I usually prefer to use words such as *worries*, *troubles*, or *problems*. One does better to use the word *scared* rather than *afraid* and *mad* rather than *angry*. Other useful words are: *mean* (rather than *cruel*), *brave* ("That was very brave of you"), *silly* (instead of *foolish*), *dirty trick*, *grown-up* (instead of *adult*), *kind* ("That was a very kind thing to do"), *big* (rather than *large*), *make believe*, *manners* ("That was very bad manners"), *mistake* ("That was a big mistake"), *pick on*, *polite* ("That wasn't very polite"), *proud* ("That must have made you very proud"), *student* (rather than *pupil*), *scold*, *scary*, *really* ("He smiled but he was really very sad inside"), *share*, *smart*, *tease*, *teenager* (the incarnation of all the desirable traits the child may aspire to acquire), *treat*, *trick*, *cry* (not *weep*), and *whisper*. When referring to other children's behavior or to a figure in a story (who may symbolically represent the patient), I have found useful such words as: *brat*, *spoiled brat*, *dumb*, *bully*, *crybaby*, *stupid*, *bad* (rather than *naughty*), *stingy*, *teacher's pet*, *temper tantrum*, *selfish*, *sissy*, *stupid*, *sore loser*, and *scaredy-cat*.

While playing a game with a child I may say such things as "Ooooh, are *you* lucky," "You're a lucky stiff," or "Boy, is this your lucky day." When things go badly for me I may exclaim: "Rats!" or "Gee, this is *really* your lucky day." And when the child wins: "And you thought you weren't good. You're really a very good player," or (while shaking the child's hand) "Congratulations. Excellent game. You played beautifully." Shaking the child's hand provides an extra dramatic touch that strengthens the effect of the message.

When a child hesitates to tell me something or tells his or her mother not to tell me, I incredulously reply: "What, keeping a secret from your *own* psychiatrist?" Emphasizing the word *own* introduces an ego-enhancing element to counterbalance the possible esteem-lowering effects of the statement. However, there is an associated quality of good humor (communicated by my gesture, facial expression, and intonations) that conveys to the child that I am not bitterly condemning him for any embarrassment over the "transgression." A stance of incredulity can help the child express thoughts and feelings that he or she might otherwise have difficulty talking about. For example, "You mean never in your *whole life* — in the seven years that you have been alive—you not once had hateful feelings toward your brother?" Emphasizing the words *whole life* tends to add a subtle dramatic quality that the children often utilize in their own talk. It is important that the therapist not be excessively condemning when expressing such surprised disbelief. It is the *quality* of the communication, more than its *content*, that will determine whether or not the message will be ego-debasing.

In a conversation in which the child expresses something that I consider maladaptive but which he or she does not recognize as such, I may say, "Do you want to know what *my* opinion is about what Robert did?" Emphasizing the word *my* tends to imply that I am not necessarily right—only that I am expressing an alternative view. The therapist's always being "right" (which is usually the case) tends to undermine the child's self-esteem and is an anti-therapeutic element in even the most well-conducted therapy engaged in by the most sensitive therapist. It is hoped that other ego-enhancing experiences will outweigh this untoward effect of the treatment. If after the ensuing discussion the child and I still differ, I do not push the point—I do not get into an argument. Rather, I say, "Well, I guess we have different opinions on that. Perhaps sometime one of us may change his(her) mind. Why don't we go on to something else?"

When a mother reports that the child has exhibited an important clinical breakthrough and is no longer exhibiting a particular pathological pattern, I will often ask the child to sit next to me (and even in my seat if he or she is small enough) and observe as I slowly and emphatically write in the chart: "I am very happy to learn that three weeks have passed now and Ronald hasn't once picked on another boy or girl. I am very proud of him and he must be very proud of himself." I may then ask him to fetch a pen from my desk (such as a Flair pen or a Magic Marker) and I then dramatically encircle the note. Sometimes I will have the child read the message aloud for further reinforcement. Similarly, when a child exhibits what I consider particularly dangerous or pathological behavior I may say, "I'm very sorry, James, but I'm going to have to write that in your chart." I will then emphatically write: "James was once again found playing with matches. I hope that I never have to write this in his chart again." These dramatically written notations serve as an added touch to whatever therapeutic approaches are being used. They add additional positive and negative reinforcement. The closer the relationship the therapist has with the child, the greater effectiveness they will have.

The Resolution
of the Transference Neurosis

Of the innumerable patterns of human interaction each person tends to select a few favorites. From earliest childhood (primarily as the result of our interaction with our parents) we develop a constellation of patterns of relating to others that are unique. As we grow older these patterns become strengthened and we tend to utilize them in preference to others that may be either absent from our repertoire or have lower priority for utilization. Some of these patterns of interaction are healthy and enhance our effectiveness in life. Others are maladaptive and often cause us significant difficulty, both personally and in our interaction with others. These patterns are strongly repetitive—almost reflexly so. Accordingly, in new situations we tend to use the old patterns even though we may suffer significantly because of our injudicious reactions.

Using psychoanalytic terminology, we tend to *transfer* onto others reactions that we had toward our parents in infancy and childhood. We tend to interact with others in a manner similar to the way we interacted with our parents. When these modes of interaction are neurotic and they exhibit themselves in the therapeutic relationship they are termed *transference neuroses*. Specifically, patients try to involve the therapist in the same pathological patterns in which they were involved with their parents and in which they try to involve others as well. Those who comply with these requests (because of their own pathological needs) maintain their relationships with the patient (they may call such individuals their "friends"); those who do not comply with the psychopathological request avoid or sever ties (and may be regarded as "unfriendly"). When the therapist refuses to involve him- or herself in the pathological pattern, the patient will generally react with resentment, anxiety, or other unpleasant thoughts and emotions. At such a point the patient may leave therapy and consider the therapist uncaring, unloving, disinterested, hostile, and so on. Or, he or she may choose to try to gain insight into what is going on and attempt to change the maladaptive pattern. Such working through is referred to as the *resolution of the transference neurosis* and is an important step in the alleviation of the patient's difficulties. It is to be hoped that once the pathological pattern of interaction is alleviated in the patient's relationship with the therapist, he or she will exhibit healthier modes of interaction in relationships with others as well.

Although child analysts differ regarding whether a child can exhibit what can justifiably be termed a transference neurosis (M. Klein, 1932; A. Freud, 1965), I believe that most children will do so if they get involved with the therapist. In other words, the deeper the child's relationship with the therapist the greater the likelihood the child will exhibit the pathological patterns of interaction and the greater the chance the child will try to involve the therapist in them. For example, a little girl who uses coyness and seductivity to get her way with adults may try to involve the therapist similarly. In response to the therapist's failure to react with the expected "affection," she may become angry, consider him or her to be mean and unfriendly, and refuse to return. However, if such a child can be engaged (and it is the purpose of this book to help the therapist accomplish this), she may be helped to appreciate and experience that there are more effective and predictably gratifying ways of relating to others. Similarly, the therapist who does not give in to a child's temper tantrums, or allow him- or herself to be bribed, or coax the pouting child, is helping the child resolve the transference neurosis.

If a good relationship is not established, the child will be less willing to tolerate the frustrations attendant to the therapist's refusal to comply with pathological requests. And the child will thereby be less likely to gain this important therapeutic benefit that can be derived from the relationship.

The Transference Cure

When patients, very early in treatment, exhibit a sudden and dramatic alleviation (and even cure) of the presenting symptoms, they are described by psychoanalysts as having exhibited a *transference cure*. Specifically, because the patient hasn't delved into the unconscious roots of the neurosis and worked out the basic problems that underlie it (something that generally takes a long time to do), the therapeutic change is usually considered specious. When this occurs extremely early in therapy (such as after the first or second session), it is understood to reflect the patient's resistance to entering into treatment:

> *Patient:* You are, without doubt, the most brilliant doctor I've ever met. Since I saw you last time, I'm one hundred percent better. I'm

feeling so good that I'm wondering whether I need any more treatment.

Therapist: But all I did was ask you some questions about your problems and get some background history.

Patient: Oh, it was much more than that, doctor. There was something about the way you asked me those questions—I don't know what it was—that made me feel so much better.

When the "cure" occurs a little later in treatment, it often relates to an attempt by patients to get the therapist to like or even love them. After all, if the primary goal of the therapist is to cure the patient then it is reasonable to assume that the therapist will love someone who helps him or her achieve quickly this goal. Of course, both of the aforementioned factors may be operating simultaneously, and others as well. Rarely is there a simple explanation for anything that occurs in psychoanalytic treatment—or any other kind of psychotherapy as well.

These specious kinds of cure are well known to most psychotherapists. Because they are generally manifestations of a pathological pattern, the term *transference cure* is generally spoken of with a certain amount of derision. This, I believe, is unfortunate because there is a useful, and often unappreciated, element in the transference cure. All patients, I believe, change partly in the attempt to ingratiate themselves to the therapist. From the very first encounter the patient has with the therapist he or she wants to be liked. (This doesn't differ in any way from all other first encounters with nontherapists.) The anxiety the patient experiences in the first session is, in part, a manifestation of the fear that he or she will be considered loathesome and unworthy because of the things that will be revealed to the therapist. As the relationship intensifies, there is usually an even greater need to be liked by the therapist. The patient has invested much time and (often) money in the project, and the reliance on the therapist to help the patient alleviate his or her difficulties is great.

I believe that one element that plays a role in patients' exhibiting therapeutic change is the desire to get the therapist to like them. Others are certainly operative. But this factor is, I believe, an important one in the early phases of alleviation of a symptom. Patients know that when they tell their therapists that improvement has occurred, the therapists cannot but feel good about themselves for their contribution to the success. (Some therapists, in accor-

dance with their theoretical position, deny having any such gratification. I don't believe them.) If the patient has it within his or her
power to make the therapist feel good, then it follows that the therapist will like the patient. After all, we generally like most those
who have the good sense to provide us with the gratifications we
seek. It is to be hoped that the new mode of adaptation will become
more deeply entrenched as the patient gains greater insights into
the causes of the symptoms and has the experience that the newer
way is the more judicious and gratifying. Then, the patient is likely
to maintain the healthier adaptation because, through knowledge
and/or experience, he or she will have developed the inner conviction that it is the preferable alternative. Ideally, the patient will then
no longer need to maintain the symptom in order to please the therapist (whom he or she will probably never see again anyway after
the treatment is over—psychological ties, fond memories, gratitude,
and other positive feelings notwithstanding).

The younger the patient the greater the likelihood he or she
will change behavior in order to please the therapist. Children are
constantly concerning themselves with the approbations of parents, teachers, and other authorities. They are constantly being told
about whether what they do and say is "good" or "bad," "right"
or "wrong." And the therapist is just another authority from whom
they usually wish to gain acceptance. It behooves the child therapist to make use of this phenomenon. It can enhance significantly
the efficacy of the treatment. Accordingly, the therapist does well
to praise the child (often profusely) for newly gained healthier
modes of behavior. It is hoped that this will help the child reach
the point where he or she engages in the healthier adaptations, both
from the inner conviction and the experience that life is much more
gratifying when he or she does so.

The Corrective Emotional Experience

In the process of working through or resolving the transference
neurosis a particularly effective therapeutic phenomenon that may
occur is the corrective emotional experience (F. Alexander and T.
French, 1946; F. Alexander, 1950). Essentially, the patient has a living
experience (often associated with a significant upheaval of emotional reaction) that alters significantly a previous pattern. For example, a girl whose father has been very punitive may generalize
and expect similar treatment from all men, including her male ther-

apist. For the therapist to tell such a child that he will treat her differently will not generally be very effective because intellectual processes only are involved in the communication. However, if the child has the living experience, over an extended period, that the therapist indeed does not react punitively then her view of men may indeed change. Her fearful reactions lessen and relaxation and trust gradually replace them. It is this combination of insight, feeling, and experience that brings about some of the most meaningful changes that can occur in psychotherapy.

When a boy cheats during a game I may say: "You know, it's no fun for me to play this game when you cheat. If you do that again I'm going to stop playing and we'll do something else." To simply discuss why the patient cheats may have some value. However, if this discussion takes place in a setting in which the patient experiences some frustration over the alienation his symptom causes, the conversation is more likely to be therapeutically meaningful. In such a discussion we might talk about whether this might be one of the reasons why children don't like to play with him, or about the futility of this way of trying to compensate for feelings of inadequacy, or about other aspects of the problem which may be of psychological significance. But, without the emotional reactions attendant to the threat of alienating the therapist and/or interrupting an enjoyable experience, such discussions are not likely to be very effective.

Identification with the Therapist

Just as children imitate their parents and acquire many of their traits (both adaptive and maladaptive), they will tend to identify with the therapist if the relationship is a good one. It is to be hoped that the personality qualities that children acquire in this way will serve them in good stead. There are those who believe that what I am saying is risky business—that such a process is dangerous and antitherapeutic. They would hold that therapists must do everything possible to present themselves as a blank screen upon which the patient's fantasies can be projected. Some believe that the therapist should encourage the child's realizing his or her "true self." Central to such a theory is that there exists such an entity—that each individual has within him- or herself a personality pattern that is blocked from free expression and that such blockage is central to psychopathological behavior. They hold that an important aspect of treatment involves helping the individual express freely these hidden personality characteristics.

Although I certainly agree that many people who are in treatment are repressed and need to be helped to express themselves (although there are many who need some repression more than anything else), I believe most people usually need to express some *specific* pent-up thoughts or feelings. I am somewhat dubious about the concept of a whole personality being hidden inside, knocking for release. Rather, I believe that certain aspects of our personality may be genetically determined (such as certain temperamental patterns as activity level, assertiveness, passivity, and curiosity); but most are environmentally induced (and even the genetic ones are subject to significant environmental modification). I see core *potentials* not core personalities. Most of our character traits, I believe, are derived from the environment—more specifically from what we learn from those in the world around us and what we acquire by imitation of significant individuals in our lives. The therapist becomes another in the series of individuals whom the child may copy, emulate, and identify with. Even the kind of therapist described above, who tries to provide the patient with a neutral atmosphere to facilitate "self-actualization," sends many subtle cues that encourage the patient to proceed in specific directions. In addition, the therapist still has a personality, and no matter how much he or she may try to suppress it, much is still revealed—much that the patient may identify with.

As mentioned, it is obviously preferable that the qualities of the therapist that patients identify with will serve them well. For example, a boy's father may have operated in accordance with the principle that admitting any deficiencies to his children will lessen their respect for him. The child, then, may take on this similar maladaptive pattern and find himself having trouble with his classwork because he cannot tolerate admitting errors. If his therapist, however, is the kind of person who can, without discomfort, admit errors when they naturally arise (to do so in a contrived situation is not only therapeutically worthless but may be antitherapeutic because it is basically dishonest), and the patient comes to see that this is a desirable and effective pattern, he may take on the quality himself. Another example. A girl may have acquired the pattern of lying (in both subtle and overt ways) as a significant part of her interactional repertoire. Observing the therapist to be one who is consistently honest and experiencing, as well, that such honesty makes the therapist's life simpler, enables him or her to enjoy the esteem of others, and has numerous other benefits, may result in the child's attempting to acquire this valuable asset herself.

Therapists traditionally encourage their patients to express their pent-up thoughts and feelings in appreciation that such expression, properly directed and utilized (not often the case [Gardner, 1968b, 1973b]), can be therapeutic. However, many therapists attempt to do this in a setting where they do little if any such expression themselves. They thereby serve as poor models for their patients and so impede the process they are attempting to achieve. Therapists who express themselves in situations where such expression is appropriate and in the best interests of the patient (and, as mentioned, without artificiality) have a much better chance of getting their patients to do so as the latter identify with them. Therapists who assert themselves and do not allow themselves to be taken advantage of serve as good models for patients who are inhibited in these areas. And it is only in the context of a good patient-therapist relationship that such salutary identifications can occur. As mentioned in Chapter Two, such identification can be risky, especially because it involves identification with the therapist's values. It is to be hoped that the therapist's values will be healthy, otherwise the therapy will do the patient more harm than good (a not uncommon occurrence, unfortunately).

The Therapist as Educator

We learn best from those we respect and admire. Disliked, hated, or disrespected teachers will teach their students little of educational value (although they may teach them something about having to tolerate a despised person in certain situations). If the therapist is basically respected, there is much that he or she can teach patients that can be of therapeutic value. One does well to compare the relationship between a therapist and a child with that between a teacher and a pupil. A teacher who is enthusiastic about his or her work and genuinely enjoys teaching will communicate to the child the message that learning can be fun. The child will thereby emulate the teacher and attempt to gain the same gratifications. In such a setting, the child will be willing to tolerate the frustrations and drudgery that are necessary if one is to truly learn. The identification with the teaching person is a central element in the healthy educational process. A teacher who basically dislikes the work is not likely to serve as such a model for children and is not likely to teach them very much. Even worse, a teacher who instills anger and fear in children not only is going to teach them little, but may very well contribute to the development of psychopathology. I believe that therapy, more than anything else, is an educational process. Although we certainly try to help our patients learn as much as they can on their own, we are also providing a significant amount of information in the course of the therapeutic process.

A. Freud (1965) strictly warned therapists against submitting to the temptation to provide child patients with information and educational communications. Such advice is like warning an internist not to submit to the temptation to provide patients with penicillin. I am in full agreement with H. Strupp (1975), who considers the central element in adult psychoanalytic therapy (and other forms of psychotherapy as well) to be what he calls "lessons in constructive living." The more competent one is in dealing with the problems in life, the less likely one will be to form symptoms in an attempt to resolve the inevitable conflicts and problems with which we are all confronted. Whether a child therapist provides such communications directly, symbolically, or through the insights into the unconscious that he or she helps the patient gain, the educational element regarding more effective living is ever there. When a therapist is admired and respected, the child will be receptive to what he or she has to say and treatment is more likely to succeed. When the therapist is bored, just putting in time to get payment, or otherwise going through the motions, little is likely to happen.

As part of the educational process the therapist helps the patient alter distortions. For example, all of us carry with us into adult life distorted concepts of the world that we blindly accept. Adherence to these dicta may cause us many difficulties and yet they may never be questioned. It is one of the purposes of treatment to help patients examine (sometimes for the first time in their lives) these premises that guide their behavior. Some of the more common ones that adult (and often child) therapists must deal with are: "No one is to be trusted," "Sex is bad," "Fun is sinful," "I must do everything to avoid criticism because all negative comments about me must be correct," "I must do everything possible to avoid anyone's getting angry at me," and "If there's a choice between another person's being inconvenienced and my being so, rather it be me." Some common dicta of childhood (which may continue throughout life) are: "Mother and father are always right," "Nice boys and girls never have hateful thoughts toward their parents," "Thoughts can harm, that is, wishing that something bad will happen to someone can make it happen," "If my mother and/or father doesn't love me very much, I can't be very good and no one can ever love me," "One fault makes you totally worthless," "There are perfect people who never make mistakes and never do anything wrong or bad," and "An unacceptable thought is as bad as an unacceptable act."

I believe that emotions related to fight and flight follow cognition and that many feelings of guilt, fear, anger, etc. can be alleviated if notions such as the aforementioned are corrected. A. Ellis (1963) holds that the correction of such cognitive distortions are the basic issues to be focused upon in psychotherapy and has coined the term *Rational-Emotive Psychotherapy* for this type of therapeutic approach. I am in agreement with Ellis that emphasis on this element is important in practically everyone's treatment, regardless of age. However, I believe that things are more complex and that many other factors contribute to symptom formation. (Although Ellis admits to other facts, he considers them far less important than cognitive distortions in producing psychopathology.)

From the earliest days of psychoanalysis S. Freud and J. Breuer (1895) considered reducing the patient's guilt to be one of the analyst's most important tasks. With less guilt, there is less repression and hence symptoms are less likely to persist. Although Freud's subsequent experience convinced him that things were far more complex (some have yet to read his later work), the concept is still valid if one considers it to be one of the possible contributing factors in some patients' difficulties. Partly by virtue of the therapist's position of authority and his or her experience in matters of things such as guilt, patients become convinced that their urges are very common, if not universal, and that the difference between themselves and others is not so much that they have the particular thoughts and feelings, but that they feel guilty over them. In essence the analyst communicates to the patient: "You're still acceptable to me, even though you have those ideas." (Condescending elements in the communication notwithstanding, the message is often helpful.)

In my work with children who need some loosening up of their superegos I will make such comments as: "Most children I know would get very angry when something like that happens. I guess you must have been pretty mad also," "I can't believe that somewhere, someplace, you weren't a little bit angry when that happened," "So what's so terrible about *wanting* to do that? You know wanting is not the same as doing."

Many children I see, however, do not need any loosening up of their consciences. They have what A.M. Johnson (1949, 1959) called "super-ego lacunae," that is, like Swiss cheese they seem to have holes in the part of the brain where the superego is (I speak figuratively, of course). Again, as part of the therapy of such children cognitive changes have to be made. Some comments that I may make in the service of this goal: "That's terrible. She really must have felt bad after you ripped up her new kite," and "I really don't think you could have felt very good about yourself getting 100% on that test after copying most of the answers from the children around you."

Most psychopathological symptoms are developed, in part, in an attempt to enhance and compensate for feelings of low self-worth. However, they are misguided solutions and usually result in the individual's feeling even worse about him- or herself than before—temporary ego-enhancement notwithstanding. The boy who feels unpopular may attempt to gain respect and admiration by boasting about various exploits, travels, etc. However, the fear of exposure and possible guilt he may feel generally result in his feeling even worse about himself than before. And if (as is often the case) others learn of his duplicity, his social position is further worsened. As part of the therapy of such symptoms the therapist does well to inform the child of the injudiciousness of his mode of compensation. For the lonely child who "clowns" in the classroom, I might say: "I know you think that clowning around in class gets the kids to like you. And I know you think that their laughing at you proves this. However, I believe that although you're good for laughs, they really don't like you in other ways. They still don't seem to invite you to parties nor do they seem to want to see you after school." To the bully, I might say: "I know you think you're quite a big shot when you beat up those little kids. But deep down inside, you know that there's nothing so great about it and that must make you feel kind of bad about yourself," "You think the kids think you're hot stuff when you go around beating up lots of kids. Some of them may; but others, I am sure, don't like you at all. They feel sorry for the children you're hitting and I'm sure you've noticed how they stay away from you." Although these comments can be very bitter medicine to swallow, they are accepted if the patient has a good relationship with the therapist. In addition, as mentioned, the therapist's attitude is more important than the content in determining whether his or her comments will alienate a patient. When benevolently communicated in the context of a firm relationship the most painful confrontations may be accepted.

All patients, regardless of their age, have to be helped in treatment to gain a clearer view of their parents. As children, we tend to operate on the principle: "If it's good enough for them, it's good enough for me." We tend to incorporate most if not all of their traits—healthy and unhealthy. We swallow the whole bag, without separating the good from the bad. Therapy, in part, involves making (often very belatedly) these vital discriminations. And the child therapist has the opportunity to provide this at a time when it can do the most good, at a time before the deleterious results of such indiscriminating incorporation and acceptance have had a chance to become deeply entrenched. Children have to be helped to appreciate that their parents, like all other human beings (including the therapist), are not perfect. We all have our deficits. Helping children become clear regarding which personality traits of their parents are assets and which are liabilities can be very useful. And the therapist is in a unique position to provide such information. (This, of course, may require some advance work with the parents; but if the relationship with them is a good one [and I will discuss in Chapter Seven the ways that may help bring this about], their cooperation can often be relied upon.

The phobic child of a phobic mother can be told: "You know that your mother has many fears that she herself realizes are not real. She knows that there's nothing to be afraid of in elevators or crowded places, but she just can't help herself. She'd prefer not to have these fears and that's why she's seeing a psychiatrist." Ideally, it can be helpful to get the mother herself to verbalize to the child comments such as these. (The reader interested in a detailed account of such parental divulgences in the therapy of a phobic child may wish to refer to Chapter Sixteen of my text *Therapeutic Communication with Children* [1971a]). The child of divorce can be told: "Your father can be counted upon to give your mother the money she needs to take care of herself and the children. However, as you know, he's not very reliable when it comes to showing up for appointments on visiting days. This doesn't mean that he doesn't love you at all. It does mean that he has less love for you than a father has who does show up all the time. This doesn't mean that you are unlovable or that no one else can love you more. You still have many people who like being with you and you can spend time with them when your father doesn't show up."

I introduce my next point anecdotally. A number of years ago Listerine mouthwash was advertised with the slogan "Your best friend won't tell you." In the typical pitch a young girl cannot understand why dates persistently reject her even though she is bright, pretty, etc. Finally, she realizes that *bad breath* is driving them away! Happily, she chances on Listerine, washes her mouth with it, and the boys come flocking. I believe that therapists should be better than one's best friend. They should be able to tell their patient things that even their best friends will hesitate to reveal. And if the therapist's motivation is benevolent and his or her timing judicious, he or she should be able to do so with only occasional difficulty or hesitation.

To put it another way. Robert Burns (1786) once wrote:

> Oh wad some power the giftie gie [give] us
> To see oursels as others see us!

It is the therapist's job to help patients see themselves as others see them. And this is one of the significant benefits that all patients, regardless of age, can derive from treatment. Patients should be able to gain, as well, what Harry Stack Sullivan (1953) called "consensual validation" of their views of the world. For example, a child can be told: "You think that the kids really like you when they play with you after you give them candy. If you think about it, I think you'll agree that they don't play with you *unless* you give them candy. I suspect you're doing things that turn them off." And if the patient agrees: "I wonder what those things might be?"

Another can be told: "You always seem to want your way when you're here in the office. You always seem to want to do only those things you want. You never seem to care about what your mother or father or I would like to do or talk about. If you act this way with friends, perhaps that's why they don't want to play with you." Another example: "You say you're sorry in the hope that a person will no longer be bothered or angry about what you've done. Although people may *say* that they accept your apology and that they're not angry, *deep down inside they really still are*. Even though you've told your father that you're sorry that you broke the television set, I think he's still angry that it's cost him all that money to

fix it." (I often suggest that children who utilize this common ma-
nipulative device [invariably taught by parents] read my story "Say
You're Sorry" in my book of psychologically oriented children's
stories, *Dr. Gardner's Stories About the Real World* [1972a].)

Part of the confrontational process involves helping children
gain a more accurate picture of their assets and liabilities (both
inborn and acquired). The child with a neurologically based co-
ordination deficit should be discouraged from intensive involvement in competitive sports (although special training and exercises
preparing for minimal to moderate involvement may be indicated).
In the earliest years children's views of themselves are acquired
from what H.S. Sullivan called "reflected appraisals" (P. Mullahy,
1970). In essence, children come to view themselves in accordance
with information about them provided by significant figures in their
lives, especially their parents. A four-year-old boy runs into the
house crying, "Mommy, the kids all call me stupid." Mother replies,
"You're not stupid. You're very smart. Although you're four you
can write your name, count to 25, and you know nickels, dimes,
and quarters. He's the one who's stupid, if he calls you stupid."
The child leaves the house reassured. As he grows older the child
generally gathers information from others (teachers, neighbors,
peers, etc.) that may modify and expand this information—which
become his criteria for judging his self-worth. It is to be hoped
that his data will be accurate and it is one of the therapist's jobs to
help correct any distortions that may have arisen.

Last, it is part of the therapeutic educational process to introduce to children alternative modes of adaptation to those
pathological and self-defeating ones that they may be utilizing.
These options may never have occurred to the child, nor may he
or she ever have been introduced to them. For example, in a boy's
family, denial of or flight from awareness of one's deficiencies may
have been the only reactions. Such a child must be helped to appreciate the value of dealing directly with one's deficits and he must
be encouraged to try this alternative to see for himself its advantages.

Intimacy and Self-Revelation

When we use the term *intimacy*, we are generally referring to a
close personal relationship. I consider a central element in the intimate relationship to be the revelation of personal thoughts and

feelings which one would generally not reveal indiscriminately to others. The revelation, however, is made in a situation where one anticipates a benevolent and/or understanding response by the listener. Without the freedom for such self-revelation the term intimacy, in my opinion, does not apply. Intimate revelations tend to bring people closer. The one to whom the information is divulged generally feels flattered by the revelation, especially because he or she has been selected from many possible listeners. Also, intimacy cannot be a one-way arrangement. Both individuals must feel comfortable with such revelations. Unilateral revelation is not properly called intimate. Accordingly, many, if not most, therapist-patient relationships are not, by the above definition, intimate. They are generally one-way arrangements in which the patient reveals all (the ideal to be achieved) and some therapists believe that it behooves them to reveal nothing (or as close to nothing as is humanly possible). Whatever benefits may be derived from such an arrangement (and I do not deny that there are some), it cannot reasonably be referred to as an intimate relationship.

This situation presents dilemmas for therapists. If they reveal more of themselves, in order to enhance the intimacy of the relationship, they are going to contaminate blank-screen associations. In addition, there is the risk that the patient's time will be used more for the benefit of the therapist than the patient, especially if the revelations focus on problems of the therapist's. This easily becomes exploitive of the patient. I believe there is some point between these two extremes where there is a proper balance of self-revelation by the therapist and self-revelation by the patient. The vast majority of the revelations should be made by the patient, but not every revelation provided by the therapist need be viewed as unnecessary utilization of the patient's time or exploitation of the patient by the therapist. Such revelations by the therapist—judiciously provided—can be therapeutically beneficial. They bring the two individuals closer, entrench the relationship, and thereby strengthen the foundation upon which therapy rests.

It is difficult to state specifically when the revelations are judicious and when they are not. There are some guidelines, however. As mentioned, a revelation made by the therapist—whose primary purpose is to use the patient for assistance in dealing with the therapist's own problems—is clearly contraindicated. Also, if a significant amount of the patient's time is used for such therapist revelations, then this too is exploitive of the patient. One of the best guidelines is that the revelation should have immediate benefit to the patient's treatment. A personal experience of the therapist's that may help the patient gain insight into his or her problems at that point would be in this category. As mentioned in Chapter Two, metaphorical, anecdotal, and experiential communications often provide a useful vehicle for communicating important therapeutic messages. And the experiences and anecdotal material provided by the therapist can very much be in this category.

Another guideline is that the divulgence of such material should not be contrived or artificial. Rather, it should flow from the natural course of the material provided in the session. Obviously, this guideline is not being followed if the therapist initiates such divulgences at the beginning of the session. The Talking, Feeling, and Doing Game (1973b), to be described in detail in Chapter Five, provides therapists with many opportunities to divulge information about themselves in a noncontrived manner. After all, the card provides the opportunity to make such revelations and, in accordance with the rules of the game, if the therapist doesn't answer the question, he or she does not get a reward chip!

There is another aspect to the therapeutic benefits of the therapist's self-revelations that is particularly applicable to child therapy. Children generally enjoy thoroughly hearing details about events that occurred in their parents' lives during their childhood. A child will commonly ask a parent, "Mommy, tell me about how things were with you when you were my age and living with grandma and grandpa." Such information is generally of great interest to children and the divulgence of it strengthens the parent-child bond. Similarly, therapists who judiciously provide such information about their own childhoods can also strengthen the therapist-patient relationship with such revelations. What is lost by the resultant contamination of the blank screen is more than counterbalanced, I believe, by the therapeutic advantages related to the strengthening of the therapist-patient bond that such divulgences create. Furthermore, the therapist is thereby serving as a model for the child to reveal his or her own feelings and will thus increase the likelihood that the child will be freer to provide such revelations. Last, when such revelations involve the therapist's describing shortcomings and deficiencies, this too can be therapeutic. It helps reduce the idealization and idolization of the therapist that can be so antitherapeutic. It makes the therapist more of a real human being who has both assets and liabilities—just like the rest of

the world. Viewing the therapist as perfect will contribute to patients' lowering of feelings of self-worth as they invariably compare
themselves unfavorably with their perfect, or nearly perfect, therapists. This too is antitherapeutic. And children, especially, already
feeling so impotent in their relationships with adults, are more
likely to benefit from such revelations.

The Role of Seduction

Generally, at some point during the introductory lecture of one of
my courses on child psychotherapy, I ask the students if they are
familiar with two main forms of reasoning: *inductive* and *deductive*.
They usually are. I then tell them that in doing child psychotherapy
one must utilize a third form of reasoning: *seductive* reasoning.

Children (and to a lesser extent, adults) do not come to therapy
motivated to gain insight into the psychodynamic processes that
underlie their problems. In fact, they generally do not consider
themselves to have difficulties. It is the parents, teachers, and other
powerful authority figures who have decided that the child has
them. If one were to ask the average child who comes to treatment
what he or she *really* wants of the therapist, he or she would probably say: "Well, doctor, if you really want to know what I want, I'll
tell you. First of all, please get those teachers off my back. Tell them
to stop hounding me to do my homework and tell them to stop
getting angry at me when I don't turn it in. And if I do turn it in,
and it's sloppy or has food stains on it, tell them to still accept it
and give me a good grade. Also, tell them to stop disciplining me
when I horse around in the classroom and don't cooperate. Tell
them not to punish me by making me stay after school and tell them
not to send me to the principal's office when I fool around in the
classroom. Get my mother and father off my back also. Tell them
to stop bugging me about turning off the television set and doing
my homework. Tell them not to punish me when I start fights with
my brother and sister. Tell them not to make me go to bed when
they want me to and let me stay up as late as I want, watching
television or doing anything else I want. Tell them to stop calling
me in off the street to eat supper. Tell them to stop making me take
baths and showers. Tell them to stop making me go for religious
training after school, to take music lessons, and other things like
that. And then, doctor, when you've done all those things for me, tell
them to stop taking me here."

Of course, there is no child who is going to be so honest, nor will most children be so articulate. However, every single cell in the child's body is giving me this message. We child therapists are continually competing with after school activities, playing with friends, television, or just "hanging around doing nothing." The competition is formidable and it behooves us to rise to the challenge and to recognize the enormous competition against which we are working. The seductive process is in the service of this goal.

But even those children who do recognize that they do have some problems do not clearly appreciate how the things we want them to do in our offices are going to bring about an alleviation of their troubles. This is not surprising, because we ourselves are not clear about the relationship between our therapeutic approaches and the changes we hope to effect with them. This book is an attempt to present my ideas about this relationship but, as mentioned, we still do best to view ourselves like the blind men and the elephant, groping for some understanding in what is a very mysterious process.

The child therapist does well to avoid trying to derive a statement from the child about the exact nature of his or her difficulties, let alone extracting a vow on the child's part regarding his or her desire to alleviate them. A. Freud (1965) considered it important to get children to the point where they had insight into the fact that they had problems before they could be considered candidates for psychoanalysis. Furthermore, once they had gained insight into this fact, she then proceeded to the step of helping them gain motivation to analyze their difficulties. She did not consider analysis to be possible before these two steps were accomplished. I am dubious about her reported successes in these areas. I suspect that many of the children who had presumably gained such insight and motivation were parroting what they believed she wanted to hear. And this, of course, is antitherapeutic in that the child is basically lying to the therapist. I do not attempt to obtain testimonials from children regarding their insight into their problems and motivations for treatment. Even when I do get such testimonials, I do not take them too seriously. Generally, I view them to be attempts on the child's part to ingratiate him- or herself to me or to comply with parental requests. One should be thankful that the child is coming and hope that, in the course of the therapeutic experience, some benefit will be derived.

Fun If children aren't coming primarily to alleviate their problems, then why else are they coming to the therapist's office? The word that answers that question better than any other is *fun*. I believe that the therapist who does not provide a significant amount of fun for the child patient (I refer only to the prepubertal child in this discussion; much of what I say here is *not* applicable to the adolescent) is not likely to keep the child in therapy for very long; or, if the child does continue to come, little will be accomplished. Children are extremely hedonistic; they are not particularly renowned for their willingness to suffer discomforts in the present in the hope of enjoying future rewards. (Adults are not particularly famous in this department either, but many of us do acquire the capacity.) In addition, the therapist is often competing for the patient's time with the child's friends and enjoyable after school recreational activities. It behooves therapists, then, to make the sessions as enjoyable as possible. This does not mean that they should reduce themselves to the level of clowns or function as playground directors. (The observer should not be able to ask: "To do this, he (she) had to become a doctor?") Rather, they must weave the therapy into the play and other enjoyable experiences provided the child. They must make the therapy an intrinsic part of the enjoyable experience. The therapy and pleasurable experience must be the warp and woof of the same fabric. They must so sweeten the medicine that there is little, if any, evidence of its sour taste. ("Just a spoon full of sugar helps the medicine go down.") If they use play therapy, it should be both *play* and *therapy*, but more therapy than play. All too often it is only *play* rationalized as therapy. It is the necessity to combine art and science (more art than science) that is child therapists' greatest challenge, but it can also provide them with their greatest gratifications.

I refer to these factors that attract children into involving themselves in the therapeutic activities as the *seductive* elements in child therapy. They not only serve to keep the child coming but, in addition, enrich the therapy and make it far more likely that the child will find the experiences with the therapist meaningful. If we compare pure intellectual insight to the words of a play on the printed page, then the true therapeutic experience would be analogous to actually having the experience. Other analogies come to mind: the difference between seeing the blueprints of a building and actually viewing and walking through the edifice, or between reading a musical score and actually listening to the music played by an orchestra, or between hearing about a sexual act and actually engaging in it oneself. To provide our patients with insight alone is to give them a relatively sterile experience compared with the deeper impact we possibly can offer them. Fromm-Reichmann put it well when she said, "The patient doesn't need an insight. He needs an experience."

Many forms of therapy attempt to provide the child with such enriching experiences. This is particularly true of the various forms of play therapy. When storytelling is a part of such therapy (whether the stories be told by the child and/or the therapist) one can gain the benefit of allegorical communication—so universally enjoyable to the child. Dramatization of one's therapeutic messages is a most efficacious way of communicating them, especially with younger children. This requires of therapists the ability to be somewhat of a "ham," as well as some degree of comfort with involving themselves in floor play, animal noises, various forms of childlike physical activity, etc. Therapists who are comfortable enough to allow themselves such regressive behavior can provide the child with highly valuable therapeutic exposures.

Humor Child therapists should commit to memory a collection of jokes that are traditionally enjoyed by children. Riddles are probably the most common form of such humor. Some examples: *Question* "Why does a humming bird hum?" *Answer* "Because it doesn't know the words." *Question* "What's *Smokey the Bear's* middle name?" *Answer* "the." *Question* "What looks like a box, smells like lox, and has wings?" *Answer* "A flying lox box." Some of these may even have a mildly scatological element. For example: *Question* "What's invisible and smells like worms?" *Answer* "A bird's fart." (Jokes such as these are a statement of the levels to which child therapists must stoop if they are to engage successfully their patients.) Humor serves many purposes. It is a pleasurable distraction from some of the heavier material often focused on in treatment. Laughing is ego enhancing, and this in itself is therapeutic. The jokes that the child learns from the therapist may be useful in improving relationships with children outside the office. They make the therapist more attractive to the child (the seductive element) and thereby increase the likelihood that the child will want to come to the office. Last, they can contribute to an entrenchment of the therapist-patient relationship via their contribution to the child's liking the therapist's personality.

The ability to introduce these elements into the child's therapeutic situation requires the acquisition of talents far above those required of the adult therapist—who need only devote his or her life to the overwhelming task of acquiring competence in helping patients gain insight and providing them with the array of other traditional therapeutic experiences.

Candy and Other Foods   There are therapists who claim that having candy and other foods available is very helpful in establishing a good relationship with the child—especially because food is so often a symbol of love (M.R. Haworth and M.J. Keller, 1964). I believe that it is important that therapists appreciate that they can provide the child with some affection (that may even be very deep), but the parents of their patients—whatever their problems, whatever their deficiencies, and whatever deprivations the child may have suffered because of them—are generally more loving of the child than they. They are the ones who are providing the child with food, clothing, and shelter. They are the ones who continually devote themselves to him or her. Generally, at least one of them is continually available to protect, guide, educate, nurse, discipline, and involve him- or herself in whatever else may be necessary to the children's welfare. The parents are the ones who suffer all the discomforts and sacrifices attendant to the children's upbringing—parental gratifications from the process notwithstanding. Their bringing their child to therapy—involving as it does sacrifices of time and money—is in itself another manifestation of their love. The therapist is getting, therefore, a selected population. Parents who have little, if any, affection for their children are not bothering, not suffering the discomforts of bringing them to treatment. It is the parents who are changing the diapers in the middle of the night, sitting with their sick children, worrying about their being scapegoated, et cetera, who bring their children for therapy. Therapists do not have these obligations. It is easier for them, therefore, to exhibit affection; but it is naive of them to think that they can provide a degree of love anywhere close to that which most of the parents of their patients are providing.

At best the therapist can provide the child with some affection in compensation for some of the privations he or she may have suffered. This, if it is in any way to be meaningful, must evolve from an ever-deepening relationship. At best, candy can play an insignificant role in bringing about such a relationship. The therapist must appreciate that food is a *symbol* for love; it is not a *replacement* for love. It is not the real thing. There are therapists who are somewhat deficient in providing that degree of affection optimum in the therapeutic situation and who may try to compensate for their deficiencies in this regard by providing food. Such therapists may be entrenching a common parental problem in which the parent uses food to compensate for deficiencies in providing genuine affection.

Central to the success of treatment is that a good relationship be established with the child. If this exists there will be no need to provide substitutes or symbols. I myself *occasionally* have lollipops or other candy available for their minor seductive value and that's all. I do not provide other foods. I would not say that providing more food is necessarily therapeutically contraindicated; rather, I believe that it doesn't help significantly and that there is a danger that it can be used, as described, in an antitherapeutic way. In short, I think that there are more disadvantages than advantages to using food as a method of engaging the child and entrenching the therapeutic relationship.

Magic Tricks   One of the most predictable ways to make oneself attractive to children is to show them a few magic tricks. It is a rare child who is so recalcitrant, uncooperative, distractible, et cetera who will not respond affirmatively to the therapist's question: "Would you like to see a magic trick?" Although not generally useful as primary, high-efficiency therapeutic tools, magic tricks can be extremely useful in facilitating the child's involvement with the therapist. Only five minutes spent in such activities can make a significant difference regarding the success of the session. The anxious child will generally be made less tense and will then be freer to engage in higher-order therapeutic activities. The child who is very resistant often becomes less so after such an "icebreaker." The uninvolved or distractible child will usually become quite interested in them and will then be more readily shifted into more efficient therapeutic activities.

In short, they facilitate attention and involvement. In addition, because they make the therapist more fun to be with and more attractive to the child, they contribute to a deepening of the therapeutic relationship which, as already emphasized, is the mainstay of the therapeutic process.

The therapist does well to gradually build a small collection of the kinds of card tricks, magic boxes and cups, secret mazes, et cetera readily purchased in many toy stores (preferably those specializing in "magic"). This small investment of time and money may have significant therapeutic dividends. My previous warning that therapists should not reduce themselves to the level of clowns still holds. I am not suggesting that the therapist become a magician for the child; rather, he or she should use such tricks on occasion, for short periods of time, for their value in facilitating more highly efficient therapeutic interchanges. The therapist interested in an excellent discussion of the use of such tricks in therapy should refer to Moskowitz's article (1973) in which he describes the aforementioned uses of magic as well as its more extensive value as a therapeutic modality.

Following the therapist's presenting a *really* good trick, a child may ask, "How did you do that trick?" To which I will generally reply, "Well, I usually don't tell people how I do my tricks. Perhaps I'll tell you, perhaps I won't. It depends on how much you're going to cooperate." I have no hesitation in utilizing such a bribe. When I talk about the utilization of seductive techniques in child psychotherapy, I can guiltlessly say that, "The end justifies the means." The child who is sitting silently refusing to talk, may be approached with a deck of cards that are fanned directly under his or her nose. To such a child I might say, "Go ahead, pick a card. You'll see I'll be able to tell you what card it was." I have never yet seen a child who will not rise to this challenge. It is difficult to imagine a child's just sitting there adamantly refusing to draw the card. Again, if the child expresses the wish to know how I did the trick, I will suggest that I may tell him or her how, depending on the degree of cooperation.

The Peabody Picture Vocabulary Test (PPVT)   The Peabody Picture Vocabulary Test (L.M. Dunn, 1965) can be a valuable "icebreaker" for involving the child who refuses to speak. The instrument tests word knowledge, which is roughly correlated with the verbal section of the WISC. The patient is presented with a series of plates, on each of which are four pictures. The examiner presents a word and the patient is asked to point to the picture that is most closely associated with the presented word. The words, of course, become progressively more difficult. The instrument is designed to assess word knowledge from age three through adulthood.

Let us take, for example, a seven-year-old boy who is sitting in my office in stony silence. This is his first session with his parents and he has informed me that he will absolutely not say a word. To such a child I might say, "You know, if you don't want to talk here, you don't have to talk here. Have you ever heard of the Constitution of the United States?" The child will generally nod affirmatively or, if not, I may take a few minutes to explain to the child the importance of this document. I will then say, "The Constitution of the United States guarantees, that means promises, that every person in the United States will have freedom of speech. And that means that a person is free to speak and say anything he or she wants. However, that doesn't mean that a person can yell 'Fire' in a crowded theater or speak in such a way that people's lives will be in danger. Anyway, freedom of speech also means freedom *not to speak*. So, if you don't want to speak, I respect your right *not to* speak, and under the Constitution of the United States you have the right not to speak!" In this way, I undermine the child's passive-aggressive gratifications which he had hoped to enjoy by thwarting me in my attempts to get him to speak.

I then proceed: "Now, because we're both in agreement that you're not going to speak, I'm going to give you this test that does not require you to speak. This is a test to see how smart you are. All you have to do is point to the picture that is closest to the word that I will say to you. Now here's the first picture." At that point I turn to the first plate of the booklet, the sample that is used for the youngest children. Generally, the instructions indicate that the examiner turns to the plate that is commensurate with the child's age and level of sophistication. My reason for starting with this first plate is to insure that the words I will be giving will not only be readily understandable to the child but significantly *below* the child's age level. The first plate (Example A) portrays a crib, an adult woman, a kitten, and a spoon. I will then say to the boy, "Please point to the *kitten*." True to form the child will sit there silently, adamantly refusing to point. I will then say, "You don't know which one is the kitten? You know, a little baby pussy cat. A little kitty cat that says 'Meow, meow.'" At this point I will utilize baby talk. As mentioned, the utilization of baby talk is contraindicative in child therapy. However, this is one exception to that rule. Here I want to *demean* the child into pointing. If the child still refuses to respond, I will incredulously say, "Gee, he doesn't know kitty cat." And then I will dramatically place a cross mark on the examiner's score sheet.

I then proceed to the second plate (Example B) on which is depicted a chair, a banana, a man hammering a nail, and a fish. Proceeding with the examination, I will say: "Now, I'm sure you'll get this one, everyone does. This is *really* an easy one. Please point to the *fish*." Again, the child will adamantly refuse to point. At which time I will shake my head, again incredulously, "Come on, you know which one is the fish. You know, a little fishy that swims around in a pond." Again, I purposely use baby talk in order to embarrass the patient into responding. If there is still no response, I will say, "Wow, seven years old and doesn't know fish. Are you sure you're really seven?" At which point the patient may nod that he really is seven. I will then turn to the parents and somewhat incredulously say, "Is that right? Is he *really* seven years old?" Again, after the parents' confirmation, I may say, "Gee, this is really something. I haven't seen anything like this in a long time. Seven years old and doesn't know fish." Then I will again dramatically place a large cross on the score sheet.

I now turn to the third plate (Example C) on which is depicted a comb, a table, a little doll, and a car. I then proceed: "I know, for sure, you'll get this one because this is *really* easy. Okay now, please point to the *doll*." Again, after no response from the patient, I will incredulously say, "Of course you know which one is the doll, a little baby dolly, that little girls play with." Again, I will utilize baby talk.

By this point, the patient is likely to say, "Wait a minute, what's going on here? What's happening?"

To which I will reply, "Well, as I told you before, this is a test to see how *smart* you are. And to be very truthful with you, you're not doing too well!"

At this point, the patient is likely to say, "Wait a minute, I know which one is the doll. That's the doll." And the patient will then point to the doll.

I will then say, "Oh, very good, I was really surprised when you said you didn't know which one was the doll. You know you're allowed to change your answers." And then I'll erase the cross and turn back to the fish and to the kitten, giving the patient another opportunity to give the answer. I have never yet seen a child who has the guts to sit there while I repeatedly and dramatically give him or her cross after cross. To date, *all*—even the most adamantly silent—have succumbed. We then proceed with the test and I get some idea about the child's word knowledge which, as mentioned, is roughly correlated with the verbal section of the WISC. With this instrument, the child is likely to involve him- or herself in the further activities. I recommend this instrument highly for its value in this regard. I also recommend it as a quick way of gaining some information about the child's general level of intelligence. (In the above example I utilize the original PPVT. In 1981 the revised edition (PPVT-R) was published [L.M. Dunn and L.M. Dunn] and although the pictures are different, it can be used in an identical manner.)

CLINICAL EXAMPLES

In the following clinical examples I demonstrate what I consider to have been good and bad therapeutic relationships that I have had with my child patients. In each case I will try to identify those factors that contributed to the kind of relationship that evolved.

The Case of George ["Can I Call You Dick?"]

When eight-year-old George's divorced mother called to make his first appointment, she told me that he was not attending to his studies and that he was fighting so excessively with peers that he had no friends. Her former husband was living in South America and although he often wrote George letters professing his intense love for him and promising future visits, the latter rarely materialized. Accordingly, George's life was fraught with frustration and disillusionment.

At the time of their first visit, when I entered the waiting room to greet George and his mother, he told me that his name was George, but that his friends called him Jojo. I asked him which name he preferred I use with him and he answered, "Jojo. What do your friends call you?" "Dick," I replied. "Can I call you Dick?" he asked. "Of course," I answered. It was clear that George was craving a close, friendly relationship. To have insisted that he call me "Dr. Gardner" or to have inquired as to the reasons why he wished to

call me by my first name would have squelched him at this vital
point and lessened the possibility of our forming a good relationship. (It is of interest that about three months later George began
calling me Dr. Gardner. I think that he was basically uncomfortable
with this "egalitarianism" and was able to give up the contrived
symbol of friendliness when we had the real thing going for us.)

Following the interchange in which we decided what names
we would use with one another, George presented me with a clay
figurine that he had made for me in school. "I made this present
for you, Dick," he said. I admired the piece of work, told him how
proud he must be to have made such a thing, and thanked him
warmly for the gift. Although there was a pathetic quality in
George's intense craving for me to like him (even to the point where
one has to consider there may have been a bribing element in the
gift), there was also a warmth and optimism communicated as he
gave me the present. To have hesitated to take the gift and/or to
have conducted a psychoanalytic inquiry into his motivations
would have compromised our already budding relationship, because such an inquiry would have robbed us of the warm feelings
being engendered in both of us. But worse, it would have been inhumane. I am not suggesting that one never question a gift given
by a patient. Rather, I am only saying that for this patient, at this
time, such a reaction would definitely have been antitherapeutic.

The Case of Henry
(An Attempt on the Therapist's Life)

Henry, a 14-year-old boy, was referred for treatment because of delinquent behavior. His defiance of authority was ubiquitous. His
father was an extremely rigid and punitive person who made Henry
feel quite impotent. From ages ten to twelve he had worked with
another therapist without too much success. Unfortunately, this
therapist had died a year previously.

When he entered his first session he smugly looked around
and said, "You shrinks are all the same . . . same stupid couch
. . . same stupid diplomas on the walls . . . same damn pictures of
your family on the desk." I understood Henry to be trying to lessen
his anxiety in this new situation. By finding similarities between
my office and that of his previous therapist he was reducing his
feelings of strangeness. In addition, he was trying to identify me
with his former therapist in order that I could better serve as his

replacement. The hostile veneer was also anxiety alleviating; acting like a tough guy is a typical teenage defense against fear. Although anger displaced from his father onto me was also contributing to Henry's hostility, I considered the anxiety-alleviating factor to be the most important at that time. To have delved into the hostility at that point would have missed the aforementioned important issues and would have robbed the patient of his defenses at a time when he was very much in need of them. Appreciating his need for reassurance that his therapist and I did indeed have many similarities, I replied, "Yes, we psychiatrists often have much in common." These comments made Henry less tense and less hostile.

In spite of a promising beginning, I cannot say that Henry and I had a very good relationship during the subsequent months. This was primarily due to the fact that I could not identify well with him when he engaged in antisocial behavior—especially when it took on dangerous proportions. I was, however, making some headway when the father angrily stated in a joint session that he was fed up with Henry's long hair and that he wanted him to cut it shorter. (This occurred in the mid-to-late 1960s when the long hair vogue [and its antisocial value] had reached a peak.) I tried to dissuade the father from putting pressure on Henry and tried to explain to him that it was one of the most innocuous forms of rebellion ever invented and he should be happy that Henry was resorting more to it and less to the more destructive and violent forms. The father was deaf to my advice. Following the session he took Henry to a barber shop. There he and a barber held Henry down while another barber gave him a very short haircut. Following this, Henry completely refused to attend school. (During the course of the therapy he had gotten to the point of attending most of the time.) In subsequent sessions it became apparent that Henry considered himself to have been castrated by his father and his rage was enormous.

About two weeks after this incident Henry came to my office with a teenage friend and asked if the latter could wait for him in the waiting room. The session was not particularly eventful. During my session with the patient who followed, she thought she smelled smoke. I didn't smell anything and neither of us thought it was necessary to investigate. At the end, when we walked out into the waiting room, I was horrified to see that attempts had been made to set my waiting room on fire. Fortunately, the curtains were made of fire-resistant material and so did not completely ignite. The bathroom toilet tissue and paper hand towels had all burned, but fortunately the flames did not spread to the walls. Had the waiting room caught on fire, my only exit would have been out the 13th-story window.

I summoned Henry and his family back for a session at the end of my day. When I asked Henry about the incident, he admitted that he and his friend were responsible. When I asked him if he appreciated that I might have been killed, he smugly replied, "Doc, you gotta die sometime." I concluded that this was not a time for analytic inquiry. Since I was discharging Henry from treatment, such inquiry would have served little, if any, purpose. Besides, I was not particularly interested in spending time helping Henry to gain insight into such things as his act being a reflection of rage felt toward his father being displaced onto me. I was just interested in getting rid of him as quickly and efficiently as possible. I called his parents in, told them about the fire incident, explained that I could not effectively treat anyone who had tried to kill me, and refused their request that I recommend them to someone else—explaining that I had too much concern for my respected colleagues to refer someone such as Henry to them. Although I recognized that this rejection might help Henry appreciate that there could be untoward repercussions to his dangerous behavior, this was not my motivation in discharging him. My intent was not to provide him with any kind of therapeutic "corrective emotional experience"; rather, I just wanted to get rid of him.

Before they left I suggested the parents give me the name of Henry's friend, so I could call his parents and inform them about what their son had done. I called the boy's father, a lawyer, whose immediate response was, "Can you prove it?" I replied, "You and your son deserve one another." And I hung up. A more blatant example of a parent's sanctioning a son's antisocial behavior (so often the case) would be hard to find.

The Case of Harry [Rebuking the Patient]

Harry entered treatment at the age of fourteen because of poor school performance, in spite of extremely high intelligence, and profound shyness. Both of his parents were professional scientists and highly unemotional and intellectualized. Their pressures on Harry to perform well in the academic area were formidable. Harry's poor school performance was, in part, a rebellion against his parents' coercions. In addition, they had a condescending attitude toward practically everyone and little meaningful involvement with anyone outside their family. Harry's shyness and uninvolvement with others was a reflection of his parents' attitudes. The family was Catholic, very religious, and puritanical in their attitudes about profanity, sex, and pleasurable activities.

After about a year of therapy, Harry joined his parochial school's computer club, where he immediately became recognized as the most knowledgeable and enthusiastic member. The activity well suited him because of his very high intelligence and his interest in activities that did not involve emotional expression. A few months after joining he began to report in session his club's new project: computerized matching of boys in his school with the girls of a nearby Catholic school. All students in both schools were to fill out a questionnaire describing various basic physical characteristics, interests, personality preferences in members of the opposite sex, et cetera. All these data were to be fed into a computer and every boy and girl would be matched to three others. A large dance was to be held, everyone was to be assigned a number, and at prescribed times each student would dance with the partner assigned by the computer.

For weeks Harry excitedly spoke of the details of this project. I was most pleased about it not only because of his enthusiasm (a rare quality for Harry to express) but because it would provide Harry with the opportunity to involve himself with girls in a way that would produce less anxiety than some of the more traditional methods of boy-girl meeting. When the week came for the students to fill out their questionnaires, Harry spoke animatedly about the large number of questionnaires being received and how happy he was that everything pointed to the program's being a success. In the context of this discussion I casually asked Harry what answers he had written on his questionnaire. Harry replied, "Oh, I'm not putting in any questionnaire. My job is to organize the whole thing and make sure that everything works well with the computer." I was astonished. For weeks we had spoken about this activity and not once did I ever consider the possibility that Harry himself would not enter. The session took place the day before the deadline for the submission of the questionnaires. There was little time to work things out, to help Harry assuage his anxieties, and to help Harry appreciate what he was doing.

Speaking more as a frustrated father than as a therapist, I told Harry that I was flabbergasted that he wasn't submitting his own questionnaire. I told him that he was making a grave error, that everybody gets nervous in such situations, and that he has to push through his anxieties if he is to enjoy the rewards of a new situation. I spoke quickly and somewhat heatedly—ending with the warning that if he came back to the next session without having submitted his questionnaire I would not only be very disappointed in him but very irritated with him as well.

One could argue that my approach was extremely antitherapeutic. I was coercing this boy; I was pushing him into an anxiety-provoking situation; I would be producing unnecessary guilt and self-loathing if he did not comply with my request; and I was jeopardizing the therapeutic relationship by such coercive and antitherapeutic tactics. I agree completely with these criticisms and I was completely aware of these dangers as I spoke to Harry. My hope was that this risk would be more than counterbalanced by Harry's appreciation, at some level, that my frustration, anger, and coercion came from a deep sense of concern; that only an uninvolved therapist could sit calmly by and allow him to pass by this wonderful opportunity. (I am reminded at this point of a psychiatric ward nurse who once reported to me overhearing a conversation among three children. The first said, "My mother's a bitch." The second, "My father's always hitting me." And the third, "My father never even hits me!" Obviously the third's situation was the worst. Having a father who never even bothers to discipline and even punish is a severe deprivation indeed.) I hoped also that the general strength of our relationship was such that he not only would comply, but that he would appreciate that I was being basically benevolent.

Harry did submit his questionnaire. On the night of the dance he "could not find" one of the girls with whom he was matched and the second "didn't show up." However, he did spend some time with the third. But because he didn't know how to dance (and forgot my suggestion that he ask her to teach him a few steps), they talked awhile and then went their separate ways. I was not surprised that no great romance developed from this first encounter with a female. One cannot expect a patient to overcome lifelong inhibitions in one evening. However, the ice was broken. Had I not reacted as I had, I believe that Harry would not have taken this step and I would have therefore been somewhat remiss in my obligation to him. I saw no evidence that Harry's relationship with me had in any way suffered because of my coercion; in fact, I believe that it strengthened. However, this improvement could not have taken place if the coercion had not occurred at a time after a good relationship had already formed. To have used such an approach very early in treatment might very well have destroyed, or seriously compromised, our relationship.

The "Amotivational Syndrome"

It is sometimes said that the patient who has been a failure in most areas of his life is likely to be a failure in therapy as well. Unfortunately, this has been my experience. I cannot say that I have had much success salvaging patients who present with massive difficulties in most areas of functioning. My best successes have been with those who have proved themselves capable of succeeding in at least some areas of functioning. One group of such difficult patients are those who present with the parents' complaint that they just aren't interested in anything—a total "amotivational syndrome." They sit in school and couldn't care less. They forget homework assignments, hand in sloppy work, daydream in class, and are generally tuned out. These are not psychotic children nor are they significantly depressed or unhappy. They just plod along. They have little, if any, interest in playing with friends. They do not seem to be in much pain and can be quite content to spend all their free time watching television. Usually they are of average intelligence (but on occasion may be a little higher or lower).

In the therapy sessions they act similarly. They just sit there—having little to talk about. There is no spontaneity, no dreams to be recalled, nothing of interest to report to the therapist. They will often go along passively with playing games, but their lack of interest becomes infectious and the therapist soon finds him- or herself yawning. I have had the feeling at times when working with such children that I have been "turning myself inside out" or "standing on my head" to draw them out—but to no avail. They may even tell stories, but their stories are often short, stereotyped, and not particularly revealing of significant psychodynamic material. One gets the feeling that they are telling the story, drawing the picture, playing the game, et cetera, in order to comply with the therapist's request as fast as possible. It is as if their main message to parents, teachers, and the therapist is: "Just leave me alone. I'm perfectly content with myself the way I am. I'm getting food, clothing, and shelter from my parents; what else should anyone want in

life?" But even this "statement" is made in such a way that both patient and therapist find themselves on the verge of falling asleep as
it is being said. Although I have been able, in most of these cases, to
delineate those factors which I believe have contributed to the formation of this type of personality disturbance, I have been uniformly unsuccessful in helping such children.

The Passive-Aggressive Child

The aforementioned children are not passive-aggressive, that is,
they are not particularly angry nor using obstructionism as a way
of expressing their hostility. The passive-aggressive represent another category of children who are extremely difficult to engage.
They are basically very angry children who express their anger by
thwarting those around them. They seem to operate in accordance
with the principle: "What he wants me to do is the very thing I will
not do." The request becomes the cue for not doing. It provides the
child with his or her weapon. It tells the child exactly what particular kind of refusal will be most effective at that particular time.
Home life provides a continuous opportunity for such negativistic
expression: they dawdle in practically everything, they forget to do
what's expected of them, they won't eat or eat very slowly or mes-
sily. Everything quickly turns into a power struggle. In school also,
where things are expected of them, they do not comply. They ex-
asperate the teacher who finds them fighting her at every point—
always silently and passively. And it is no surprise that they react
similarly in the session with the therapist. The child is asked to talk;
so the child has nothing to say. The therapist asks the child to play
games; the reply: "not interested," "can't think of a story," "I don't
like to draw," et cetera.

The therapist who is willing to spend weeks, months, and perhaps even years sitting silently and not falling into the child's trap
of reaching out and then being thwarted may be providing such a
child with a therapeutically beneficial experience. I, however, like
myself too much to endure such boredom for the sake of a patient.
In fact, the resentment I would feel in such sessions could not but
be antitherapeutic. In addition, my experience has been that the
child who is willing to sit silently as a gratification of passive-aggressive needs knows that the therapy is costing his or her parents
money and so the therapist's participation in such sessions makes
him or her an ally in the child's acting out—an obviously anti-

therapeutic situation. I have sometimes tried to work with such children in family sessions. I take the tack: "We are talking here about you and it behooves you to participate in this discussion because we'll be making decisions that concern you." I try to draw such children into the discussion to get their opinions—especially when it may behoove them to talk in order to argue against a decision's being made that may make them uncomfortable. Again, I cannot say that this approach has been particularly successful either.

The Case of Carol [The Hostile Parent]

The parent who is actively antagonistic to the therapist and who still brings the child (for a variety of pathological reasons) impedes and even prevents formation of a working therapist-patient relationship. Torn between the two, the child usually sides with the one who is most important: the parent. A good example of such interference occurred with Carol, a nine-and-a-half-year-old girl with stuttering, insomnia, and poor peer relationships, who was placed in just such a difficult bind quite early in treatment. Her mother, a very angry woman, became increasingly hostile toward me and tried to get the patient to side with her against me. She would interrogate the patient after each session in an attempt to point out what she considered to be my defects. On one occasion, after two months of treatment, the following dialogue—related by the patient and confirmed by the mother—took place:

> *Mother:* (in a tone of biting sarcasm): So what did you and Dr. Gardner talk about today?
> *Patient:* We talked about a nightmare I had. I dreamed monsters were chasing me.
> *Mother:* And what did *he* think about *that?*
> *Patient:* He thought I had a lot of anger in me that I was scared to let out.
> *Mother:* I think he's full of shit!

Following similar reports by the patient, I arranged an interview with the parents. I told them that the likelihood of therapy succeeding was small as long as the mother continued to try to undermine Carol's relationship with me. My invitation to the mother to air her complaints to me directly, in the hope that at least some of the difficulties might be resolved, was greeted with a barrage of invective. Attempts to help her gain insight into her reactions were futile. She did agree, however, to consult with another therapist regarding treatment for herself. It was also decided that if, after another month, there was still no appreciable difference in the mother's attitude, treatment would be discontinued.

One month later the mother, although in treatment, was as hostile as ever toward me, and it was agreed that there was no point to my working further with the child, who had been in treatment for three months. The parents also decided not to seek treatment elsewhere for the child at that time.

The Case of Greg (Death of a Boy's Father)

This 11-year-old boy's father died suddenly of a heart attack at the age of 39, two days after my initial two-hour evaluation. Over the next few months, every session with Greg was spent talking about his father and helping him work through his reactions to this tragedy. The sessions were deep and meaningful to both of us, and I believe that his involvement with me at that time contributed significantly to his adjustment to the loss.

During his seventh week of treatment he presented me with a piece of paper and stated that he had written a poem about me. We sat down together and read the poem (errors retained):

> I KNOW A MAN
> written in honor of
> Doctor Richard Gardner
>
> I know a man that
> tries to help others
> as much as he Poss-
> ibly can, With a
> desire to find and
> see out you're prob-
> lem, and cure it
> to the best of his
> ability. His quest;
> to follow through on
> his everlasting path
> overcoming all obstac-
> les in his way. His
> kind and understand-
> ing personality, and

self convidence,
with a mind that
expresses great
contributions
towrd his feild.
wich all help to
guide him through
lifes endless
passage, accomp-
lishing more than
most any man
could ever dream.

Following my reading of the poem I told him how touched I was by it and how pleased I was that he had taken the trouble to write it for me. I told him that I was glad to see that he appreciated that I can only *help* people with their problems to the *best of my ability*, but that their help is important also if their problems are to be reduced. I then asked him if he would like to read a poem that I had written which was hanging on the wall. We went over and he began to read:

To Children

    whose infectious joie de vivre
elates us,
    whose ingenuousness
refreshes us,
    whose guilelessness
embarrasses and teaches us,
    whose undiscriminating love
flatters us,
    whose optimism
gives us hope,
    and who, as our progeny,
provide us with our most meaningful
link to immortality.

There were a number of words that the patient did not understand and I explained their meaning to him. When we got to the end we discussed the last line: "and who, as our progeny, provide us with our most meaningful link to immortality." I then said to him: "This last line reminds me of your father. Although he is dead,

I am sure that when he was alive you were a great source of pride to him. When people have such fine, bright, and good-natured children it makes it easier for them to die because they know that they are leaving something good and wonderful behind—something that they have helped to create—something that they have helped to grow."

Both the patient and I found the experience quite meaningful. There was an extra dimension to the experience that went beyond our discussing his father and our feelings about one another. The interchange—especially the feelings that existed between us while talking—created a closeness that I find extremely difficult to describe exactly. There was a mutual sense of respect and admiration. We were joined together in our sorrowful feelings over the loss of his father. This mutual experience in which we both felt the same emotion at the same time contributed to the richness of the experience. I believe that such experiences are among the most ego-enhancing that an individual can have, and they serve as the most powerful antidote to psychopathological processes and the most effective prophylactic against their formation.

The Case of Timmy
(Revelation of the Therapist's Defect)

During my initial consultation in which I discussed the treatment of Timmy, a ten-year-old boy, I informed the parents that they should contact me if they knew that they could not keep any of their appointments. I told them that if I could fill the session there would be no charge; however, if I was unable to do that I would charge them. In addition, I told them that I usually spend about three hours collating all the data from my intensive evaluation of themselves and their child, as well as reports from the schools, psychological tests, and so on. For this time, I informed them, I charge for two sessions.

One morning, about a half hour prior to the patient's final evaluative session, the mother called me and told me that she would be unable to bring her son for his session. With such short notice it was impossible to fill the appointment. Accordingly, at the end of the month there was a charge for the missed session, as well as the two sessions' time for the preparation of my final report. A few days after sending out the bill I received an angry note from the father asking me why I could not have used his son's session time toward the preparation of my final presentation. The letter arrived on a morning when I was under great pressure taking care of many last minute details prior to leaving on a lecture tour to the west coast. I quickly dictated a letter to my secretary angrily informing the father that I charge for my time, that his son had not shown up for his session, that it was too late for me to fill it, and that my bill still held.

When I returned from my trip full payment had been sent with another angry letter from the father claiming that he still felt that his criticism was justified. I found myself getting angry at the man and then began questioning myself very seriously as to whether there was some justification for his complaint. I had to admit that I had used his son's time for telephone calls and that there *was* some justification for his complaint.

Accordingly, during the next interview in which I was to see the patient *with* his parents and two brothers, I took the opportunity to apologize to the father for having charged him and explained that I'd been somewhat greedy in doing so. Although I described the pressure of my final preparations for my trip to have contributed, I openly admitted that I was not for one minute claiming that this was a justifiable excuse. The apology was made at a point in the discussion when the patient's older brother was describing how Timmy was unable to tolerate deficiencies. Timmy suffered with a mild learning disability and reacted violently whenever his learning deficiencies were exposed. Following this discussion I apologized to the father. We then discussed the father's feelings about me, and he described admiration for my willingness to admit a deficiency. Of course, as part of my apology, I informed the father that he would be credited for the cost of the charged session in his next bill. In a subsequent discussion, I believe that Timmy was helped to appreciate that admitting a deficiency might bring one more respect than covering it up. The fact that I, his therapist, could have a deficiency was also of therapeutic value to Timmy, in that it contributed to his feeling less loathsome about his own defects.

Other Assorted Examples of a Good Therapist-Patient Relationship

Some children have collected the prizes that they have won playing *The Talking, Feeling, and Doing Game* (1973a) (Chapter Five) and the *mutual storytelling technique* derivative games. Some children will amass collections, others merely save special prizes that have particular significance. A number of children have developed special psychological relationships with certain books of mine. This is especially the case for *The Boys and Girls Book About Divorce* (1970, 1971b). On occasion, I will see parents who are contemplating separation or divorce in order to counsel them regarding the best way to tell their children about the forthcoming separation. In the course of the consultation, I will recommend that they give the children a copy of the book as a present from me. I am especially prone to do this when I suspect a child might become involved in therapy. Reading the book provides a useful transition in that a relationship is already established via the book.

My *Stories About the Real World* (1972a) has also proven a useful vehicle for entrenching the relationship. A number of children have related so strongly to the book that they develop a psychological tie with it and actually put it under their pillows when going to sleep. One boy with many fears took the book along with him when he went for his swimming lesson. He was particularly absorbed with the story of Helen (the girl who wouldn't try, a girl who was fearful of entering new situations). He actually took the book along to his swimming lessons, clutched it as he approached the pool, and gave it to his mother just before he entered the pool. It clearly served as a kind of security blanket.

Joel lived in the same town as I and belonged to the same community swim club. One day, as I was walking at the edge of the pool, he yelled from the other side of the pool to a boy in the water, about halfway between us: "Hey, Benjy, look over there (pointing to me). That's Dr. Gardner. He's my psychiatrist!" Although the boy's mother (who was standing next to him) cringed beyond description, he beamed with pride as many in the pool looked at me as I waved to Joel. About one year after the completion of his treatment Joel, then age ten, came up to me at the pool one day and said: "Dr. Gardner, I know you're off duty. But I had this dream last night that bothers me. Would you help me analyze it? I don't have much money; but I can pay you fifty cents." I told him that there was no charge for postgraduate dream analyses and we sat down together and discussed the dream.

Michael, whose divorced father rarely visited, when he sat opposite me often put his feet up on the ottoman between us—in obvious imitation of me. At times, he would place the soles of his feet against the soles of mine and we would continue talking in this way. This was never discussed. To have done so would have robbed the experience of some of its beauty and import. There are certain times in therapy when talking about something robs it of therapeutic benefit—and this is one such example.

One day, Bernard, during his sixth month of treatment, saw a clock in my wastepaper basket. When he asked if he could have it I told him yes, but informed him that it was broken and that was why I had thrown it away. Two years later, during our last session, his mother said to me: "Doctor, do you remember that clock from the wastepaper basket you once let Bernard have?" Since it had never been mentioned again, I had a little difficulty recalling it, but the patient soon refreshed my memory by describing the incident in which I had given it to him. "Well," she continued, "I don't know whether you know it or not but he sleeps with that broken clock under his pillow every night."

One girl asked if she could bring her own cassette tape recorder and tape her sessions—especially the stories we told—so she could bring them home and listen to them. I readily agreed, and it was from this request that I ultimately suggested that all patients do so because it provides such a good opportunity for reiteration of the therapeutic messages and in many cases an entrenchment of the relationship with me.

Sally came to the session the day after Christmas and wanted to take my picture with her new camera so that she could show all her friends what I looked like. Helen, age 12, came to her second session with a notebook entitled: "Secret Things to Tell Dr. Gardner." And Susan's younger sister is reported to have told her mother, "I wish that I had a problem so that I could go and see Dr. Gardner too."

As is obvious, forming a good relationship with the child has more benefits than just helping the child's therapy. It can be extremely gratifying for the therapist in its own right. My hope is that the methods described in this book will prove useful to therapists in helping them form such satisfying and enriching relationships themselves.

FOUR

Parental Involvement
in the
Child's Treatment

Considering the primitive state of the art/science we call
psychotherapy, therapists need all the help they can get.

R.A. Gardner

For many years I practiced in the traditional manner and saw my
child patients alone. Usually the mother rather than the father was
available to bring the child. My procedure was to have the mother
bring the child and then sit in the waiting room. However, I did
not strictly refrain from involving her in the treatment. I would
intermittently bring her in to discuss certain issues with the child,
and also had occasional separate sessions with her and/or the father.
In my initial evaluation, I would see the mother and father, both
individually and together. In addition, during the initial evaluation,
I would also have a session or two with the child and the parents
together, and even occasionally bring in one or more siblings. However, the basic therapeutic program after the initial evaluation was
that the child and I were alone in the room. As is true of most
trainees, I automatically accepted as optimum the methods of treatment used by my teachers and supervisors. I believed that being

with the child alone was crucial to the development of a good therapist-patient relationship, and that to the degree that I brought third parties into the room, to that degree I would compromise our relationship. In addition, I believed that it was very important to have a confidential relationship with the child, a relationship in which he or she would have the security of knowing that I would not reveal to the parents anything he or she told me.

Over the years I became increasingly dissatisfied with this procedure. When something would come up in a session that I thought would be important for the mother to know about (nothing particularly confidential), I would bring her in and, in the last few minutes of the session, quickly give her a run-down of what had happened and then would make some recommendations. Most often this was done hurriedly; however, on occasion we would run overtime because I considered it important that she fully understand what had happened in the session and what my recommendations were. My usual experience was that the mother had little conviction for the recommendations, primarily because she had not been witness to the situation that brought them about. When I started keeping the mothers in the room for longer periods, I found that the children generally did not object and, in addition, the mothers had greater conviction for my recommendations because they had been witness to the situations that had brought them about. They not only had the opportunity to observe directly the events that resulted in my suggestions, but they had ample time to discuss them with me in detail. This resulted in their much more frequently and effectively carrying out my recommendations. To my surprise, the children did not express any objections. They had not read the books that I had read—books that had emphasized the importance of my seeing the child alone and the crucial role of the confidential relationship.

In this chapter, I discuss in detail the ways in which I utilize parents in the treatment of children. I generally refer to my approach as *individual child psychotherapy with parental observation and intermittent participation.* Although this title may appear cumbersome, it states exactly what I do. In addition, I will often indicate to the parents that they are my *assistant therapists.* This designation communicates the point that their active participation in the therapeutic process will be utilized.

Before discussing the ways in which I use parents in the child's therapy, it is important for the reader to learn about my views on confidentiality in treatment, especially in the treatment of children. I will describe my position on confidentiality, therefore, before I present descriptions of the ways in which I enlist the aid of parents in the child's treatment.

THE ISSUE OF CONFIDENTIALITY AS IT RELATES TO THE PARENTS' INVOLVEMENT IN THE CHILD'S TREATMENT

Many therapists believe that the active involvement by a parent(s) would significantly compromise the child's confidentiality, and this they believe is crucial if there is to be meaningful therapy. I believe that such therapists are placing too much weight on confidentiality. The patient is coming primarily for treatment, whether the patient is a child or an adult. The patient is not coming primarily for the preservation of confidentiality. I believe that to the degree that the preservation of the confidential relationship serves the ends of treatment, to that degree it should be respected. If it is a choice between confidentiality and doing what is in the best interests of the patient therapeutically, then, I believe, the therapeutic indications should be given priority over the confidences. One must not lose sight of the primary aim of therapy: to do what is in the best interests of the patient. In order to describe my position more specifically, I will consider the confidentiality issue as it pertains to the treatment of the adult, the adolescent, and the child. Although there are differences with regard to confidentiality in these three areas, there are basic similarities that hold for all three categories.

Confidentiality in Adult Therapy

If the adult is to have a successful therapeutic experience, he or she must have the feeling that the therapist will not disclose to others what is revealed during the course of treatment. Otherwise, the freedom to reveal will be significantly compromised—to the point where therapy may become meaningless. Most therapists would agree, however, that there are certain situations in which strict adherence to the confidentiality may be antitherapeutic. Such is the case when there is a strong suicidal or homicidal risk. Basically, when a human life is at stake, concerns about confidentiality are reduced to the point of being trivial. If the patient is suicidal, it behooves the therapist to enlist the aid of family members and close friends to do everything possible to protect the patient. This usually involves their active participation in hospitalizing the suicidal patient. It would be unconscionable, in my opinion, to "respect" such a patient's request that the suicidal danger not be divulged to the nearest of kin. Similarly, when there is a homicidal risk, the therapist should do everything possible to warn the potential victim.

When a patient in treatment raises the issue of confidentiality, I will openly state that he or she can feel secure that I will not reveal what is divulged—with the exception of situations in which there is a homicidal or suicidal danger. In most cases, the patient is thereby reassured that confidences will not be divulged because neither of these eventualities seems likely. On occasion, however, a depressed patient will be told that I might divulge the suicidal danger. In such cases I will reassure the patient that everything will be done to avoid such disclosure. However, I inform the patient that there might be an occasion in which I might divulge the suicidal risk, if such divulgence might prove lifesaving. Interestingly, most patients are not upset by this. Some healthy part of them appreciates that they could conceivably "go crazy," and that at such a time they might impulsively commit a self-destructive act that could cause irreparable damage and even death. My position provides reassurance that should such a situation occur some healthy and stabilizing intervention will take place. My experience has been that this is usually reassuring.

In recent years there have been a number of cases in which the litigation has centered on this issue. Psychiatrists were sued for malpractice because they preserved patients' confidences, and there was a resultant suicide or homicide that could conceivably have been prevented. The usual defense was that the therapist was respecting the patient's confidentiality and acting in the highest ethical traditions of the medical profession. Even in former years, I did not subscribe to this view. It is not in the highest ethical tradition of the medical profession to sit by and do nothing when there might be a suicide or homicide taking place. It is in the highest interests of the medical profession to protect human life. Fortunately, the courts and ethical committees in medical societies are shifting in the direction of supporting divulgences in such cases. This is a good trend.

Confidentiality in Adolescent Therapy

It is not uncommon for me to have the following conversation with an adolescent:

> *Patient:* Everything I say to you is just between me and you. Right? You'll never tell my parents anything I tell you. Right?
> *Therapist:* Not right.
> *Patient:* You mean you're going to tell my parents everything I tell you?
> *Therapist:* No, I didn't say that either.
> *Patient:* But my friend goes to a shrink, and his shrink told him that everything they speak about is strictly confidential, and his shrink says that he'll never tell my friend's parents anything about what goes on in a session.
> *Therapist:* Yes, many psychiatrists work that way. But I don't. Let me tell you how I work. As long as you don't do anything dangerous, to either yourself or others, you can be quite sure that what we speak about here will be held strictly confidential. I'm in full appreciation of the fact that it's important that you have the feeling that what we talk about is strictly confidential. However, there are certain exceptions. And these exceptions hold for anyone, regardless of age. My policy is the same for all. It's not just for teen-agers. It's the same whether you're 5 years old or 85 years old. The basic policy is this: As long as you're not doing anything dangerous, you can be sure that I won't reveal what you tell me. However, if you're doing something that's dangerous, I reserve the right, at my discretion, to reveal to your family whatever I consider important to reveal to help stop you from doing the dangerous thing. I may need their help. What do you think about what I've said?

At that point the patient may ask me to tell him or her what things I would reveal. I will not then provide "food for thought." I do not wish to give the youngster suggestions for various forms of antisocial and/or self-destructive behavior that may not have entered his or her head. Rather, I ask the adolescent to tell me what things he or she might do that might warrant such divulgence. I may then use this as a point of departure for a therapeutic inquiry. However, I do have a "list." It includes: heavy use of drugs (not occasional use of marijuana), heavy use of alcohol, dangerous driving (especially when under the influence of drugs or alcohol), criminal behavior, and for girls, a desire to have an out-of-wedlock child (occasional sexual intercourse is not a reportable item). I also impress upon the adolescent the fact that should one of these dangerous situations be arising, I will not automatically discuss the problem with the parent. Rather, I will exhaust all possibilities of discussion with the patient and the adolescent group before divulging the risk. Usually, such discussions are enough. However, when they are not, the youngster usually knows beforehand that I am going to divulge the information.

There is another aspect of the confidentiality issue in adolescence which warrants comment. The parents have a reasonable right to know whether there is a significant risk of dangerous behavior. When this issue is broached, generally in the initial evaluation, I will tell them that they should know that "no news is good news," that is, that I will divulge dangers to them, and if there are no such divulgences, they can feel assured that no great risks are imminent.

I am fully appreciative of the fact that the adolescent needs a special, separate relationship with the therapist. This is part of his or her developmental need to establish a separate identity from that of the parents. This autonomy is necessary if the adolescent is to grow into an independent, self-sufficient adult. Active participation of the parents in the adolescent's therapy can compromise this goal. However, the goal can still be achieved by some participation on the part of the parents. Occasional joint sessions in which the youngster is seen along with the parents need not interfere with this goal. There can still be a significant percentage of sessions devoted to the adolescent, him- or herself, and the confidential relationship can also serve the purpose of enhancing separation and autonomy. The potential divulgence of a dangerous situation also need not interfere with this sense of autonomy so important to the adolescent's development.

Confidentiality in Child Psychotherapy

By child psychotherapy I am referring to the treatment of children between the ages of about four and ten. In my opinion, the confidentiality issue has little if any place in the treatment of most of these children. There are many therapists who will say to such children something along these lines: "Whatever you tell me here in this room is just between you and me. I promise I'll never tell your mother or father what you tell me. You can trust me on that." Many children might wonder exactly what the therapist is referring to.

They know of no great secrets that they have from their parents. And this is especially the case for younger children. The parents know quite well that the child is soiling, stealing, lying, truant, and so on. They more than the child are aware of these problems, and it is they who initiated the treatment. So the statement must be confusing and even irrelevant to many children.

In addition, the statement sets up a structure in which there are "we" (the therapist and the patient) and "they" (the parents). "We" and "they" can easily become "we" versus "they." And this concept can introduce schisms in the family. The family has enough trouble already; it does not need an additional problem brought about by the therapeutic program. The system also impedes open communication. Generally, communication impairments contribute to the development of and perpetuation of psychopathology. The confidential relationship with the child is likely to increase the communication problems of the family. The thrust of the therapy should be to encourage open expression of the issues that are causing people difficulty. A conspiracy of silence usually serves only to reduce communication and defeats thereby an important therapeutic goal.

The therapist should attempt to create an atmosphere in which there is an open pool of communication—an atmosphere in which all things pertinent to the child's treatment are discussed openly with the parents. I do not make any statements about this; I do it as a matter of course. I make no mention of the confidentiality. If the child says to me that he or she does not wish me to tell his parents something, I will get very specific about what it is he or she wishes me not to divulge. Almost invariably it is an issue worthy of being discussed with the parents. Usually, the child fears repercussions that are unreal and exaggerated. Encouraging the child to express to the parent(s) the forbidden material, either in my presence or at home, is usually therapeutic. It can teach all concerned that the repression (unconscious) and suppression (conscious) of thoughts and feelings is likely to perpetuate problems; whereas civilized discussion is the best way to resolve family problems.

A boy, for example, will say to me that he doesn't want me to tell his parents something. On further inquiry the issue almost invariably is one that should be discussed with the parents, and the child's fears of what will happen if such information is disclosed are unrealistic. Encouraging the child to express the forbidden material to the parents can teach him that the hidden thoughts and feelings are not as terrible as he considered them to be and the anticipated consequences are not forthcoming. The therapist can serve as a catalyst for such expression, and his or her presence can make the atmosphere a safer one for the child to first make such revelations.

There is an aspect of S. Freud's famous Little Hans case (1909) that is pertinent to my discussion here. During the one joint session that Freud held with Little Hans and his father, Hans expressed some hostility toward his father that he had not previously revealed. I believe that it is unfortunate that Freud did not direct his attention to this in his report of the case. I would speculate that the reason why Hans had not expressed the hostility previously was that he was afraid to do so because of fears of his father's retaliation. However, in the presence of "Professor Sigmund Freud," a man of whom both the patient and his father were in awe, Hans could safely reveal his anger because of his awareness that his father was not likely to react with severe punitive measures in Freud's presence. I suspect that Hans' having had the living experience that his father would react to his hostility in a civilized manner made it easier for him to express his resentments elsewhere. And this, I believe, was a contributing factor to the alleviation of his symptoms. Later in this chapter I will discuss in greater detail this and other aspects of the Little Hans case.

Classical psychoanalysts, in particular, are strict adherents to the confidentiality principle. It is they, more than other therapists, who make it a point at the outset to emphasize to the child that they will respect confidences. It is of interest that Freud did not consider confidentiality to be an important issue in his treatment of Little Hans. Hans' father was the therapist and Freud was the supervisor. When reading the transcript of the treatment, one observes that Hans revealed just about every intimacy one can imagine a child might have: bowel movements, urination, masturbation, interest in observing his mother's toilet functioning, sexual fantasies toward his mother, and so forth. If he were indeed hiding material that a child might be ashamed to reveal, I would find it hard to imagine what such material might be. Little Hans knew that his father was revealing their discussions to Freud. In the one joint session that Freud had with Hans and his father, there was open discussion of these intimacies. Classical analysts often point to the case of Little Hans as the proof that Freud's theories of infantile sexuality, the Oedipus complex, and castration anxiety are valid.

Libraries have been written on these theories—which are supposedly proven by the Little Hans case. However, the structure of Freud's therapeutic program is often ignored by the same psychoanalysts. They do not utilize the parents as assistant therapists (as did Freud), and they enter into a strictly confidential relationship with the child (which Freud did not do). In both cases, I believe, they do the child and the family a disservice.

REASONS FOR PARENTAL AMBIVALENCE REGARDING A CHILD'S TREATMENT

Parental involvement in a child's treatment is at best tenuous. Although parents may profess commitment to the therapeutic process, there are many reasons why they are generally quite ambivalent and their mixed feelings about the treatment may interfere significantly with its progress and even result in their prematurely terminating therapy. In this section I discuss some of the more common reasons for impaired parental commitment to the therapeutic process. An understanding of these factors can be useful in increasing the likelihood that the therapist will be able to engage the parents more successfully and thereby increase the likelihood of the child's involvement in treatment. Some of the more common ways in which parental resistance exhibits itself: lateness to the sessions, canceling sessions for frivolous or weak reasons, forgetting to follow through with the therapist's recommendations, complaining to the child about treatment (its cost, time consumption, et cetera), and withholding payment (one of the most predictable ways to ultimately bring about a cessation of treatment).

One of the most important reasons for compromised parental commitment to therapy is the financial privation that it often involves. This is especially the case when the child is in private treatment. Whereas the parents may agree initially to commit themselves to the cost of the treatment, when the bills start coming they often have a change of heart and remove the child prematurely from treatment or support the child's resistances, which are inevitably present. There is also a time commitment in that the parent who brings the child (more often the mother) will generally think of better ways of spending her time than bringing the child to a therapist. If she has other children and cannot afford housekeepers, then bringing the child to treatment may become an additional burden.

Here again, these extra pressures compromise her commitment to the therapeutic process.

Most parents experience guilt when the therapist advises them that their child needs treatment. They consider it proof that they somehow failed in the child's upbringing (H.S. Lippman, 1962). A common way that parents use to assuage such guilt is to rationalize withdrawal of the child from treatment. This is done either overtly or covertly. After all, if they can justify removing the child from treatment, especially if they can believe that he or she does not need it, they thereby absolve and even obviate their guilt. Therapists should tell such parents that they appreciate that at every point in the child's development the parents did what they considered to be in the child's best interests (usually the case) and that through misguidance and/or unfortunate circumstances, and/or the unavoidable effects of their own difficulties, their child developed psychiatric problems. Furthermore, the therapist does well to advise such parents that, at the present state of our knowledge, we do not understand all the factors that contribute to a child's psychiatric difficulties. Thus, even if they themselves had no psychiatric problems, and even if there had been no detrimental circumstances, and even if they had assiduously followed the best available advice, their child might still have developed difficulties (J.W. Kessler, 1966). Moreover, they must be helped to appreciate that innate temperamental factors may be contributing significantly to the child's problems (A. Thomas, S. Chess et al., 1963). My experience has been that a discussion of these factors can often be useful in reducing parental guilt and thereby increasing the likelihood that they will support the child's therapy.

Many parents become jealous of the child's intimate relationship with the therapist and may act out such feelings by undermining the treatment. They may consider themselves to have been the ones to have done all the "dirty work": changed the diapers, taken the child to pediatricians at all hours of the night, and made the hundreds of other sacrifices necessary for successful child rearing. Yet the therapist is "the good guy" who is viewed by the child as benevolent, kind, and sympathetic. Often the parents are threatened by the anxiety-provoking revelations about themselves that inevitably emerge in the child's treatment, and the desire to avoid these can contribute to their impaired commitment to the process.

One of the most effective ways of reducing parental guilt and the resistances that emerge from it is to have the parents participate actively in the child's treatment. Parents who believe that they are somehow at fault in bringing about the child's disorder can assuage their guilt by actively contributing to the therapeutic process. They are thereby helping "undo" what they have "done." By working closely with the parents, the therapist is more likely to develop a good relationship with them. The child will sense the parents' feelings about the therapist and will then be more likely to develop such involvement him- or herself. When parents have a good relationship with the therapist, they are more comfortable expressing resentments and disagreements. The failure to express such differences and complaints is one of the most common sources of parental resistance to the child's treatment and removal of the child from it.

Therapists who believe that it is their role to protect child patients from the indignities suffered at the hands of their parents are likely to alienate parents. The preferable position should be one of impartiality. The therapist should be viewed by all family members as someone who criticizes the parents when such criticism is warranted and, similarly, criticizes the child, again when such criticism is warranted. His or her criticisms, however, should be benevolent and he or she should not "keep score" regarding who is getting more or less. The therapist neither takes the side of parent or child; rather, he or she supports the side of healthy behavior regardless of who exhibits it.

Another common source of parental resistance to treatment derives from the situation in which the parent may not genuinely want the child to be relieved of his or her presenting symptoms, despite protestations to the contrary. The child's problems may play an important role in the family equilibrium. For example, the overprotective mother may want her child with separation anxiety disorder to stay at home and may undermine the therapist's efforts to get the child back to school (R.A. Gardner, 1984). Parents of delinquent youngsters often gain vicarious gratification from their children's antisocial acting out (A.M. Johnson, 1949, 1959; R.L. Stubblefield, 1967). Parents may ostensibly want their child to do better academically but, unconsciously, may undermine the treatment because they fear that the child will surpass them educationally and socioeconomically.

It behooves therapists to appreciate these and the multiplicity of other factors that may contribute to parental undercommitment to the therapeutic process and even removal of a child from treat-ment. The therapist should try to detect these compromising fac-tors during the initial evaluation and deal with them at the outset. Otherwise, they may cause a compromise and even a cessation of the therapy. In this chapter I discuss the ways in which parents can be utilized in the child's treatment. Such utilization has many ben-efits for the child's treatment and is one of the predictable ways to obviate, circumvent, and avoid the aforementioned potential com-promises in the child's therapy.

WAYS IN WHICH PARENTS (USUALLY THE MOTHER) CAN BE USEFUL IN A CHILD'S THERAPY

Gradually my procedure evolved to the position of informing the parents that they would be my therapeutic assistants in the child's treatment. Recognizing that it would most often be the mother who would be bringing the child, I invited the father to feel free to at-tend, without any prior notification, any session when he was available. My experience has been that this occurs from 5 to 10% of the time. For ease of presentation I utilize the term *mother* when I refer to my therapeutic assistant. However, it should be under-stood that fathers are available on occasion to serve in this role. My usual procedure is to have the mother come into the session with the child at the outset, and then to keep her in the room as long as I consider it warranted. This ranges from five to ten minutes to the full session.

The mother can be useful in a number of ways. The younger the child, the less likely that he or she is going to be able to recall many of the important events that occurred since the last session. This is especially the case if the child is seen only once a week. My usual experience is that when I ask a child at the outset what has gone on since I saw him or her last, there is no response. It is al-most as if the child were frozen in ice or transfixed in space since the previous session. Knowledge of these events is often vital for the understanding of many of the child's therapeutic productions. The mother, almost invariably, is a ready source of this important information. I have mentioned that the more knowledge the ther-apist has about the child, the greater will be his or her capacity to respond with a meaningful story utilizing the mutual storytelling technique (Chapters Eight and Nine). These stories, like dreams, often relate to important events that have occurred in the day or two prior to their creation. The child is often not in touch with these events, nor will he or she readily provide them. Many mothers, when hearing the child's story, offer these vital data. It is important for the therapist to appreciate that the mother knows the child far better than he or she. Although not trained as a therapist, her hunches about the meaning of a story may be better than the therapist's—regardless of the number of years of psychoanalytic training the therapist has had. In the post-story discussion period, as well, the mother's input can prove most valuable.

In analyzing the dream the mother's assistance can also be invaluable. The child may include in the dream a figure who is entirely unknown to the therapist. The therapist certainly should obtain as many associations as possible from the child. This, of course, is the best way of ascertaining exactly what the dream figure symbolizes for the child. However, most children provide only a paucity of associations to their dream symbols, and the mother's input can be extremely valuable. She can ask the child leading questions about the figure, and she can often be a better interrogator than the therapist because she has some hunches about what may be important. And, when this fails, her specific and direct comments about the dream figure can often provide the therapist with useful information for understanding the dream.

The presence of the mother in the room enables the therapist to observe mother-child interactions that would not have otherwise be seen. The mother's observations of the ways in which I handle the child, especially when he or she is being difficult, can be useful to her in that it provides her with a model for handling these situations herself. (I am not claiming that I always handle every situation in the most judicious fashion. However, I believe that I do so more frequently than most of my patient's parents.)

The effects of parental participation on the treatment are important and may be even more important than the specific way in which a parent can be useful to treatment. Whereas originally I was taught that such participation would compromise my relationship with the child, my experience has been just the opposite. It is hard to have a good relationship with someone who is a stranger, and whose only or primary contact is the monthly bill. Not only is such a situation likely to produce some alienation, but the paucity of contact increases the likelihood that negative distortions and misinterpretations about the therapist will not be corrected. Having the mother in the room provides her with the opportunity to air her grievances, express her resentments and disappointments, ask questions, and so on. This is the best way to prevent or resolve such problems. Both parents' feelings toward the therapist are extremely important in determining what the child's feelings will be. A parent's animosity toward the therapist frequently, if not invariably, will be picked up by the child. If there is a dispute between the therapist and the parents, the child will have a loyalty conflict. Most often he or she will side with the parent. After all, the parents are providing the food, clothing, and shelter; they are the ones who are with the child the remaining hours of the week. The child knows where his or her "bread is buttered," and it is extremely unlikely that the child will, over a period of time, basically support the therapist's position when it is in conflict with the parents'. Accordingly, anything that can improve the relationship between the therapist and the parents is likely to strengthen the tie between the therapist and the patient.

Parental participation can strengthen the therapist's relationship with the parents in other ways. Seeing the therapist "in action" enables the parents to know firsthand exactly what is going on in the sessions. They are not left in the dark about the therapeutic procedure. In the traditional method, parents are ignorant of what is going on, and this can be a source of irritation and alienation. This is especially the case when the parents are paying for the treatment. When they know what they are spending their money for, they are less likely to harbor negative distortions and criticisms. Of course, if the therapist is spending significant amounts of time with traditional play therapy—which is much more play than therapy—then the parents may have a justifiable criticism and may reasonably consider themselves to be wasting their money. The play techniques that I use are, I believe, much more *therapy* than play. I believe that one of the main reasons child therapists often hesitate to allow parents to observe them is that they are basically ashamed of what they are doing.

Parents most often feel ashamed of the fact that they are bringing their child for treatment. No matter how much the therapist may try to assuage their guilt, they generally feel that they were at fault. And even though the therapist may initially say to the parents that they did their best and that they should not feel guilty, he or she then proceeds to ask questions that are basically designed to elicit information about what the parents did wrong. And the acquisition of this vital information cannot but entrench and enhance guilty feelings. The facts of the matter are that the parents did make mistakes, or else the child would not have developed psychogenic difficulties. As benevolent as were their motivations, as dedicated as they may have been to the child-rearing process, they were indeed deficient in certain areas and that is why the child is coming for treatment. Platitudes and gratuitous reassurances regarding the inappropriateness of such guilt are not likely to work. One way of genuinely reducing such guilt is to invite the parents to be active participants in the therapeutic process. In this way they become directly engaged in reducing and alleviating the very problems that have brought about their guilt. And the working-together process produces a sense of camaraderie with the therapist which also entrenches the relationship with him or her.

In the field of psychiatry, people like to give labels and names. I am often asked what I call this therapeutic approach. It is not family therapy because it is rare for all family members to be present. In addition, when I do have family sessions, they are primarily during the diagnostic phase. While I do practice family therapy in certain situations, that is not what I am describing here. It is more than parental counseling, which is also part of my therapeutic process, because the parent is actively involved in the child's treatment. The name that I use for the method is *individual child psychotherapy with parental observation and intermittent participation*. Although this name is somewhat cumbersome, it describes accurately what I do. It focuses primarily on the child and the techniques that I utilize are primarily designed for child therapy. Accordingly, it is a form of individual child psychotherapy. However, there is parental observation in that the parent (usually the mother) observes directly the therapeutic process. In addition, she actively participates to the degree that it is warranted during the session. To date I have not come up with a better name for this procedure.

I wish to emphasize again that the presence and participation of the parents do not usually compromise the therapist-patient relationship with the child—although this is what I had been taught, and this is what many still believe. The basic determinant of the relationship between the therapist and the child is their own personalities. A healthy mother does not believe that her relationship with her first child will be significantly compromised by the appearance of the second or third. No competent therapist would advise a parent to have only one child, lest the relationship with the first be compromised by the appearance of a second. No healthy mother strictly excludes the father's presence on those occasions when she is with her child, with the argument that it will compromise her relationship with her son or daughter. It is not the presence of one or a few others in the room that is the primary determinant of the relationship between two people. The relationship depends more on qualities that exist within and between the two of them. Therapists who strictly adhere to the traditional view may be providing the child with an antitherapeutic experience. This view expresses, both explicitly and implicitly, the notion that exclusivity is crucial for a good relationship. This can only engender possessiveness, egocentricity, intolerance for sharing, excessive dependency, and other untoward reactions.

SITUATIONS IN WHICH THE PARENTAL PRESENCE IS CONTRAINDICATED

It would be an error *always* to involve a parent throughout all of the sessions. In my view, this would be substituting one inappropriate therapeutic procedure for another. Those who strictly refrain from parental involvement are providing their patients with what I consider to be a significantly compromised form of treatment. Similarly, those who would strictly adhere to the opposite, that is, insist that a parent be present in every session—throughout the session—are imposing an equally rigid and, on occasion, antitherapeutic treatment procedure. What I am suggesting is that the therapist have the flexibility to tailor each therapeutic program to the particular needs of the patient. Most, but not all, patients do best with active parental participation. However, there are some children for whom the active parental participation is contraindicated. And it is these situations that I discuss here.

First, there is the issue of the child's age. I generally do not treat children below the age of about four. There is no strict cutoff point at the fourth birthday. There are children who are younger than four who are psychologically older than four, and these may be good candidates for treatment. And there are children who are older who still might not be candidates for direct therapy. But generally, it is around the age of four that the average child becomes a potential candidate for a meaningful therapeutic endeavor. Prior to that age my therapeutic focus is primarily on work with the parents, with intermittent interviews with the child, both alone and with the parents. I want to establish familiarity and groom the child for treatment if the counseling does not prove to be adequate to relieve the problem(s).

At about the age of 11, children may start revealing confidences that should not justifiably be communicated to the parents. (As I will discuss later, below that age I do not believe that most children have a significant amount of material that warrants the special confidential relationship so frequently utilized by many therapists.) Also at about the age of 11, many children begin to appreciate that their projected fantasies are revealing of their own problems, and they may become defensive about utilizing such techniques. In fact, children at this age generally consider traditional play therapy approaches to be beneath them. Accordingly, after the age of 11 or thereabout a high degree of parental involvement in the treatment may be contraindicated. Again, there should be no sharp cutoff points here. It depends upon the child's maturity and the nature of the information being discussed.

When an overdependent child is in a symbiotic relationship with an overprotective mother, the therapist would not want to utilize the mother to a significant degree in the therapeutic process. To do so might only entrench the pathology. Such a child needs "breathing space" and the freedom to develop a separate relationship—separate from that which he or she has with the mother. To actively involve the mother in the treatment may defeat this goal. However, this does not mean that the mothers of such children should be strictly excluded from all aspects of the child's treatment. No harm is done, in my opinion, by having the mother come in during the first few minutes of the session in order to apprise the therapist of the events that have occurred since the previous session. In addition, she can be kept in the waiting room to be "on call" should her further participation be warranted. (This is standard procedure for me. I do not support a mother's going shopping or attending to other activities while the child is being seen. I emphasize to her the importance of her being available, at a moment's notice, during the session. And this can only be accomplished by her remaining in the waiting room.) Even when a child is suffering with separation anxiety disorder, some active participation with the mother can be useful. Here again one would not want to keep her in the room for significant amounts of time.

There are some parents who are so psychologically fragile that they cannot tolerate the criticisms and other forms of negative feedback that would come their way during the therapeutic session. This is especially the case for parents who are psychotic or borderline. Such a parent may be so defensive that he or she would not be able to handle many of the therapeutic revelations, even though expressed symbolically. Were the parent to sense the underlying meaning of a hostile symbol, it could be ego-debasing and precipitate psychological deterioration. Exposure of such a parent to the child's therapy could be considered cruel and would be likely to alienate significantly both the parent and the child. Any benefits that the child might derive from the parent's presence might be more than offset by the compromise of the therapist-patient relationship that such exposure might result in. In addition, such benefits might also be obviated by the parental psychiatric deterioration and its resultant compromise of parenting capacity. This is not a common situation, but I mention it because it does occur.

There are parents who are extremely hostile, and such hostility might be exhibited toward the therapist. No matter how hard the therapist tries, such parents never seem to be satisfied. No amount of explanation or discussion seems to reduce the hostility. Yet, such parents may bring their children. When they are invited to participate actively in the child's treatment, they may use the opportunity for the collection of ammunition, for example, "Is this what I'm spending all my money on?—to hear you tell those stupid stories?" "How is answering questions about whether or not he touches his penis going to help him obey me at home?" and "My husband is right: psychiatry is just a lot of bullshit!" Such parents tend to "cramp my style" when I am working under their observation and scrutiny. I have the feeling that everything I am doing is going to be used as ammunition against me. Attempts to discuss their negative attitudes have often proved futile. Accordingly, I have found it in the child's best interests to have such parents sit in the waiting room. Although I am deprived of their input, such loss is more than counterbalanced by the enhanced efficiency of the individual therapeutic process with the child. It is the lesser of the two detrimental alternatives. Therapy, like life, often boils down to such a choice. If there were a better option, I would utilize it. So I work under these compromised circumstances.

One might ask the question: "What about the overbearing mother who is always intruding in the child's therapy? Shouldn't she be kept out of the room?" My answer to this question is: "Not so quickly." Let us take, for example, the following situation. I am in session with Jimmy and his mother. I ask Jimmy a question. His mother answers. At that point I consider myself to have a golden opportunity for a meaningful therapeutic interchange—an opportunity that would have not been possible had the mother been out of the room. At that point I will say to Jimmy, "Jimmy, what just happened?" Jimmy may respond, "You asked me a question." And I will respond, "And what happened then?" Hopefully, Jimmy will respond, "My mother answered you." To which I will respond, "Right! And what did you do?" Jimmy may answer, "I didn't do anything." To this I will respond, "Yes, Jimmy, that's right. You didn't do anything. But I believe that you had certain thoughts and feelings when your mother answered my question and didn't give you a chance to answer it yourself. What exactly did you think at the very moment she answered? Exactly what were you feeling at that time?" Here, of course, I will try to get the child to express the thoughts and feelings that he must have had about his mother's intrusiveness. It is generally easier for the child to do this in the therapist's presence. The child recognizes that the therapeutic situation reduces the likelihood that the mother will react with severe punitive measures in the therapist's presence. The child may fear that there will be "hell to pay" when he or she gets home, but the child also knows that there will be at least some protection in the consultation room. If the therapist can encourage such expression during the session and use it as a point of departure for a therapeutic approach to the mother's intrusiveness, it will have served a very useful purpose in the child's treatment.

As mentioned, the richest therapy is that which provides experiences. When the parent is in the room, there is a much greater likelihood that significant experiences will take place. The therapist should view such experiences as golden opportunities, to be grabbed onto and milked to their utmost. They are the most meaningful aspects of the therapeutic process, and they should be cherished. Accordingly, I do not quickly remove intrusive parents from the room. I can conceive of the possibility of a parent being so compulsively intrusive that I would not have the opportunity for such interchanges, and that no living space would be provided the child. However, this has not yet occurred, and I have been successful in utilizing the situations in which the intrusiveness was exhibited as a step toward a reduction of the problem.

This same principle is operative in the more common situation where the child is fearful of expressing hostility toward a parent, hostility engendered by a wide variety of parental deprivations and maltreatment. In a session in which there is the implied therapist's protection the child can be most comfortable in first expressing his or her resentment. Having done so under protected conditions, the child will generally feel more comfortable doing so outside of the session.

I had an experience a number of years ago that demonstrates this point quite well. A boy repeatedly complained to me in sessions that his father insisted that he finish every morsel of food at every meal. His father would be extremely angry at him if he did not eat every speck of food. I asked him if he had expressed to his father the resentment he felt over this. The patient stated that he was afraid to do so. I knew the child's father in that I had interviewed him on a couple of occasions during the evaluative process and, in addition, had seen him on two occasions in joint session with the mother and the child. I knew that he was not as punitive as the patient viewed him to be, and that although he was indeed insisting that the child finish all the food on the plate, he would not have reacted anywhere nearly as violently as the patient anticipated. Accordingly, I felt comfortable encouraging the child to express his resentment. I would not have done so had the father been more punitive. In that case, I would have tried to work more directly with the father himself.

Each week I encouraged the child to express his resentment and told him that I would be asking him in the next session what had happened. Each week he returned with some excuse: "Oh, I forgot to tell him this week." "I was very busy this week." "I had a lot of homework to do this week." I knew that this could go on for months and contribute to the perpetuation of the symptomatology that was a derivative of the pent-up hostility the child was feeling. Accordingly, I had a family session during which I encouraged the child to express his feelings about the mealtime situation. He hesitantly did so and had the *living experience* (again that important concept) that his father did not react as punitively as he had anticipated. We all recognized that he was expressing his anger in a safe situation, with the implied protection of the therapist. However, it was following that session that he became freer to express resentments in other areas and to assert himself more generally. Had I not brought the father into the room, it might have taken a much longer time to achieve this result.

A rarer, but nevertheless very important situation in which the parent's presence is generally contraindicated, is the one in which the parent is suffering with an incurable disease. If the parent is openly discussing the disease, then the parental involvement can be salutary for both the child and the parent. However, if the parent is using denial and other related defense mechanisms as a way of dealing with his or her reactions to the illness, then participation in the child's therapy can be detrimental to the parent. One would not want to have such a parent exposed to the child's working through his or her reactions to the inevitable death of the parent. Such exposure can be cruel and inhumane. Having the parent there will probably lessen the likelihood that the child will reveal his or her true feelings because of the appreciation (depending upon the child's age, sophistication, and intelligence) that his or her revelations may be detrimental to the parent.

CLINICAL EXAMPLES

Freud's Case of Little Hans [The Boy Who Feared Horses]

Here, I will present as my first clinical example Freud's case of Little Hans. Although all the other case examples in this book are derived directly from my own clinical experience, I have chosen to discuss Freud's case of Little Hans here because it lends itself well to demonstrating some important points made in this chapter as well as other sections of this book. However, I will only focus on certain aspects of the case that pertain to issues focused on in this chapter: confidentiality and the utilization of the parent (in this case the father) in the child's treatment. For those readers who may not be familiar with the details of the case and for those who may wish to refresh their memories, I present this brief summary:

> At the age of four-and-three-quarters Hans developed the fear that if he went out into the street, a horse might bite him. Accordingly, he dreaded leaving his house and preferred staying at home with his parents and sister Hanna, who was born when he was three-and-a-half. He was especially fearful of a horse's falling down, "making a row" with its feet, and possibly dying. Large dray horses, especially those pulling heavy wagons, were particularly frightening, as were

horses with black muzzles around their mouths and flaps around their eyes.

Freud did not conduct the analysis; rather, he instructed the father in the analytic method. The latter conducted the treatment and brought back to Freud detailed notes of his interchanges with his son, and these are recorded verbatim in the article. Freud saw the boy only once during the four months of therapy. The interview with the child and father together took place a little less than three months after the onset of the phobia.

Freud considered Hans' symptoms to be manifestations of oedipal difficulties. The horse symbolized his father, who he feared would castrate him (bite off his penis) in retaliation for his incestuous wishes toward his mother. Horses with black muzzles and flaps around their eyes were particularly reminiscent of his father, who had a black mustache and wore glasses. His fear that the horse might fall down and die was a reaction formation to his wish that his father would die—thereby leaving him the uncontested possessor of his mother.

Freud was presented with a child who exhibited neurotic symptoms. There were many ways in which Freud could have involved himself with his little patient. As mentioned, he had no guidelines. From all the possible alternative methods, he chose to have the father serve as therapist. It would have been more consistent with his previous pattern for Freud himself to have seen the child. Freud gives us his reason for this dramatic departure (p. 149):

> No one else, in my opinion, could possibly have prevailed on the child to make any such avowals; the special knowledge by means of which he was able to interpret the remarks made by his five-year-old son was indispensable, and without it the technical difficulties in the way of conducting a psycho-analysis upon so young a child would have been insuperable.

It is of interest that Melanie Klein, Anna Freud, and the child psychoanalysts who followed them—although basically accepting the Freudian theory (the differences between them notwithstanding)—did not generally utilize the parents in the treatment process. In fact, at the present time most classical child analysts, although they may get a history from the parents, confine their treatment exclusively to the child. They recognize that involvement with the parents may have therapeutic benefit; but the greater such involvement, the less they consider the treatment to be justifiably called psychoanalysis—which they consider to be the most definitive, reconstructive, and therapeutic form of therapy for those patients for whom it is the indicated treatment. Yet there is no question that Freud considered Hans to have been psychoanalyzed. A strange paradox.

Many therapists (not only classical child analysts) do not involve the parents directly in a child's treatment because they believe that disclosure of the child's revelations to the parents would compromise the therapy. Many hold that having the parents present in the session would restrict the child from freely expressing important material. Many believe that it is important to establish a special relationship with the child which is "all his(her) own." The preservation of the child's confidentiality is looked upon as an important prerequisite to effective treatment. From the outset this is communicated to the child. At the first meeting he or she alone is brought into the therapist's office (most often with tremendous anxiety and resistance) while the parent or parents are left in the waiting room. One purpose of this separation is to communicate this special relationship at the onset. In addition, the child is often told, quite early in treatment, that what is said to the therapist will not be revealed to the parents.

Although Freud was a strong proponent of confidentiality for his adult patients, there were no such considerations for Little Hans. His deepest and most humiliating secrets were to be directly revealed to his father, the person with whom one would think he would be most hesitant to discuss them. There is little evidence that Hans felt the need for confidentiality or that the therapy was an "invasion of his privacy." There is little reason to believe that Hans' treatment was in any way compromised or otherwise interfered with by his being asked to reveal himself to his father. Even in Freud's one interview with Hans, the father was present. Yet, the more ardently and strictly the classical child analyst adheres to the Freudian theories, the less the likelihood he or she would have such an interview.

Most therapists, regardless of their therapeutic orientation, would not instruct a parent in the therapy of his or her own child. First, to be a therapist requires many years of exacting training and experience. Because parents (with rare exception) have not had such training, they are ill-equipped to conduct such therapy, and to teach them to treat their own children would be a disservice to the patients. In addition, the child's parent cannot have the objectivity which the therapist must have toward the patient if the therapy is to be successful. Yet Freud seems to have ignored these considerations. I. Stone, in his novel on Freud (1971), states that Hans' father was one Max Graf, a graduate in jurisprudence, a doctorate in music, and an editor. He was one of the members of Freud's weekly discussion group and therefore had some familiarity with psychoanalytic theory. Neither Freud nor Stone described him to have had any previous experience as a therapist. But even if he did, Freud did not believe that he would be impaired enough by lack of objectivity to disqualify him as an effective therapist (which he apparently proved to be).

Whereas the theoretical conclusions that Freud came to in his work with Little Hans have often been too literally and even rigidly adhered to, the implications of Freud's mode of conducting the analysis have been largely ignored by the classical analysts. And this, I believe, has been most unfortunate.

Had Little Hans been working with Freud alone (with Freud having no therapeutic contact with the parents, and his "respecting" Hans' right to confidentiality) and had Freud encouraged him to discuss his sexual and hostile feelings with his parents, I believe it would have taken Hans far longer to do so. In the single interview with Freud Hans was encouraged to talk about these matters, and there was, I believe, the implied protection of a man who had already achieved formidable stature in Hans' eyes. Even prior to this interview, Hans knew that everything he said could be brought back for Freud's consideration, and in this way too Hans was reassured (from what had been communicated to him about Freud) that he would get Freud's benevolent protection. Further, I believe that the repeated discussions of the anxiety-provoking material with the father served to desensitize Hans to them in a way that would not have been accomplished as quickly had Freud himself seen the boy alone. Hans repeatedly had the *living experience* that the terrible retaliations he anticipated from his father did not occur.

Four months is a very short time for an analysis. One of the reasons for its short duration was, I believe, the intensive experience which Freud provided the child with his father; the father was the person for whom the horse stood in the first place—the person to whom Hans had to learn to desensitize himself, as well as the person with whom he had to work out the other problems he had in his relationship with him. This experience was a significant (and largely unappreciated) element in Hans' cure. *Hans was afraid of horses, and Freud had Hans work with the "horse."* Whether Freud did this by choice, hunch, intuition, or chance, we will probably never know. It is indeed unfortunate that Freud did not tell us more of the reasons for his decision (if there were any). If his followers had heeded this aspect of the case as diligently as the more theoretical, the whole course of child psychoanalysis might have taken a different path.

What factors, then, were instrumental in bringing about Hans' cure? The most important, I believe, was the improvement in Hans' relationship with his father. To conduct the analysis, the father assiduously noted all of Hans' comments which he considered relevant. This new attention and interest was a potent antidote to his previous deprivations and traumas. The analysis provided Hans with the opportunity to have the *living experience* that his father was more benevolent than he had believed and that his father did not, in fact, retaliate for Hans' hostility in the way that he had feared. This was most rapidly and conveniently accomplished via Freud's choice of the father as the child's therapist. To go further with this, I believe that the psychoanalytic experience—working together in it—provided the father and son with a new intimacy that they probably did not previously enjoy. Mutual revelation of inner feelings, in a benevolent setting, invariably brings people closer together. For a boy who was suffering some deprivation of affection in his relationships with his parents, this experience was clearly therapeutic. I do not think that *what* was said (in fact, the father made some hostile comments and a number of analytic blunders) was nearly as important as the experience of spending time alone together in a mutually enjoyable and productive endeavor. Regarding this issue, Freud stated (p. 285): "the only results of the analysis were that Hans recovered, that he ceased to be afraid of horses, and that he got on to rather familiar terms with his father as the latter reported with some amusement." Freud described Hans' improved relationship with his father as a fringe benefit of the treatment; I consider it a crucial contributing factor to the cure.

Another critical factor in Hans' cure relates to his relationship with Freud. The parents' admiration of Freud, which must have been formidable, could not but have been transmitted to Hans. He was repeatedly told that Freud was going to cure his phobia; therefore, the suggestive element, I believe, was strongly operative (although Freud denied this). In addition, the single interview with Freud must have had a powerful influence on the boy, observing as he had the awe and respect his parents had for "the Professor." It is reasonable to assume that everything that happened during this interview (pp. 184–185) must have considerably affected Hans. These suppositions are well substantiated by Hans' comment to his father upon returning home (p. 185): "Does the Professor talk to God?" Hans' fantasies of Freud's omnipotence and omniscience were reinforced during the interview by Freud's statement to him (p. 185):

> Long before he was in the world, I went on, I had known that a little Hans would come who would be so fond of his mother that he would be bound to feel afraid of his father because of it; and I told his father this.

Following the interview Hans expressed to his father his amazement that (p. 185) "he can tell all that beforehand." It is reasonable to assume that all that Freud told Hans, either directly or through his father (but especially directly), was received with greater receptivity and was held onto more tenaciously than if he had been in treatment with a more mortal and fallible therapist.

Also, there was uniform agreement between the father and Freud. At no point did Freud describe any differences of opinion between himself and the father. Only on the question of whether Hans should be told about vaginas and sexual intercourse was there the faintest possibility raised of the father's not following through with Freud's suggestions. Other than this possible exception, the father dutifully followed all of Freud's advice. Few therapists enjoy such cooperation on the part of a parent. More often than not parental jealousies, resentments, and other neurotic problems interfere with our work and place the child in the position of being torn between us and the parents—no matter how hard we try to establish a good working relationship with them. Hans had no such conflicts—and this, I am sure, was one of the reasons why his therapy proceeded so rapidly. However, such cooperation on the father's part was not without its drawbacks and dangers. His credulous attitudes caused him to transmit many communications which were not valid or relevant to Hans (Gardner, 1972b). Hans, however, got better in spite of this misinformation. In addition, the father did not serve for Hans as a good model for independent thinking and healthy self-assertion, so slavishly dependent was he on every one of Freud's words.

I think that the most important thing that happened in the interview was Freud's making it easier for Hans to express his angry feelings toward his father. Freud stated (pp. 184–185):

> I then disclosed to him that he was afraid of his father, precisely because he was so fond of his mother. It must be, I told him, that he thought his father was angry with him on that account; but this was not so, his father was fond of him in spite of it, and he might admit everything to him without fear.

Soon after this comment Hans reported that his father had hit him. Hans had unexpectedly butted his head into his father's stomach, and the latter had responded with a "reflex blow with his hand" (p. 185). Hans had not previously mentioned this incident, and the father then "recognized it as an expression of the little boy's hostile disposition towards him" (p. 185). It is reasonable that Freud's comments not only made it easier for Hans to express his hostility toward his father but made him feel less guilty about his anger. He was able to test his father's reaction in Freud's presence and gain thereby Freud's implied protection from any retaliation on his father's part. Such an experience, I believe, made it easier for Hans to express his hostility in subsequent situations when Freud was not present—contributing thereby to Hans' cure. Three days after the interview Freud described the (p. 186) *"first real improvement"* in Hans' phobia.

I do not believe it an oversimplification to state that all psychogenic symptoms are, in part, the result of a lowering of one's self-esteem and that, in a misguided and often self-defeating way, they attempt to enhance compensatorily one's feelings of self-worth. Therefore, helping a patient improve self-esteem is one of the most predictable ways to alleviate psychopathological symptomatology. There were a number of things which happened to Hans that enhanced his feelings of self-worth and in this way contributed to his cure. The improved relationship with his father (especially the greater attention he was receiving) must have made him feel better about himself. There is a self-deprecatory element in guilt ("How terrible I am for these thoughts, deeds, etc."). With an alleviation of the guilt Hans felt over his hostility toward his parents came a corresponding enhancement of his self-worth. Lastly, the attention that Hans was getting from the famous Professor must have also made him feel very important. The reader who is interested in reading further my comments on the case of Little Hans might wish to refer to my article on the subject (1972b). Therein I discuss other aspects of the case, aspects that go beyond those discussed in this chapter, namely, confidentiality and the use of the father in the child's treatment.

The Case of Jack
["Daddy, please take me fishing"]

The way in which a mother served well as an assistant therapist is well demonstrated by the case of a boy whom I will call Jack. He was six when he entered treatment. The chief complaint was stuttering. I consider stuttering to have a strong neurophysiological basis; however, I also believe that psychogenic factors can affect the stuttering in that in tense situations the stuttering is more likely to be worse. Accordingly, my psychotherapeutic approach with such patients is to make every attempt to reduce their tensions in the hope that the benefits to be derived from such reduction will ameliorate the stuttering symptomatology as well. I therefore explore other areas of difficulty, especially those that may produce tension and anxiety. In Jack's case, such difficulties were not hard to find. He was significantly inhibited in asserting himself, especially with his father. He was particularly fearful of expressing resentment toward his father and expected dire repercussions for such expression. His father, unfortunately, was very insensitive to Jack. However, he would not have responded with the terrible punishments Jack anticipated. In those situations in which Jack squelched his anger, his stuttering would predictably increase. Jack's anger-inhibition problem was so profound that he was generally viewed as a "model child" by his teacher, parents, and the parents of his friends.

One Monday afternoon (the day is pertinent) Jack began the session with his mother (whom I had learned could be an extremely valuable "assistant therapist"). He said that he had nothing much to talk about and asked if he could draw something with crayons. Suspecting that he had something important to "say" with this medium, I readily agreed. First he drew a blue pond. Then he drew grass and trees around the pond. Lastly, he drew some fishes in the

pond and then put down the crayon. When I asked him if the picture was finished, he replied that it was. I then asked him to tell a
story, and he stated, "A boy went fishing there, and he caught a
few fish." When I attempted to get him to elaborate upon the story,
he flatly denied that there was anything more to the story. I told
him that I considered him an excellent storyteller, and that I was
sure that he could do better. Again, he stated that there was nothing
more to the story. When I asked him if there was anything else he
could add to the picture, he again stated that the picture was completed. I noted that there were no figures in the picture, either human or animal, and suspected strongly that this had some
significance. However, it would have been antitherapeutic to suggest that he place figures in the picture, in that this would have
been a significant contaminant to the purity of his fantasy.

I turned to Jack's mother and asked her if she had any ideas
regarding the meaning of Jack's picture and "story." She responded
strongly in the affirmative, and then turned to Jack and began an
inquiry. She first asked him if he recalled what he had asked her
on arising the previous morning, which was a Sunday. Jack had no
recollection. Upon further urging he did recall that he had asked
her to ask his father to take him fishing. She then asked him what
her response was, and Jack replied, "You said that Dr. Gardner said
that it's a bad idea for you to be my messenger boy, and that if I
wanted to ask Daddy something, I should ask him myself." The
mother agreed that that was what happened, and then asked him
to continue telling what had happened. Jack replied, "I asked Daddy
if he would take me fishing, and he said that he wouldn't take me
now, but that he would take me later." In the subsequent inquiry
by the mother it was revealed that for the next five hours Jack repeatedly asked his father to take him fishing, and the father repeatedly said that he would do so, not then but later. Finally, by
midafternoon, Jack's father told him that it was too late to go fishing.

The mother then described how Jack's stuttering immediately
became severer. Whereas earlier in the day the stuttering had been
relatively mild, it became so bad following this final rejection that
Jack was practically unintelligible. And the increased severity was
still present when I saw him the following day. The picture and its
associated story now became completely understandable. It clearly
represented the fantasy that had existed in Jack's mind throughout
the previous day. There was a pond that he hoped to visit. The story

about the boy who went fishing represented his wish that he were indeed to have gone, but he never did. In the egocentricity of the six year old, if he is not there fishing, then no one is there—thus the conspicuous absence of human figures. In this situation, I decided not to tell a responding story but to use the picture and the associated inquiry with his mother as the point of departure for further discussion.

I then asked Jack what his thoughts and feelings were after what had happened with his father the previous day. Jack denied any resentment at all over the rejection. He reiterated his father's statement that it was really too late, in such a way that it was clear that he considered his father's excuse to be justified. I responded incredulously that I could not believe that there wasn't even a little bit of anger over what had happened. In the ensuing discussion Jack did admit to some anger and then we went on to discuss what he feared would happen if he were to express his resentment. I reassured him that his father, although insensitive at times, was not the kind of person who would be as punitive as Jack anticipated. I then suggested a joint session with the father in which the whole issue could be discussed.

In the following session Jack hesitantly and with some fear did express his disappointment over his father's rejection the previous Sunday. The session proved to be a meaningful one, and was the first of a series in which Jack *had the experience* (that word again) that expressing resentment did not result in the terrible consequences he had anticipated. If Jack's mother had not been present in the session, I would not have known what the picture meant, and we would not have then gone on to the series of meaningful and therapeutically useful discussions that focused on issues that were at the core of Jack's anger-inhibition problem.

The Case of Howie
(Nude Bathing in New Zealand)

Howie came to treatment at the age of eight with chief complaints of severe tics of the face and occasionally of the shoulders. No verbal tics were ever present, and I did not consider him to be suffering with Gille de la Tourette's syndrome. In addition, there was a stuttering problem. He was an extremely tense boy and the combination of tics, stuttering, and tension was interfering with his properly attending to his school work. He could not state exactly what distracted him while in the classroom but he found it extremely difficult to concentrate there. At home, as well, he was always "on edge," and would "fly off the handle" at the slightest frustration or provocation.

By the time five minutes had passed during my initial interview with Howie and his parents I had a fairly good idea about an important contributing factor to Howie's symptoms. His mother was the most sexually seductive woman I have ever encountered off the movie screen. Not only did her perfume precede her into the room but her breasts were so propped up that they might more probably be referred to as torpedoes. So prominent were they that the rest of her body appeared almost as an afterthought that trailed after them as they entered the room. They seemed to me to defy the laws of gravity. Just about every movement, every gesture, and every vocal intonation oozed sexual seductivity. In accordance with the important therapeutic principle that the therapist should attend to distracting stimuli that appear to be interfering with what are ostensibly the issues under consideration in the interview, I recognized immediately that a likely cause of Howie's symptoms was the anxiety he was suffering over the sexual excitation he was constantly exposed to in the presence of his mother. His tics and other tension manifestations related to his fears of expressing directly his sexual thoughts and feelings. (I did not know at that time about how great these fears were and what the special situations were in the household that made these formidable.) Were I to have had a deeper therapeutic relationship with the family, I would have brought the mother's sexual seductivity up at that point. However, I considered it more judicious to suppress my distraction and proceed with the interview (as best I could).

In the course of my evaluation I learned that Howie's mother considered herself to be "liberal and modern" with regard to the undressing situation in the home. Specifically, she considered it unnatural to do anything but undress in front of her children and husband. She also considered it "natural" to take baths and showers with Howie and/or his sister. When I suggested to her that this might be sexually titillating to Howie, she scoffed and accused me of being old-fashioned.

Howie's parents both complained about the fact that Howie's mother was frequently propositioned by men. Typically, she would report the experience to her husband who invariably would go into a raging fit with threats such as, "I'll kill the bastard," "Just wait till I lay my hands on that son of a bitch," "I'll cut off his balls," and "There ought to be laws that can get guys like that thrown in jail." The parents had described how on a number of occasions they had been invited to dinner parties where a man would make sexual advances toward the mother. Typically, Howie's mother would respond with a loud shriek: "How dare you make sexual advances to me. Imagine, a married man and your wife is only standing a few feet away!" Needless to say, the room was generally completely silent by the time she reached the end of this little speech. Invariably, Howie's father would go into one of his fits and on a few such occasions physically assaulted the man who had made passes at his wife. As might be expected, Howie heard about what had happened and on many occasions was witness to his father's rage outbursts and threats.

I mentioned elsewhere (Gardner, 1968a, 1983a) my belief that when children exhibit oedipal symptomatology there are most often specific family influences that are likely to produce the oedipal constellation of symptoms, specifically sexual titillation by the mother and/or castration threats by the father. Howie had an extremely seductive mother. He had a father who literally threatened to kill those who had illicit sexual designs on his wife and to "cut off their balls." Howie could not but place himself in the category of those who were not only titillated but who risked being castrated and/or murdered for their sexual excitation. It was no surprise that Howie was an extremely tense boy who stuttered and ticked. His situation and symptoms certainly warrant being viewed as oedipal.

Early in therapy I recommended that Howie's mother discontinue the practice of undressing in front of and bathing with him. She was most unreceptive to my recommendation, claiming that I was "old-fashioned." However, she finally agreed to follow my recommendation with the response, "Well, you're the doctor." My experience has been that this comment invariably reveals lack of conviction for compliance. In the following session Howie's mother described how she had "really" followed my advice. She had gone to the bathroom to take a shower and made sure to tell Howie that he was not permitted to come into the bathroom. However, when she got out of the shower she realized that she had "forgotten" to bring in a towel. Accordingly, she called to Howie and asked him to bring a towel into the bathroom; but warned him that he should cover his eyes with his hand and be very sure not to look through the slits between his fingers. Unfortunately, I was totally unsuccessful in my attempts to get his mother to appreciate the seductivity of what had gone on. She merely accused me of "having sex on the mind all the time, just like all men." She also told me that she had heard about psychiatrists who find a sexual interpretation to everything and she was beginning to suspect that I was like the rest of them.

One day, early in treatment, Howie came into the waiting room and his ticking was significantly bad. When I asked what had happened the mother replied, "I can't understand it Doctor, he was perfectly fine until he came to this office." It is not uncommon for therapists to be accused of making symptoms worse. I replied by asking the mother exactly *when* things got worse.

She replied, "I don't know Doctor, he was fine while we were riding over here in the car. And he was fine when we got into your waiting room. It happened while we were sitting down there waiting for you." I then asked her what she and Howie were doing while waiting.

She responded, "We weren't doing anything Doctor. We were only reading a magazine together. It was Time Magazine." I asked her to bring the magazine up and I sat the two of them down on the couch and requested that they try to reconstruct the situation as carefully as they could. I asked them to try to recall the exact page where they had started reading the magazine together, to go through the pages one at a time, and try to recall the discussion that ensued. The magazine was brought up; they sat down together and began perusing the magazine.

Finally, after four or five minutes, Howie said, "Mommy, I think you said something funny when we were looking at this picture." He pointed to a *Qantas Airlines* advertisement in which was depicted a beach scene. The advertisement read: "It is not generally known that Australia and New Zealand have among the most beautiful beaches in the world. Call your travel agent. *Fly Qantas.* Come and see for yourself." I then asked exactly what the conversation was around this advertisement.

The mother responded, "I don't think anything happened, Doctor. All I said to Howie was 'I wonder whether they have nude bathing there in Australia and in New Zealand?'" Again, my attempts to get Howie's mother to appreciate that she was introducing sex into a situation where others would not have had a sexual association proved futile. She again accused me of being a sex maniac.

As the reader might expect, my efforts to help Howie failed completely. Both the mother and the father had too great an investment in the mother's seductivity to give it up so quickly or easily. It was the mother's primary source of attention and ego enhancement. Over many years this woman had devoted significant time and energy to perfecting her seductive skills and talents. In addition to providing her with an inordinate amount of attention, her seductivity served as a hostile outlet. She tantalized men and not only rejected them herself but could rely upon her husband to attack them as well. For her husband, having such an attractive wife was a source of ego enhancement. In addition, having a wife whom other men appeared to prefer in preference to their own wives was also a source of pride. And his wife's complaints about those who propositioned her provided him with an outlet for his own pent-up hostility. After a few months' treatment the family discontinued therapy and informed me that they were going to find another psychiatrist—one who "didn't have so much sex on his mind." I wished them luck in their quest for such a psychiatrist.

The Case of Walter
("Stop touching the walls")

Walter was referred to treatment at the age of ten because of a touching compulsion. Specifically, he felt compelled to run his hands along walls as he walked past them. The movements were executed with his finger tips in the vertical direction. Not only was he compelled to perform these motions indoors, but outdoors as well. Accordingly, his finger tips would often become irritated to the point of bleeding and in recent months many had become callused. In the classroom, as well, Walter was compelled to touch the walls. The compulsion was so strong there that he could not restrain himself from getting up out of his seat during lessons and going over to the side of the room to touch the walls. And this of course interfered with his learning in school. He was getting poor grades in spite of high intelligence. He was also the subject of ridicule in the classroom because of this symptom, so much so that at times he would resist going to school entirely. I had never before encountered this particular symptom (and I never have since, for that matter).

By the time we reached the end of my two-hour consultation with Walter and his parents, I still did not have the faintest idea why Walter had this unusual compulsion. As we stood near the door making the next appointment, wherein I was going to explore the matter further, the reason for the compulsion immediately became apparent. As the four of us stood talking, Walter was stroking his mother's breasts with both hands. The movements were identical to those used when he executed his compulsive ritual. The parents appeared to be completely oblivious to what was going on and carried on the conversation as if nothing unusual was happening.

In accordance with my belief that it is very important to give serious consideration to certain therapeutic "distractions," I interrupted the conversation and asked the parents if they had noticed anything unusual going on while we were talking. They both replied in the negative—even though Walter was still stroking his mother's breasts. I then directed their attention to what was happening and the mother laughed and said, "Oh he does that all the time. It doesn't mean a thing." The father agreed that this was a common occurrence but considered it harmless.

As is clear, Walter's symptom certainly could be explained along oedipal lines. As is clear, as well, there was obvious maternal seductivity that was a primary contributing factor. In Walter's case, the therapy proceeded well. I did not have too much difficulty impressing upon the parents the relationship between Walter's symptoms and the mother's titillating him. The mother did not have difficulty complying with my suggestion that she no longer permit Walter to caress her breasts. Within a week there was a marked reduction in the symptomatology. The parents had some sexual problems (as the reader might have guessed), and I was successful in effecting some improvement in that area. And this, of course, lessened the mother's need to gain her gratifications from her son. Walter had other problems as well and these were dealt with successfully so that by the end of the five months of treatment he was asymptomatic.

The Case of Tara
[Your Brother's in Heaven]

The way in which the educational element and parental involvement can combine to effect dramatic improvement in a child's symptoms is well demonstrated by the case of four-year-old Tara, who was referred because of phobic symptoms of about six months' duration. When Tara was two, her brother Kevin (then 16) was found to be leukemic. During the next one-and-a-half years, Tara's mother was swept up in the care of her oldest child. Her mother's involvement in the care of Kevin was so extensive that little time was left for Tara. Tara was never told that her brother's illness would be fatal; at the time of his death she was simply told that he had gone to heaven, where he was very happy. The family was European, and the father had been temporarily assigned to his organization's office in the United States. At the time of Kevin's death, the family returned to their native country for the burial. Unknown to Tara, her brother's body was in the cargo compartment of the airplane. When they arrived in their native country, Tara was quickly sent to stay with friends while her brother was buried.

Upon returning to the United States, Tara began exhibiting the symptoms that ultimately brought her for treatment. Whereas previously she had attended nursery school without difficulty, she now refused. When the doorbell rang, she panicked and would hide under the bed. Whereas previously she enjoyed visits at the homes of friends, she now refused. She seemed comfortable only when she was close to both of her parents and would scream hysterically if they left. Although her parents had told her that Kevin was in heaven, she repeatedly asked questions about her brother. Apparently she was not satisfied with the answer her parents had given her. Observing Tara to be so upset by her brother's absence, the parents decided to destroy most of his personal possessions and stored away the remainder.

My inquiry with the patient confirmed my initial speculation that Tara's symptoms were the direct result of the way in which the parents had handled Kevin's death with regard to Tara. From Tara's viewpoint, people, without explanation, could suddenly disappear from the surface of the earth. Accordingly, there was no safety because one never knew why such disappearances occurred. It might be that someone came to the door and took children away; or perhaps it occurred at nursery school; or maybe one was abducted from the homes of friends and relatives. No place was really safe. In addition, there was no point in trying to get explanations from one's parents as to how such disappearances occur, because their answers would also prove unsatisfactory.

With this speculation regarding the origin of Tara's symptoms, I asked the parents what their genuine beliefs were regarding the brother's whereabouts. Both claimed that they had no conviction

for any type of existence in the hereafter and their religious convictions were not particularly deep. They said it was their view that
telling Tara that her brother was buried in the ground would be
psychologically deleterious. I told the parents what I considered to
be the source of their child's problems. I explained to them that
although their explanation was benevolently motivated, I considered it to be doing her more harm than good. I suggested that they
return home and tell Tara exactly what they believed happened to
their son—as simply and as accurately as possible. I suggested that
they give her one of her brother's few remaining mementos and tell
her that it would always be hers. Although initially reluctant, they
finally gained some conviction for my suggestion and decided to
follow my recommendations.

I then explained to them the psychological importance of
mourning and described how Tara had been deprived of this important salutary experience. I suggested that they encourage Tara
to ask the same questions that she had asked in the past and to
recognize that the repetition of these conversations was an important part of the mourning and working-through process. Further, I
suggested that they slowly urge her to face once again the various
phobic situations and to reassure her each time that she, unlike
Kevin, would not be taken away. I suggested that they impress upon
her the fact that Kevin was sick and that he died of physical illness.
She, however, was well, and there was no reason to believe that her
death was anything but remote.

Within one week, there was a dramatic improvement in Tara's
condition. After having been told about the true circumstances of
her brother's death, Tara cried bitterly. As I had suspected, Tara
repeatedly questioned her parents during the next few days, and
this time the parents responded in detail and with patience. She
was given a picture of her brother, which she carried around at all
times and proudly showed to friends and relatives. With such presentations, she would once again discuss in detail her brother's
death. Concomitantly, there was a marked diminution in all of
her fears. Within a week she was again attending nursery school
without difficulty. She no longer cowered at the ringing of the doorbell and once again began visiting friends. Moreover, she experienced only mild fear when her parents went out at night. No further
sessions were scheduled, and the parents were advised to contact
me again only if there was a need for further consultation. Six

months later, I learned through the referring colleague that Tara had remained asymptomatic.

This case demonstrates well the value of education in treatment and how active participation by parents can be extremely useful in child therapy. Although seeing Tara alone might have ultimately brought about the same alleviation of her symptoms, I believe that active work with the parents and my "educating" them caused the therapy to proceed much more rapidly than it would have had I seen the child alone.

The Case of Mack
[The Baseball Hall of Fame]

Mack entered treatment at nine and a half because of disruptive behavior at school and home. There was a basic organic deficit characterized by hyperactivity and impulsivity. His father had left the home about one year previously and was most unreliable regarding his visits. When he was home he was frequently condescending toward Mack. And the anger Mack felt in response to these indignities was being displaced onto siblings, peers, his mother, and his teacher.

Near the middle of his eighth month in treatment, Mack spoke about his father's visit to the home that previous weekend. Although he tried to speak enthusiastically, it was quite clear that he was forcing the impression that the experience was pleasurable. Mack's mother, however, related how he had followed his father around all weekend "like a puppy dog." She stated that it was pathetic to see how Mack would not resign himself to his father's lack of interest. She described how whenever Mack would try to elicit his father's attention or interest he would be responded to with a "shut up" or "don't bother me." Mack became upset by what his mother said and denied that there was any validity to it.

He then described two dreams. In the first he was in a hotel in Cooperstown, New York, the site of the National Baseball Museum. (Mack was an avid baseball fan.) There he was trying to get onto a cable car of the kind seen in San Francisco. The patient could not figure out the meaning of the dream. He did describe, however, a pleasurable experience at Cooperstown with his mother and teenage siblings a week previously but could provide no further associations. Mack's mother then offered further information. She described how the whole family had gone to San Francisco when Mack was about five and this had been one of the high points of his life. This occurred long before his father had left the home and Mack often referred to the experience with great pleasure. The meaning of the dream then became clear: In response to the frustrations that he had experienced with his father the previous weekend Mack was dreaming of a return to happier days with his father in San Francisco. The more recent experience with his mother in Cooperstown was marred by his longing to regain the joys of the San Francisco trip with his father (as symbolized by his trying to get on the cable car). However, he is not successful in getting onto the cable car. This reflected his appreciation, at some level, that his father could no longer provide him with the kind of gratifications he had given him in the past.

Had the mother not been in the room I would not have understood the meaning of this dream. Its analysis is a good example of the vital role that a parent can play when actively participating in the child's therapy. Both the mother and I agreed that the aforementioned interpretation was valid. When it was presented to Mack he admitted that it might be possible, but I did not get the feeling that he accepted our explanation with much conviction.

Mack then went on to relate his second dream. In it he was walking to school with a classmate and they were going to be late. There was a bus ahead and Mack wanted to run ahead and catch the bus. His friend, however, was resistive to the idea. The dream ended with neither boy reaching the bus. Rather, there was a confused discussion regarding whether they should have boarded it. Again, Mack was unable to ascertain the meaning of the dream and I, myself, could offer no specific suggestions. Mack's mother, however, stated, that in her opinion, buses appeared to be the symbol of Mack's father. When he lived at home, Mack's father commuted into New York City and returned each day in a bus to the suburban New Jersey home where the mother and children lived. Especially when he was younger, Mack would often ask if his father was on a passing bus. With this new information the dream became clear. It reflected Mack's ambivalence about joining his father. On the one hand, he desperately wants to catch up to the bus (as symbolized by Mack's pursuing it); on the other hand, he does not anticipate acceptance by his father or gratifying experiences with him so lags behind (as symbolized by his friend's [Mack's alter ego] resistance to such pursuit).

Again, when Mack was offered this explanation for the dream he passively accepted its interpretation, but I did not feel that I was "hitting home." However I did have the feeling that there was some receptivity, that some seeds were planted, and subsequent experience bore this out. Had Mack's mother not been present these advances would have been much more slowly achieved.

CONCLUDING COMMENTS

I believe that the traditional practice of seeing children alone while mothers are in the waiting room compromises seriously therapeutic efficacy. My experience has been that children's treatment proceeds much more rapidly when there is active participation by parents. I believe that thousands (and possibly even millions) of hours have been wasted by having mothers sit in waiting rooms reading magazines while their children are being seen alone by their therapists. In many cases such therapy is basically a waste of time. I am referring here to therapy that is primarily play. If the parents are paying for this, they are paying for a very expensive playmate. But even when the therapy is providing the child with a richer experience, it is still not as efficient nor as effective as it might have been if there were more active parental involvement. Throughout the rest of this book, I will be describing the techniques I believe can be useful in the treatment of children. Throughout I will be describing also the ways in which parental participation has been useful in their treatment.

FIVE

The Talking, Feeling, and Doing Game

When the One Great Scorer comes to
write against your name—
He marks—not that you won or lost—
but how you played the game.

Grantland Rice

The mutual storytelling technique proved useful in facilitating children's telling self-created stories and providing other fantasy material that was of value in therapy. There were, however, children who were not free enough to tell stories using the relatively unstructured format of "Dr. Gardner's Make-up-a-Story Television Program." It was for these children that the derivative games were devised. However, there were still some children who were so inhibited, constrained, or resistive that even these more attractive modalities did not prove successful in getting them to reveal themselves. It was for these children that *The Talking, Feeling, and Doing Game* (Gardner, 1973a) was devised. This game proved useful in engaging the vast majority of such children. In addition, for children who were free enough to reveal their fantasies, it proved useful in another therapeutic modality.

THE BASIC FORMAT OF THE TALKING, FEELING, AND DOING GAME

The game is similar in appearance to the typical board games with which most children are familiar (Figure 5.1). It includes a playing board, dice, playing pawns, a spinner, a path along which the pawns are moved, reward chips, and cards that are drawn from the center of the game board. This familiarity, as well as the fact that it is a game, reduces initial anxieties and attracts the child to the therapeutic instrument.

To begin the game both the therapist and the child place their colored pawns at the START position. Alternatively, they throw the dice and move their pawns along a curved path of squares which ultimately end at the FINISH position. For younger children, one die can be used. A pawn can land on one of a number of squares: white, red, yellow, SPIN, GO FORWARD (a specific number of squares), and GO BACKWARD (again, a specific number of squares). If the pawn lands on a white square, the player takes a Talking Card; on a yellow square, a Feeling Card; and on a red square, a Doing Card. If the pawn lands on SPIN, the player spins the spinner and follows the directions. Generally, these provide gain and loss of chips, or forward and backward movement of the playing pawn. Similarly, landing on GO FORWARD or GO BACKWARD squares results in movement of the pawn. The spinner and movement squares are of little, if any, psychological significance. They are included to insure the child's fun and relieve some of the pressure associated with a high frequency of drawing only the aforementioned three types of cards.

Of course the core of the game is the directions and questions on each of the cards. As their titles imply, the Talking Cards instruct the player to make comments that are primarily in the intellectual and cognitive area. The Feeling Cards focus primarily on affective issues. The Doing Cards usually involve play acting and/or some kind of physical activity. The child is given a reward chip for responding to each of the cards. Although a token reinforcement is provided, the game is by no means a form of behavior therapy. Positive reinforcement is not being given for behavioral change

Figure 5.1

at the manifest level. Rather, the child is being reinforced for providing psychodynamically meaningful material for psychotherapeutic utilization. The child's and the therapist's responses are used as points of departure for psychotherapeutic interchanges.

There is no actual time limit for the game. Both the therapist and the patient play similiarly, and each responds to the cards. The first player to reach the FINISH position receives five extra reward chips. The second player continues to play until he or she also reaches the FINISH position. If the game is interrupted prior to one player's reaching the FINISH position, the player who is closest to that position receives three extra reward chips. The therapist should discourage active competition on the child's part for the acquisition of chips. The game should be played at a slow pace, and each response should serve as a point of departure for psychotherapeutic interchange.

There are 104 cards in each stack. I always randomize them and have never "stacked the deck" with specific cards that I hope the child will draw. The cards are so designed that any card will be relevant to any player. About five percent of the cards in each stack are so simple and nonthreatening that just about any child will respond. These are basically placed there for the extremely fragile child who would be threatened by the cards that will touch on basic problems of living. These simpler cards insure that the child will get chips and thereby remain motivated to participate in the game. The most liberal criteria are used when deciding whether or not a child should be given a chip for responding. Again, the therapist wants to do everything possible to draw the child in and maintain his or her interest. Some typical low-anxiety cards: "How old is your father?"; "What's your lucky number? Why?"; "What is your telephone number?"; "What is your address?"; "What's your favorite flavor ice cream?"; "What present would you like to get for your next birthday?"; "What's your favorite smell?" "Make believe you're blowing out the candles on your birthday cake."; and "Make a funny sound with your mouth. If you spit, you don't get a chip."

The remaining questions and directions are far richer psychologically and are at the "heart" of the game. These are not as anxiety provoking as a request to make up a story that will reveal free fantasies; however, they provide highly meaningful therapeutic material. Some typical cards: "All the girls in the class were invited to a birthday party except one. How did she feel? Why wasn't she invited?''; "Everybody in the class was laughing at a girl. What had happened?''; "A boy has something on his mind that he's afraid to tell his father. What is it that he's scared to talk about?''; "What's the worst thing a boy can say to his mother?''; "Suppose two people were talking about you, and they didn't know you were listening. What do you think you would hear them saying?''; "What things come into your mind when you can't fall asleep?''; "If the walls of your house could talk, what would they say about your family?''; "Tell about something you did that made you proud.''; and "What's the worst thing that ever happened to you in your whole life?''.

The child's responses are usually revealing of the psychological issues that are most relevant to him or her at that point. The questions and instructions cover the wide range of human experiences. The material elicited is likely to be relevant to the etiology of the child's disturbance. The questions are designed to direct the child's attention to the basic life conflicts which are being resolved in inappropriate and maladaptive ways by the symptomology. They direct the child's attention to the issues that I referred to previously, that is, the basic life conflicts that are at the foundation of psychopathological processes. As mentioned, each response serves as a point of departure for therapeutic interchanges. The therapist does not merely provide the child with a chip and then race on with the game to see who can reach FINISH first. Rather, the therapist tries to get "as much mileage" as possible from each response, using his or her discretion in deciding how much discussion is warranted for each patient. Highly defensive and resistant children will not be able to tolerate the kind of in-depth discussion in which the healthier child can readily participate.

The therapist answers the same questions as the child. The greater the therapist's knowledge of the child's problems, the more judicious will be his or her responses. Obviously, it is not the therapist's role to provide answers relevant to his or her *own* life problems. Rather the responses should be designed to provide therapeutic messages pertinent to the child's difficulties. I always respond honestly. Often I will provide a response that will relate to an experience of mine in childhood that is relevant to the patient's problems. Children generally enjoy hearing about the events of their parent's lives that occurred at that time in the parent's childhood that corresponds to the age of the child at the time of the conversation. Such discussions draw children closer to their parents. The same principle holds in therapy. Such revelations, then, can contribute to a deepening of the therapist-patient relationship. As mentioned, a good relationship is crucial if therapy is to be successful. Without it, there will be little receptivity to the therapist's messages and practically no identification with him or her.

Many therapists, especially those with a classical psychoanalytic orientation, may take issue with the freedom with which I reveal myself. They would argue that I am contaminating terribly the therapeutic field and making the patient's free associations practically useless. I am in full agreement that such revelations contaminate the patient's free associations. I am not in agreement, however, that the classical approach is without its drawbacks. It does indeed provide the so-called "blank screen" for the purest projections. However, the acquisition of such information is done in a setting which, I believe, is antitherapeutic. It creates a distance between the therapist and the patient that compromises the development of a good therapist-patient relationship. The patient's thoughts and feelings about the therapist become distorted and divorced from reality. The situation increases the likelihood that the patient will develop delusions about the therapist and will idealize him or her. It will widen the gap between them as the patient comes to view the therapist as perfect. We can love most those whom we know nothing about—but such love is more delusional than real, based as it is on a paucity of information. What is gained in the way of pure free associations is more than counterbalanced, I believe, by the losses of a compromised therapist-patient relationship and the antitherapeutic experience of the patient comparing him- or herself negatively with the therapist. *The Talking, Feeling, and Doing Game* provides the therapist with the opportunity to reveal defects in a noncontrived and nonartificial setting. He or she thereby becomes more human to the patient, and this is generally salutary for the therapist-patient relationship. In addition, my revelations are not those that would compromise my own privacy and that of my family. Even with these restrictions, there is enough that has gone on in my life to provide me with a wealth of potential information for revelation.

I uniformly answer all questions. Some highly defensive children, however, may find it difficult to do so. Sometimes, I will inform such children that failure to answer the question will result in their not getting a reward chip, and this will lessen the likelihood that they will win the game. Some children are motivated by this "threat" and try to respond to the card. On occasion, a child will refrain from answering most cards but still involve him- or herself in the game. Many of these children listen attentively to my responses and, I believe, gain thereby from the game. Although I am working here in a partial vacuum because I am not getting as much information from the child as is desirable, my knowledge of the child's history and background provides me with enough information to give responses to the cards that are meaningful to the child and pertinent to his or her problems.

The question is sometimes raised about winning and losing when playing therapeutic games with children. *The Talking, Feeling, and Doing Game* obviates this problem. It may not be immediately apparent to the therapist that the main determinant as to who wins the game is *luck*. If each player answers each card, the determinant as to who wins the game is the dice. If a player obtains many high thows, then he or she will reach FINISH earlier and thereby acquire fewer chips. If a player obtains a larger number of low throws, more chips will be acquired when going from START to FINISH. Because low and high throws average out for each player, the number of wins and losses also average out over the course of treatment.

Although *The Talking, Feeling, and Doing Game* was originally devised to engage resistant children in therapy, it has proved useful for less defended children as well. In fact, it has proved to be the favorite therapeutic activity of the children in my practice. Many other therapists have informed me that this has been their experience as well. This therapeutic boon is not without its drawbacks, however. One danger of the game is that it will lure the child (and, unfortunately, the therapist) away from utilizing techniques that are more likely to elicit "deeper" psychodynamic material. Dealing with this material is also important in therapy. Accordingly, the therapist should not injudiciously "respect" the child's wishes to devote the entire therapeutic experience to this technique. The game is generally useful for children over the age of five or six, the age at which they begin to appreciate the give and take structure of board games. At that age, of course, the therapist may have to read the cards to the child (or read along with the child), but this is not an impediment. Whereas the mutual storytelling technique and its derivative games are generally not useful above the age of 11, one can get a few more years mileage from *The Talking, Feeling, and Doing Game*. My experience has been that it can be useful up to the age of 14 or 15.

Although primarily designed to be used in the one-to-one therapeutic situation, the game can be used in child group therapy as well (preferably for small groups of three to five children). When so utilized the therapist can use a child's response as a point of departure for group discussion. The game is particularly useful in child group therapy because it provides intrinsic structure in a situation that traditionally tends to become unstructured (the children tend to become playful, rambunctious, distracted, etc.). In addition, it facilitates discussion of problems in a setting in which such conversations are usually difficult to accomplish because of the reticence of most children to engage in them.

Generally, the material elicited when utilizing the Mutual Storytelling Technique is closer to pure dream and free fantasy than that revealed in *The Talking, Feeling, and Doing Game*. The "Make-up-a-Story Television Program" is so structured that there are no specific stimuli around which the stories are told. Traditional play materials such as dolls and puppets, although valuable and frequently effective catalysts for story elicitation, do contaminate the story and tend to "draw" the child's projections into specific directions. The cards in *The Talking, Feeling, and Doing Game* are similarly contaminating. However, I believe that the "push" of the unconscious material to be released in a form specific for the child's needs at that particular time is far stronger than the "pull" of the evoking stimulus and its power to significantly alter the projected material. Accordingly, the "channeling" of the projections is not very significant.

First, I will describe some common responses I provide for each of the three categories of cards. Then I will present some clinical vignettes in which I demonstrate my utilization of the game in the treatment of children.

EXAMPLES OF CARD RESPONSES

Talking Cards

Human behavior lends itself well to being divided into thoughts, feelings, and actions. It was from this observation that I decided to name this game *The Talking, Feeling, and Doing Game*. Furthermore, the sequence here is also important. Thoughts generally precede feelings, and feelings precede actions. Certainly, the sequence is applicable for fight-flight reactions. One sees a danger. A possible emotional reaction is fear. In response to the fear one flees. Another possible emotional reaction is anger. Then, one fights and the anger enhances one's efficiency in protecting oneself from the attacker. For emotions such as sexual arousal and hunger, feelings may precede thoughts. One feels hungry, then one experiences thoughts related to food acquisition. Then one takes action and attempts to obtain food. Because therapy is more likely to deal with fight-flight emotions then those related to eating and sexual arousal (not that these aren't involved in treatment at all), I decided to place *talking* before *feeling* in the name of the game.

The Talking Cards encourage the child to speak about his or her opinions on a wide variety of subjects. The questions are designed to elicit information related to the fundamental problems of life with which all children are confronted. As discussed in Chapter Three the solutions to these problems can either be adaptive or maladaptive. We refer to a maladaptive solution as *symptomatic*. The game is designed to elicit discussion of these issues in the hope that the child will learn how to deal better with these problems of life and thereby not have to resort as frequently to the pathological adaptations.

It is vital for the therapist to appreciate that *there are no standard answers for the therapist to provide*. Rather, each response must be tailored to the particular child with whom the therapist is playing the game. Accordingly, it would be an error for the therapist to use the responses I provide here in the models I have created for the therapist's answers. Rather, they should be viewed as selected examples of the *kinds* of responses that I might provide and as guidelines for the therapist's own responses. Just as the therapist's responding story in the mutual storytelling game is tailored to the patient's story, the therapist's answers in this game are also designed to fit the patient's needs.

Question: What sport are you worst at?

Response: I never really was very good at sports. So there are a lot of sports I am pretty bad at. Of the sports that were commonly played in my neighborhood when I was kid, I would say that the one that I was worst at was basketball. I guess that I didn't try hard enough. It's not that I was born a klutz; I just think that I didn't work at it enough. I used to feel pretty bad when kids would choose up sides and I was the last one to be chosen. Had I worked harder at it, it probably wouldn't have happened to me.

The card "What sport are you worst at?" essentially forces the therapist to reveal an area of weakness. Even if the therapist were an olympic decathalon champion, he or she would still be provided with the opportunity to talk about a sport in which there is weakness. Besides providing the aforementioned benefits of such revelation, I use the response to put in a plug for the work ethic. The response also provides the child with the knowledge that I too had my rejections and that I too was not chosen for involvement in various activities when I was a child. This is a universal phenomenon, and it is helpful for the child to know that the therapist too suffered such rejections. It contributes to a sense of communion with the therapist and this cannot but be therapeutic.

* * *

Question: What things come into your mind when you can't fall asleep?

Response: If I had let someone take advantage of me during the day and didn't do anything about it, it would tend to linger on my mind. I would keep thinking about what I should have done and how I didn't do it. This might interfere with my falling asleep. I would keep thinking of the thing over and over again—especially how I might have said something or done something, but I didn't say or do anything at the time. I'm sorry then that I didn't speak up or do something. But later, it was too late. And there may be nothing that I can then do about it. So I have trouble falling asleep because I keep thinking about what I should have done. Sometimes however, there is something I can do about it and then I do it at the time. Then I get it off my chest. Then I feel better. Then I can fall asleep more easily. I did the thing that I was supposed to do.

For example, something happened when I was a young kid that caused me to lose a lot of sleep for a few nights. I was in junior high school at the time. I was walking out of a classroom. Some kids in the class made some kind of a smoke bomb and threw it into one of the desks. The teacher wasn't there and as they left the room the smoke started to pour out of the desk. I was scared that the desk would catch on fire. I wanted to run over and pull everything out of the desk because I was so scared that the whole school might burn down, but I was afraid that the other kids would call me "chicken." So I walked out of the classroom with the others. About five minutes

later I heard a fire alarm bell and I wasn't surprised. It was a big
school with almost 1000 kids. And we all quickly left the building.
As we got outside I could see the smoke coming out of the classroom.
The fire engines came and put out the fire. Fortunately, it was caught
in time and no one was hurt. Also, the fire didn't spread too far. The
kids who lit the smoke bomb were kicked out of school.

I was really sorry that I hadn't had the guts to pull the stuff out
of that desk and stomp on it. I think there were other kids in the
classroom that wanted to do the same thing, but none of us had the
guts. For the next three nights I kept thinking about how much trouble I would have saved everybody—especially those boys—if only I
had done what I knew was the right thing. I know some kids probably would have laughed at me, but I would have known I was doing
the right thing. It was a big mistake. And I still remember it after all
these years, even though I only lost some sleep for a few nights.

Although my response at the beginning is designed to be general, the example I give makes particular reference to self-assertion.
In particular, I focus on the importance of doing what one considers to be "right" even though it may be the unpopular thing. I try
thereby to encourage self-assertion. Such comments are especially
helpful to children with self-assertion problems. The pent-up resentments that such children cause themselves can distract them
from learning in school. It also contributes to their becoming tar-
gets for bullies and scapegoaters. And this too can interfere with
learning as the child comes to dread school attendance.

* * *

Question: What's the best story you ever heard or read? Why?

Response: Of all the books that I ever read when I was young, the
one that I remember to have been the best was the one describing
the life of Thomas A. Edison. As you probably know, Thomas A.
Edison was one of the greatest inventors who ever lived. Although
he wasn't the only man to work on these things, his inventions were
important—giving us the electric light bulb, the phonograph, and the
moving picture camera. He was a poor boy who lived in Ohio. He
was a very hard worker and was an extremely curious person. He
was immensely interested in how things work.

He had a laboratory near his home and it is said that he would
sometimes work most of the night on his inventions. He loved learning about how things work, and he loved trying to figure out better
ways of doing things. To this day, people all over the world use his

inventions. To this day, he is remembered as having given mankind some of its greatest inventions. He must have really felt great about himself because of all the good he did for mankind. It is mainly his curiosity and hard work that did these things both for himself and for others. It was Thomas A. Edison who said: "Genius is 1 percent inspiration and 99 percent perspiration." Do you know what that means?

Edison epitomizes the gratification and fame that can come to someone who is strongly committed to the work ethic. I emphasize here the great benefit that can come to others from the efforts of a strongly motivated person. My aim here is to engender some desire on the child's part to view Edison as an admirable figure worthy of emulation and inspiration. Obviously, one such message is not going to achieve this goal. However, the seed is planted and with reiteration over time it is quite possible that Edison will become incorporated into the child's psychic structure and join with other introjects to serve as a model for identification and emulation. Younger children, obviously, will not understand the quotation about genius and perspiration. However, even they can be engaged in a discussion of it if the words they do not understand are explained.

* * *

Question: Suppose two people you knew were talking about you and they didn't know you were listening. What do you think you would hear them saying?

Response: I might hear the people saying that I'm the kind of a person who is direct and honest. Although people might disagree, at times, with what I've said, they would agree that I am direct about what my opinions are and don't pussyfoot about them. They know that when they ask me a question, they'll get an honest and direct answer with no hedging, beating-around-the-bush, or saying things that aren't true. I am not saying that they would say that I never lied in my whole life and that I never will, only that they are pretty confident that I'll be honest with them. You see, I believe that there is truth and wisdom to the old saying that "honesty is the best policy." If you tell a lie, you have to go around worrying that people will find out that you've lied. Also, lots of people feel bad about themselves when they lie, they feel guilty about it. And when people find out that you've lied, then they don't trust you even when you've told the truth. So these are the main reasons why I find it better to tell the truth, rather than to lie. What's your opinion on this subject?

Identification with the therapist and modeling oneself after him or her is an important part of the therapeutic process. This is very similar to the educational model in which the child learns, in part, because of identification with the teacher and the desire to gain the same gratifications that the teacher enjoys from learning. The therapist not only serves as a model for learning, but should be serving as a model for other desirable attributes as well, for example, healthy self-assertion, sensitivity to the feelings of others, feelings of benevolence toward those who are in pain, handling oneself with dignity, and honesty. This card enables the therapist to provide examples of such traits. However, the therapist should select traits that are particularly relevant to the child's problems. Furthermore, the therapist must avoid presenting these with a flaunting or holier-than-thou attitude.

* * *

Question: Make believe that you're looking into a crystal ball that can show anything that is happening anywhere in the whole world. What do you see?

Response: I'm looking into a crystal ball. There's a cloud there, and I can't see anything now. Wait a minute . . . wait a minute . . . it's starting to clear. I think I can see something now. Oh, yes, it's a big auditorium. In the front rows are lots of children, school children. In the back rows are all the parents. There's something happening on the stage. There are teachers sitting up there and, oh yeah, there's the principal. He's standing in the front and he's giving something to a child. It looks like he's giving her an award. She certainly looks proud. Now the principal is shaking her hand and everybody's clapping. Now he's making another announcement. And here comes another child up on to the stage and everybody's clapping. He's then giving her an award and the principal's making a little speech about her. There's a big smile on her face. Obviously she's also won a prize or award. Now she's walking off the stage and everyone's clapping.

My message here is clear. I am trying to help the child gain an appreciation for the rewards of successful school work. I focus on the internal reward, the sense of pride and gratification. I also describe the external rewards: the applause of the audience, the speech of the principal, and the prizes. The dramatic element here serves to enhance the child's interest and increase the chance that my messages will be heard.

* * *

Question: Tell about something you did that you are ashamed about?

Response: I had an experience many years ago, when I was a medical intern, that was very embarrassing. It was so embarrassing that I still remember it clearly to this day. It happened when I was an intern. An intern is a young doctor just out of medical school. Well, one Friday morning the resident, the doctor who was my boss, told me that I should prepare a speech about one of the patients that I was treating. He told me that I was to give it the first thing the following Monday morning. He told me to look over the patient's present and past charts as well as to study all the old X-rays. The patient had been sick for many years, and there was a lot of material to cover. He told me that it was important that I do a good job because this was the biggest conference of the month and that all the doctors in the hospital would be there. The hospital had over 200 doctors and it was a very important conference.

Anyway, Monday morning I got to the hospital and started to work with my patients. I noticed that none of the other doctors were there and wondered where everyone was. Suddenly, the telephone rang and I answered. It was the resident. He was very upset and he asked me why I wasn't at the conference. I was so surprised and shocked that I almost fainted. I realized that I had totally forgotten about the conference. I had prepared nothing! I was sick to my stomach. I immediately grabbed the patient's chart, the two X-rays that I could find, and rushed to the conference room.

What I should have done was to publicly announce that I was unprepared and to express my apologies. However, I tried to get away with it. I tried to go through the chart and give a speech about the patient, when I had very little information. I didn't lie or anything like that. I just tried to take a little information from one place and a little from the next but it didn't hang together. Finally, one of the older doctors who organized the conference interrupted me and suggested that we discontinue the conference. I was humiliated. But I was also relieved. I certainly learned an important lesson that day. And I have never again forgotten to prepare a speech. That event took place many years ago, and although it was painful and embarrassing, I learned an important lesson.

The question "Tell about something you did that you are ashamed about" again requires the therapist to reveal an area of imperfection. In the vignette that I selected, I also provide a message about preparing things in advance, thinking ahead, and thereby protecting oneself from humiliation. This message is likely to be of some relevance to most children in treatment.

* * *

Question: If you became mayor of your city, what would you do to change things?

Response: If I became mayor of my city, I would do everything in my power to bring about the passage of two laws. One would prohibit smoking in public places and the other would fine people large amounts of money for letting their dogs crap in the streets. Let me tell you my reasons for saying this. I, personally, find cigarette smoking disgusting. I'm not saying this because smoking causes cancer of the lungs. I'd say this even if smoking *cured* cancer of the lungs. I'm just saying it because I find smoking nauseating. I think that if anyone is stupid enough to smoke, that person should be required to do it privately, in his or her own home. Many people who smoke don't care about other people's feelings. As far as they're concerned, other people can choke or even croak on their smoke. They don't think about the feelings of the people who are suffering because of their smoking. Unfortunately, a lot of people don't speak up and say how the smoke bothers them. But more and more people are doing this.

The other law, about there being big fines for people who let their dogs crap on the streets, would be for the same purposes. People who let their dogs do this don't think about how disgusted others feel when they step in the dog shit. It's really a disgusting thing to have to wipe dog shit off your shoes. It's too bad there are so many people in this world who don't think about other people's feelings. What do you think about people who smoke and people who let their dogs crap on the streets?"

The major thrust of my responses here is to help an insensitive child appreciate how one's acts can affect others and that those who don't think about how they are affecting others are generally scorned. Included also in my response was a message about self-assertion regarding nonsmokers in their relationships with smokers.

* * *

Question: What was the worst punishment you ever got in your whole life? What had you done wrong?

Response: I remember my worst punishment quite well. I was about seven or eight years old at the time. My brother and I had gone off and were playing in an empty lot a couple of blocks from my home. I lived in an apartment house in the Bronx, in New York City. One of the things we liked to do was to make bonfires. We would gather some wood and papers and build a fire. We built them in safe places, not in buildings. We didn't want to burn anything, we just wanted to have some fun building the fire and then throwing garbage and other things into it and watch the stuff burn. Anyway, on this day, we got so involved with the fun of the fire that we didn't realize how late it was. In fact, it was getting dark and we thought that was even greater fun because we could then watch the fire during the night. We were having so much fun that we completely forgot about our parents and how worried and upset they might be because we hadn't come home.

Well, anyway, at about 8 o'clock at night we finally got home. We were supposed to be home about 5:30 or 6 o'clock. Although our parents were very happy to see us, they were also very angry. They were very worried; so much so that they had already called the police to look for us. The police hadn't started to look for us yet; they just said wait a little while longer.

Anyway, my father hit us both with a strap to help us remember never to do such a terrible thing again. They were not only upset about our building fires—which was more dangerous than we had realized—but about our not having thought about their feelings and about how worried they were when we didn't come home. They were scared that we might have wandered off and gotten lost. They were also scared that we might have been kidnapped or even been killed. And they were extremely upset that we hadn't thought about their feelings. Do you know what lessons I learned from that experience?

My hope here is that the story will engender some appreciation in the child of the effects of antisocial behavior on other people, how other people might feel who suffer from or who are otherwise inconvenienced by the child's antisocial behavior. In addition, it emphasizes the point that there were personal repercussions for my behavior. I received a severe spanking that I remember to this day and I also risked being burned by the fire.

* * *

Question: What do you think about a boy who curses at his father?
Response: It's perfectly normal to think curse words about a father. In fact, practically every child I have ever seen will, at times, have such thoughts in mind—especially after something happens that gets the child angry at his or her father. However, if instead you *politely* talk about the things that are getting you angry, then your father is more likely to listen and maybe then you'll be able to solve the problem. Maybe your speaking politely will help, and maybe it won't. However, there's a greater chance it will help solve the problem if you don't use curse words than if you do. And the worst thing is to say nothing at all when you're angry. Then, you won't solve anything and things will probably get worse.

* * *

Question: What do you think about a boy who sometimes wished that his brother were dead?
Response: It's perfectly normal to have thoughts once in a while and even wishes that one's brother were dead. This is especially the case in the middle of a fight. But having a thought once in a while and having a wish once in a while and *really wanting* the brother to be dead are two separate things. Most children are comfortable with the idea that they could think it and wish it once in a while and that there is nothing wrong with them. They know that there is a big difference between having a wish once in a while and *really* wanting it to happen.

There are some children who have such thoughts once in a while who believe that they are terrible to have such thoughts. They believe that only the worst kinds of children would have such thoughts about a brother. They feel terrible about themselves for having such thoughts and try to blot them out of their minds when they start thinking about such things. If such children knew that these thoughts, once in a while, are perfectly normal they might feel better about themselves. They might not feel so guilty about these thoughts and then they would be happier people.

There are some children who have these thoughts once in a while who become very frightened of them. They think that the thought can actually make the brother die. That's silly. A thought can't make anything happen. In fact, no matter how hard a child thinks something, the thought itself can't make the thing happen. Even if the brother wished very hard that the other brother would die, that wouldn't make it happen. If such children changed their minds and realized that thoughts can't make things happen, they would become less afraid of the death wishes. They would then become more comfortable with themselves over them.

My aim here is to reduce guilt in children who believe that occasional hostile thoughts and feelings, especially death wishes, are terrible to have. I inform the child that such thoughts and feelings are commonplace. Many children with such guilt harbor the notion that they are alone in the world or that only the most lowly individuals would harbor such heinous thoughts and feelings. I also attempt to dispel the notion that a thought has magic powers and can bring about an event. This notion is often intrinsically associated with excessive guilt over such thoughts and feelings.

* * *

Question: A girl was very angry at her father and wished that he would be hit by a car. Later that day he was hit by a car. How did she feel? What did she think?

Response: The girl felt very sad. She was not only sad because her father was hit by a car and had to go to the hospital, but she was also sad because she thought that her thoughts had actually caused the car to hit her father. She thought that an angry idea could actually make a thing happen. This of course, isn't true. That would be magic and there is no such thing as magic. A thought cannot make anything happen. Things happen by people doing things. The man who drove the car that hit her father was the one who was responsible for the father's being hurt. Probably it was an accident. If anyone was at fault it was he, not the girl who had the thought and wished that her father would get hit by a car.

The girl didn't realize that everyone has thoughts like that once in a while. She was very angry at her father and, at that time, she had the wish that he would die. It isn't that she *really* wanted her father dead. It's just that when she was very angry, such wishes came into her mind. Fortunately, this girl discussed the whole thing with her father after he came out of the hospital. He told her that he wasn't angry at her for the accident. He told her that her thoughts were normal and to have them once in a while, when a person is angry, is normal. He told her that he didn't blame her for his having been hit by the car. He didn't even blame the man who drove the car.

He did blame the man who fixed the car, because he had done a poor job. Her father had gotten a lawyer and he was going to sue the mechanic, the man who fixed the car, for the hospital bills as well as the money he lost from work when he was in the hospital. Her father discussed with her her feelings that her thoughts might have made the man in the car drive into her father. He told her that this was not the case. He told her that her thoughts could not make the thing happen. It was the car mechanic's fault and not hers. He told her also that her thoughts could not make the car mechanic make his mistake. After that, she didn't feel so bad. After that she realized that thoughts can't make things happen. Then she felt better about herself.

I deal here in detail with the issue of thoughts having magic power as a central element in guilt over anger. It is important to note that this factor is much more likely to be operative in children under the age of five or six. Prior to that time it is normal for children to believe in the magic of their thoughts. The sicker the child the greater the likelihood this notion will persist beyond the age when it should no longer be believed.

Sometimes I will enhance the efficacy of this message by bringing out the play dolls. I may take the little girl doll and the father doll and play act that the little girl is wishing very hard that her father will die. The dialogue may go something like this:

And the little girl wished very, very hard that her father would die. But no matter how hard she wished, her father just didn't die. She was very angry at him because he had done such terrible things to her. She hoped that if he would die then he would no longer abuse and hurt her. So she kept wishing and wishing that he would die. But it just didn't work. He just went on living. (I then move the father doll around as if he was carrying out various activities—demonstrating thereby that he is still alive.) No matter how hard she wished, he just didn't die.

I might then bring into the story a teenage brother (or some other powerful authority figure) who asks the little girl what she's wishing for. In the ensuing discussion the teen-ager also emphasizes the theme that her wishes cannot bring about her father's

death. He may, however, enter into a discussion with her about
what else she might do to improve her situation.

* * *

Question: If a fly followed you around for a day and could then
talk about you, what would it say?

Response: I followed Dr. Gardner around all day and I noticed
that the people he is with hardly ever have any doubt in their minds
about what he thinks. He's not afraid to tell people what's on his
mind and to express his thoughts and feelings. He avoids a lot of
trouble this way. If people had to wonder what he thought, there
would be a lot of confusion and trouble. He also gets many things
accomplished that he wouldn't have if he didn't speak up.

For example, during his lunch break one day, he went to a res-
taurant with a friend. He asked to be seated in the *No Smoking* section. After they were there awhile, a man sat down at the next table
and started to smoke. Dr. Gardner immediately complained to the
waiter and the man was asked to either put out the cigarette or sit
in the *Smoking* section. He quickly apologized and put out the cigarette. Some people probably would have sat there and said nothing.
However, Dr. Gardner didn't. By speaking up, he stopped a person
from doing something that was making him uncomfortable.

During the evening he went to the movies with his wife. The sound
was on much too loud and lots of people were bothered. However,
no one was doing anything about it. Dr. Gardner got up, went out
to the lobby and asked for the manager. He asked the manager to
lower the volume of the sound. At first, the manager didn't believe
him, so he asked the manager to go into the theater and hear for
himself. The manager did so and realized that Dr. Gardner was right.
He then lowered the volume and then everyone was more comfortable. Again, he saved himself and other people a lot of trouble by
politely and firmly expressing his thoughts and feelings. Of course,
every once in a while, he may not express his thoughts and feelings
and this usually causes some trouble. This helps him remember that
the best thing, most often, is to tell people about things that bother
you—but to do so in a polite way.

This is another example of my view that it is useful for therapy
to help the patient learn important principles in living which can
be applied to specific situations as they arise. Clearly, my hope here
is that this description will impress upon the child the value of self-
assertion. My hope also is that my own ways of dealing with these
problems will serve as a model for the child.

Feeling Cards

The Feeling Cards, as their name indicates, encourage primarily the expression of feelings. Many therapists view such expression to be the primary goal of the therapeutic process. These therapists will frequently ask such questions as: "How did you feel about that?" and "That must have made you feel very angry (sad, happy, etc.)." Others speak of therapy primarily as a place where the child can let out or get in touch with his or her feelings. Some pride themselves on their skill when a boy, for example, expresses the anger he feels toward his father by hitting the head of the father doll with a toy hammer. I believe that this view of therapy is naive. I consider the expression of feelings to be a first step toward the alleviation of difficulties. Feelings serve in part to enhance one's efficiency in reaching a goal. When we are frightened, we run faster; when we are angry, we fight harder and more effectively. When sexually excited we make love more ardently. When hungry we eat, sometimes voraciously. And when tired we sleep more deeply.

The therapist's goals should be that of helping patients express their thoughts and feelings at the earliest possible time that is reasonable and appropriate. At such times, the feelings are generally at a low level and can be used most effectively. When feelings build up to high levels they are likely to interfere with their effective utilization. When we are irritated we can use our irritation to attempt to remove the noxious stimulus that is evoking our frustration. If, however, we do not express ourselves early, the angry feelings build up to levels of rage and even fury. When expressed under these circumstances the anger is not likely to be focused on the particular source of frustration. When expressed in a wild and even chaotic fashion, we are not likely to remove expediently the source of irritation. Furthermore, when feelings reach an extremely high level their gratification may become an end in itself, with little further purpose. A murderer, for example, will generally accomplish his or her goal with one or two stabs in the chest. The murderer who continues to stab the victim is no longer using the anger in the service of killing the victim. The same phenomenon applies to sexual gratification, eating, sleeping, and drinking.

As is true of the other cards, the child's reactions should serve as a point of departure for therapeutic interchanges. The examples given here do not present such discussions. Later in this chapter I will provide clinical examples in which sample interchanges are presented. Again, there are no "right" answers to the questions and instructions on the Feeling Cards. Rather, my responses presented here may serve as guidelines for the therapist's responses when playing the game.

* * *

Question: What do you think happens to people after they die?

Response: No one knows for sure. Some people think that there is some kind of life or existence after death. Some believe that there is a soul or ghost that remains after we die. Some people believe that we actually come back to life in another form. And some people believe that there is absolutely nothing that happens after you're dead. They believe that your body just rots away in the ground and that there is no such thing as a soul or ghost or spirit or anything else. They believe that that's just the end of it all forever. That's my personal opinion as well. I don't believe that there is any kind of life or existence after you die. I'm not 100 percent sure, but it's the theory that seems most reasonable to me.

Therefore, because I believe that I only have one life, I try to make it the best life possible. I try not to do things that will foul me up. I work hard so that I'll be able to get the things I want in life. This doesn't mean that I don't take out time to have fun. I do that as well. I try to balance them out and spend time both at work and at fun. However, some of my work is also fun. And some of my fun is also work. The two tend to get mixed up at times. For example, writing books is work, but it's also fun for me. Hiking is fun for me, but it also involves some effort and work.

I think one of the worst things that can happen to a person is to reach the end of his or her life and look back and realize that most of it has been wasted. To avoid this, it is important for people to do those things each day that make life as good as possible. No matter what people believe about what happens after death, most of them agree that it's important to make the one life they have the best possible one. Do you think you're doing this for yourself?

Like many of the questions, the brighter the child, the greater the likelihood the post-response discussion will be rich and meaningful. Although we may enter into a somewhat philosophical discussion, my main purpose here is to help the child gain a sense of the sanctity of life and the importance of doing the best one can for oneself at any point along the way. I believe that people who have a greater appreciation of this unhappy fact are more likely to be motivated to make the most of the relatively short time we have here.

* * *

Question: What's the happiest thing that ever happened to you?

Response: I've had many happy days in my life. Three of the happiest were the three days on which each of my children were born. Of course, that happened many years ago, but I still remember the days clearly. I was so happy on each of those days that I cried. They were tears of joy. I still have those warm feelings when I see little babies. It's hard for me not to touch them and sometimes I'll even ask the mother to let me hold the baby so I can cuddle and kiss the child. Although my children, like all children, may give me trouble at times, they also give me great pleasures. And the pleasures are certainly greater than the pains.

We speak often of the importance of the therapist-patient relationship in therapy. However, the factors that contribute to the development of a good relationship in this area have not been well delineated. This question can be used to help foster a good patient-therapist relationship. My hope here is that the child's relationship with me might improve (admittedly in a small way) by the recognition that children produce warm responses in me. The response conveys the notion that I have the capacity for such pleasure with children in general and this response is not simply confined to my own children.

* * *

Question: What's something you could say that could make a person feel good?

Response: One thing you could say that could make a person feel good is to compliment the person on an accomplishment, that is, on something he or she did very well. For example, if a boy worked very hard making a model airplane, and it turned out very well and looked very good, then I'd say to him, "That's a beautiful job you did!" That would make him feel very good about himself. Or, for example, if a girl started the school year as a very poor student and then improved significantly, she would also feel very good if someone complimented her on her accomplishment. If, for example, she was spending a lot of time in the early part of the year goofing off and fooling around, then she wouldn't feel very good about herself. Let's say that she then begins to study much harder. After a lot of work over a period of time the teacher might say on her report card: "Congratulations, Sarah, you have really improved. Whereas you were once a pain in the neck because you never tried or did your homework, now it's a pleasure to have you in the classroom. It's a pleasure to be your teacher. You've really come a long way. Keep up the good work." Now that's the kind of thing that would make the girl feel good about herself. What do you think about what I've said?

When I congratulate a child on an accomplishment, I generally focus my attention primarily on the deed or the act and direct the child's attention to the good feeling he or she must experience over the accomplishment. I secondarily mention other people who may be pleased over the child's accomplishment and/or external rewards such as high grades, certificates, awards, and so on. Also included here is the notion that hard work is necessary if one is to enjoy these benefits.

* * *

Question: Say three curse words. What do you think of people who use these words?

Response: Shit. Crap. Fuck. I think these words are okay to use if you're having a fight with someone outside your home. They serve a useful purpose. They get out anger without *actually* hurting the other person. However, it's a bad idea to use these words in front of parents, teachers, and other adults. They usually get very upset and angry and will tell you that it's not proper to use these words in front of others. So, it's often best to use words that are *more polite* than these if you want to get something accomplished, especially with an adult. There are times when these words are the best words to use. If another kid speaks to you with such words, it can often be useful to use similar words back. There's an old saying, "Sticks and stones may break my bones, but names will never hurt me." This tells very well what I said before about dirty words helping you use anger without actually hurting anyone.

This card is designed for the child who is inhibited in the proper use of profanity in socially acceptable ways and situations. The child may be initially astounded to hear me use such words—believing that it is inappropriate for a doctor to utilize profanity. Obviously, this is not the response I would provide for the child

who has an antisocial behavior disorder and uses such words indiscriminately. Rather, I would provide a response that attempts to
induce guilt and/or embarrassment over the use of such words.

* * *

Question: What is the best kind of job a person can have? Why?
Make believe you're doing that job.

Response: I think the best job a person can have is one in which
that person earns money doing something that he or she finds enjoyable. Normally, the more education a person has, the greater the
likelihood he or she will have such a job. People who don't have
much education, or who drop out of school early, are not likely to
have such jobs. It's more likely that they'll have a miserable or lousy
job that they hate.

Less important than the fact that they'll earn less money than the
more educated person, is the fact that they hate what they're doing.
And this is a bad way to spend one's life. It's much better to get
education and training. Then, it's more likely that the person will be
able to earn money doing something that he or she enjoys. Therefore,
my answer to this question is that there is no one best job. My answer
then is that it's any job that the person enjoys doing. And there are
hundreds of different kinds of jobs different people can enjoy doing.
What kind of thing would you like to do when you grow up?

My hope is that my response will contribute to the child's appreciation that what he or she is doing now is going to play an
important role in his or her future life. In addition, my hope is that
the response will contribute (admittedly in a small way) to the
child's motivation to think about the future and be willing to spend
some effort toward gaining greater knowledge and skill.

* * *

Question: What do you think is the most beautiful thing in the
whole world?

Response: Watching a beautiful sunset, whether it be from the top
of a mountain or at the seashore, is to me one of the most beautiful
things in the world. It makes me feel relaxed and happy to be alive.
Sometimes I read poetry while watching such a scene. And the
poems also make me think of beautiful things that help me appreciate
how beautiful the world can be if one is willing to stop and enjoy

them. Sometimes I will bring along a tape recorder and play a tape of some calm, beautiful music while watching such a scene. This is indeed one of the great pleasures of life.

* * *

Healthy pleasure is well viewed to be a general antidote for just about all forms of psychogenic psychopathology. When one is enjoying oneself in a healthy way, one is at that time not suffering the psychological pain attendant to psychiatric disorder. In addition, the pleasurable feelings are esteem enhancing. Because feelings of low self-worth are often involved in bringing about psychopathological reactions, any experience that can enhance self-worth can be salutary. And aesthetic pleasures are in this category. Accordingly, anything a therapist can do to enhance a child's appreciation of beauty is likely to be therapeutic.

* * *

Question: What do you think about a boy who sometimes plays with his penis when he's alone?

Response: I think that it's perfectly normal—as long as he does it when he's alone. Of course, there would be something wrong with him if he did that in the open, in public; but as a private thing I think it's normal. In fact most teenage boys do it a lot, and many kids play with their penises when they're younger as well. There are some kids, however, who think that playing with their penises is a terrible thing. They think it's sinful, or wrong, or dirty. I completely disagree. Those kids are the ones that have a problem, and not the ones who play with their penises once in a while in private. What's your opinion on what I've just said?

* * *

Question: What do you think about a girl who sometimes plays with or rubs her vagina when she's alone?

Response: I think it's perfectly normal for her to do that when she's alone. Of course, that's not the kind of thing that one would generally do in front of other people. It's a private matter. What do you think?

For the sexually inhibited child these responses enable the examiner to approach a forbidden subject in a noncontrived way. Discussing the subject is in itself therapeutic in that it provides the child with the living experience that such discussions do not result in dire consequences. That which is unmentionable is far more anxiety and guilt provoking than that which is spoken about. The child whose parents never speak about sex will generally become far more inhibited than the parent who preaches often about the sins and evils of sex. Of course, the latter approach is likely to produce guilt as well, but probably not as much as the guilt produced by the situation in which the subject is unmentionable. For the child who is excessively guilty, I might add:

> There are some children who think that touching themselves is a terrible sin or crime. They think it's the worst thing a person can do. This is a strange idea because touching oneself is perfectly natural and normal. It only becomes a problem if the person does it most of the time and then doesn't do other things, or if the person feels very bad or guilty about it. Feeling that it's a terrible sin or crime is then the problem, not doing it. What are your opinions on this subject?

* * *

Question: A boy's friend leaves him to play with someone else. How does the boy feel? Why did the friend leave?

Response: Bob invited Frank to play with him at his house. But Bob was selfish. He wouldn't share. Frank was his guest. He should have known that it's important to be courteous to a guest. He should have known that it's important to be nice to a guest. Anyway, Frank wanted to share Bob's toys with him and Bob refused. Also, Bob always wanted to decide which game they would play. Finally Frank said that if Bob wouldn't play nicely with him and share, he would leave and go play with someone else. Bob's mother overheard the boys talking and took Bob aside into another room. She didn't want to embarrass Bob in front of his friend Frank. She told Bob, while they were alone, that he wasn't playing nicely with his friend and that he wasn't thinking about how his friend felt. She told him that Frank would go home soon if he didn't start to share with him. She told him that Frank had another good friend, George, whom he could go play with if he wanted. What do you think happened? Do you think that Bob listened to his mother? Do you think that his mother was right or wrong in this case?

Some children have great difficulty sharing. They have difficulty putting themselves in the position of their peers and fail to recognize that the child with whom they refuse to share is likely to be alienated. Some of these children have neurologically based learning disabilities that interfere, on a cognitive level, with their capacity to project themselves into other people's position. Other children may have reached the developmental level where this is possible, but have psychological problems in the realm of egocentricism and narcissism that interfere with healthy functioning in this realm. For children in both of these categories, certain Talking, Feeling, and Doing Cards can be useful.

* * *

Question: Make believe you're reading a magazine showing pictures of nude ladies. What do you think about such magazines?

Response: Boy, there really are some exciting looking women in some of those magazines. I think they're great to look at once in a while. They have some of the most beautiful and luscious women in those magazines. Some people are ashamed to admit that they're interested in looking at those women. I don't think there's anything wrong, bad, or sinful to look at those pictures. I don't agree with those people. I think it's natural and healthy. It's only a problem if the person doesn't want to have anything to do with real people and wants to spend a lot of time looking at those pictures. What is your opinion on the subject?

This response is the one I provide for boys who are uncomfortable expressing sexual interest. Obviously, I attempt here to convey some of the excitement that most boys and men have when looking at pictures of nude women. I also attempt to lessen any guilt the child may have over such interest. My hope is that the child will be receptive to my opinions on the subject and will identify with my attitude.

* * *

Question: A boy was laughing. What was he laughing about?

Response: This boy was not only laughing, but he was cheering. He was just jumping up and down with joy. He had just gotten his eighth grade report card and learned that he had gotten into three honors classes in the ninth grade. He was very happy. He had worked very hard in order to make the honor classes and had hoped that he might make one or two of them. But he didn't think that he would get into all three. He was very proud of himself and couldn't wait to get home and tell his parents. His teacher had written a note on the report card that said, "Robert, I am very proud of you. Good luck in high school." He was also very happy because he knew that, when he applied to college, having been in three honors classes would look very good on his record and this would help him get into the college of his choice. And so he ran home from school laughing and singing all the way. It was really a happy day for him. What do you think about what I said about that boy?

This is the kind of response I provide for children with low academic motivation. My purpose here is to enhance their school interest by demonstrating the joys and ego-enhancement that are the potential benefits of such commitment to the educational process.

* * *

Question: Tell about an act of kindness.
Response: A good example of an act of kindness would be visiting someone who is sick in the hospital and giving up a fun thing that you'd prefer to do. Let's say that a boy in a class was in an automobile accident, injured his leg, and had to be in the hospital for six weeks. Even though his mother and father visited him often, he was still very lonely. His really good friends were those who were willing to give up fun things like playing baseball, or watching their favorite television programs, or just hanging around and relaxing, and instead went to visit him in the hospital. He was very grateful when they came to see him. And they felt good about themselves for their sacrifices. Visiting the friend was an act of kindness. Do you know what the word sacrifice means?

This is the type of response I provide self-centered children, those who have difficulty putting themselves in the position of others. In the ensuing discussion, I would try to help the egocentric child appreciate the feelings of loneliness suffered by the hospitalized child. I would also try to engender in the child the feelings of self-satisfaction and enhanced self-worth that comes from benevolent acts.

* * *

Question: Was there ever a person whom you wished to be dead? If so, who was that person? Why did you wish that person to be dead?

Response: During my childhood and early teens there lived a man in Germany named Adolph Hitler. He was a madman. He was insane. He was the leader of Germany during World War II and was personally responsible for the deaths of millions of people. He was one of the greatest criminals in the history of the world. He used to murder people whose opinions, skin color, or religion differed from his. He not only had them shot but he gassed them to death and burned their bodies in ovens. Millions of people died this way. When I was a boy, I used to wish that he would die. I wished that someone would kill him. I hoped then that maybe all this crazy murdering would stop. To this day, I and many other people in the world feel sorry for the millions of people he killed and all the millions of friends and relatives that also suffered because of his murders. Even though the war ended in 1945, there are still millions of people who are suffering because of the terrible things Adolph Hitler did. These are the people who were put in his prisons and concentration camps and escaped, or were fortunate enough not to have been killed. And these are also the people who are the friends, relatives, children, and grandchildren of those who died there. He was a very cruel man. I really hated him, and I often wished he would die or be killed. Finally, in 1945, he committed suicide. If he hadn't killed himself he would have been captured and executed for his terrible crimes.

This question can be particularly useful for children with antisocial behavior disorders who have little sensitivity to the pains they inflict on others. My hope here, by elaborating on Hitler's atrocities, is to engender in the antisocial child a feeling for the pain that criminal behavior causes others. It is important for the reader to appreciate that when responding to Feeling Cards the therapist does well to try to dramatize as much as possible his or her responses in order to bring about a kind of resonating emotional response in the patient. To engender these feelings in the child who is out of touch with them or who has not experienced them to a significant degree is one of the goals of treatment.

* * *

Question: Say something funny.
Response: Okay, I heard a funny riddle. "What's invisible and smells like worms?" (Generally, the patient does not know the answer. In such cases I will give it.) "A bird's fart!" (This joke generally goes over quite well, except among the most inhibited. Incidently, it

is a statement of the low levels to which the child's therapist may have to stoop in the service of his or her calling.)

The joke may be useful for the child with sexual-inhibition problems as an icebreaker. Sexual and scatological issues often get fused and inhibitions in the sexual area often extend to this area as well. By telling the joke the therapist serves as a model for what I consider to be healthy, normal sublimation. It may contribute to the lessening of sexual inhibitions. The child may reason: "If it's okay for him to talk this way, it's okay for me." In addition, the introduction of some levity into the therapeutic experience is also useful. It lightens the session, makes the therapist more human, and increases the likelihood that the child will become involved. It is part of the seductive process, so important in child therapy.

Doing Cards

The Doing Cards involve physical activity in association with the child's responses. These cards, more than the Talking Cards and Feeling Cards, involve a fun element, and this serves to make the session more enjoyable. My purpose here is to counterbalance some of the less pleasurable aspects of treatment that are likely to reduce the motivation for treatment of even the most highly involved child. Some of the Doing Cards involve modeling and this can also be therapeutic. There are some therapists who consider role modeling and physical activity to be a central part of therapeutic process. I am not in agreement. Often, there is an artificial quality to role modeling, and this makes it less therapeutic than actual experiences or imitations that are spontaneously derived from a situation. Accordingly, I most often use the Doing Cards as a point of departure for direct discussion. My hope is that in the course of such discussions the child will have emotional reactions and experiences that will contribute directly to therapeutic change.

* * *

Question: What is the most selfish thing you ever did? Make believe you're doing that thing now.

Response: Well, the most selfish thing I ever did was a long time ago—it was right after the Second World War—it was in 1946 or 1947. I was looking for a way to earn money to pay for my education in college. It was very hard to get jobs after the Second World War. All the war factories were closing down, and people were fired from their jobs. They didn't need them anymore to make tanks, and guns, and things like that. And all the soldiers were getting out of the Army. And everybody was also getting out of the Navy and Air Force. There were millions of people trying to get jobs. And I finally got a job selling magazines to the wives and mothers of the soldiers who had been in the war. I told the people how important it was to buy the magazine because it would help the veterans, the people who fought in the war. After working a few days I found out that this magazine was kind of phony. A lot of people weren't getting the subscriptions they were paying for, and I felt very guilty about what I was doing.

I was preying on people's sympathy. I was saying that this was very important for the parents and the wives of the soldiers who were killed or who had fought in the war, and it was a kind of phoney organization. I didn't realize it when I got the job, but after I started working I realized it, and I soon quit. But I felt very guilty, and I think I worked a day or two too much because I needed the money. Do you know what I mean? I should have quit as soon as I realized it. There was so much money to be made, and I needed the money so badly that I stuck with it awhile, but then my guilt overcame me and I quit the job. It was a selfish thing to do. Sometimes when people are hungry, when they need money a lot, then they do things that they would never want to do. I was ashamed of myself when I did that. Do you want to say anything about that?

As mentioned, *The Talking, Feeling, and Doing Game* provides therapists with the opportunity to reveal their own deficiencies in a noncontrived and natural way. This lessens the likelihood that the patient will idealize the therapist. It makes the therapist a more real human being. It lessens the likelihood of the development of the unfavorable comparison in which the patient views the therapist as perfect, and views him- or herself as a bundle of psychopathology. The particular incident was chosen because it demonstrates how guilt can be useful in preventing a person from engaging in antisocial behavior. This is the kind of response I provide for patients who do not have enough guilt over their antisocial behavior. My hope is that the vignette will contribute to the development of a slightly stronger superego.

* * *

Question: You're standing in line to buy something and a child pushes in front of you. Show what you would do.

Response: Let's say I'm a kid and I'm standing here in line and some kid pushes himself in front of me. A part of me might want to push him away and even hit him. But another part of me knows that that wouldn't be such a good idea. I might get into trouble or he might hit me back and then I might get hurt. So the first thing I would do would be to say something to him like, "Hey, I was here first. Why don't you go back to the end of the line and wait your turn like everybody else." If that didn't work I might threaten to call some person like a parent, teacher, or someone else around who is in charge. But sometimes there are no other people around to call, so I might just say that it's not worth all the trouble and that all it's causing me is the loss of another minute or two. If, however, the person starts to push me, then I might fight back. But that would be the last thing I would try. Some people might think that I'm "chicken" for not hitting him in the first place. I don't agree with them. I think that hitting should be the last thing you should do, not the first. I don't think that people who hit first are particularly wise or brave; rather, I think they're kind of stupid.

This is the type of response I am likely to provide the antisocial child. As is obvious here, I am trying to educate the antisocial child to the more civilized option that individuals have learned to use in order to bring about a more relaxed and less threatening society. These options may not have been part of the antisocial child's repetoire. Whatever the underlying factors there are in such a child's antisocial behavior (and these, of course, must be dealt with in the treatment), such education is also a part of the therapy.

* * *

Question: You're standing in line to buy something and an adult pushes in front of you. Show what you would do.
Response: I would tell the person that this is my place in line and that I would appreciate his going to the back of the line and waiting his turn like everyone else. If the person looks like he's crazy, someone who might do dangerous things, I wouldn't make a big deal out of it. There are times when it's smart not to speak up and fight for your rights, but most often it's wise to do so. The important thing is to size up the situation, and get a lot more information before acting. Otherwise, you may find yourself in a lot of trouble.

Obviously, the response to this card should be different from the previous one. It is unreasonable and even injudicious to encourage a child to respond in the same manner to both a child and an adult who pushes him- or herself in line in front of a child. My main point here is that there are times when it is appropriate to assert oneself and other times when it is judicious not to.

* * *

Question: Make believe you're doing something that makes you feel good about yourself. Why does that thing make you feel so good?

Response: As you know, I like to write books. I have already given you one of the children's books that I've written. As I'm sure you can appreciate, writing a book takes a lot of work. It's a very hard job. Sometimes I may work over many years on one single book. However, when I finally finish, I really feel good about myself. I feel that I've accomplished a lot. Although I may be very tired over all the work I've put in to it, I'm very proud of what I've done. And then, when the final printed book comes out, that really makes me feel good about myself. I have what is called a "sense of achievement." Do you know what I mean when I say "sense of achievement"?

I use this response for children who are academic underachievers. After clarification of the meaning of the term "sense of achievement," I might ask the child to tell me things that he or she has done that have provided him or her with similar feelings of accomplishment. My hope here, obviously, is to provide the child with some appreciation of the ego-enhancing feelings that one can enjoy after diligent commitment to a task.

* * *

Question: Make believe you're smoking a cigarette. What do you think about people who smoke?

Response: First of all, I want to say that I have not once in my whole life ever smoked a single cigarette. I remember when I was about 14 years old I went to a party. Some of the kids there were smoking. One kid gave me a cigarette. I really didn't want to smoke it, but I felt that if I didn't take it, all the kids would think that I was "chicken." So I took the cigarette, and I lit it, and I took one puff. I then gasped and started to choke. It really made me sick to my stomach. I then put out the cigarette and said to the guy that had given it to me, "I can't really believe that anybody can like this shit. The only reason that you guys are smoking is because you want to look like big shots. It must take a long time to get used to smoking this filthy weed." And that was the first and last time I smoked a cigarette in my whole life.

Now, if I'm to get a chip, I've got to make believe that I'm smoking a cigarette. Okay, here I go! (imitates cigarette smoking) Egh, is this terrible. (starts coughing heavily) This is disgusting. This is nauseating. (more heavy coughing) Egh, I can't stand this any longer. I hope I've done enough of this to get my chip. It's a heavy price to pay for a chip. People who smoke cigarettes must be crazy. Not only is it a disgusting habit but it can give you all kinds of terrible diseases like lung cancer, heart disease, and diseases of your blood vessels.

I think kids start to smoke because they want to act like big shots. It makes them feel like adults. Then they get hooked on cigarettes and they can't stop. When they get older, and begin to appreciate how really terrible it is, they still can't stop. It's a heavy price to pay for looking like a big shot. Also, it's no great stunt to smoke. If you really want to feel big you have to *do things*, over a period, that makes you feel good about yourself. Thinking that you're going to feel good about yourself by putting a cigarette in your mouth is simple minded. It just doesn't work that way. What do you think about what I've just said?

The response, of course, touches on the most common pathological mechanisms that contribute to children's beginning to smoke. It is quite likely that the antisocial child subscribes strongly and somewhat blindly to these sick values. Not having basic competence in meaningful areas, he or she is likely to embrace quick and superficial methods for enhancing self-esteem. Of course, the utilization of smoking in this regard is strongly promulgated by the advertising of the cigarette industry. Cigarette manufacturers know well that they will increase sales if they associate cigarette smoking with sexual attractiveness and adult "maturity." My response also directs itself to the peer pressure element in the initiation of cigarette smoking. As mentioned, I do not create stories when responding to the cards in *The Talking, Feeling, and Doing Game*. The experiences I relate in my response actually occurred and my reasons for not smoking are those that I genuinely hold.

* * *

Question: Make believe someone grabbed something of yours. Show what you would do.

Response: I would first try to use talk before using action. I'd tell the child to give it back and threaten to grab it back if he or she doesn't return it. If the child was my size or a little taller, I'd try to grab it back, providing it wasn't something that could break. If it was something that could break and/or the person was bigger, I would threaten to call the teacher or my parent(s) if it wasn't given back immediately. I might ask a friend or two to help me get it back. But I wouldn't just stand there, say nothing, and let the person get away with it.

* * *

Question: Make believe you've just met a bully. Show what you would do.

Response: If he were my size I'd let him know that I'm not going to let him get away with taking advantage of me. Even though I might be a little scared, I would fight back. If he called me names, I would call him names back. And if he threatened to hit me, I would threaten to report him to the teacher or to his parents. Or, I would tell him that I'll hit him back twice as hard.

Most bullies are usually frightened kids, and they usually try to pick on kids who won't fight back. The best way to get rid of a bully is to fight back. If you keep letting him take advantage of you then he'll keep picking on you.

These cards are especially useful for children with self-assertion problems. My response provides advice regarding the sequence of steps one does well to follow when one's rights are being infringed upon.

* * *

Question: Make believe you're speaking to someone on the phone. Whom are you speaking to? What are you saying?

Response: I'm speaking to the principal of a school. He's asking me whether I think that a certain girl, let's call her Ruthie, should be promoted. He's telling me that she got Fs in most of her subjects, but that he fears that she'll feel very bad about herself if she's left back, that is, if she has to repeat the grade. He fears that she'll be very embarrassed and humiliated. He's telling me that if she has to repeat the grade, she'll be the oldest one in the class and bigger than anybody else in the class and this will make her feel very bad about herself. He's calling to ask my advice regarding what he should do.

Now this is the answer I'm going to give him. "I think that she should be left back. She really isn't ready to go on to the next grade.

She's failed most of her subjects. She'll feel embarrassed if you leave her back. But if you promote her, she'll feel embarrassed in her new class anyway. If you leave her back, she'll be ashamed for a few days or for a few weeks and then she'll probably get over it and get used to her new class. If you promote her, she'll not only be embarrassed all year but will continue to be ashamed as long as you continue to promote her. In addition, she might end up a drop-out because she'll get so far behind that she'll never be able to catch up. It's a choice between feeling bad now for a short period or feeling bad for many years, or possibly even the rest of her life. That's why I'm telling you that I think she should be left back." What do you think about the advice I gave the principal?

There are schools that give the parents veto power over a decision to have a child repeat a grade. This is a terrible disservice to the child. The reasons for my saying this are basically presented to the child in the aforementioned response. The advantage of retention far outweigh its disadvantages, the embarrassed feelings the child suffers notwithstanding. My main purpose here, of course, is to help the child appreciate that there can be consequences if one does not fulfill one's academic obligations, and one of these consequences is being required to repeat the grade and suffer the attendant embarrassment associated with such repeat. In addition, I point out that even if the child does not repeat the grade, there will be humiliations associated with continually being in a classroom where he or she is behind the other students.

* * *

Question: Make believe you're playing a dirty trick on someone.
Response: I don't think I'm going to get a chip on this one. I don't like playing dirty tricks on people. I remember when I was a kid how badly I felt if someone played a dirty trick on me. And I used to feel sorry for those kids who had dirty tricks played on them. I remember once a kid in my class used to like stealing other children's books and hiding them. He thought it was very funny. Actually, it was cruel. Then the kid whose book was stolen would go home and not have a book to do his or her homework. He or she would have to go to a lot of trouble to borrow someone else's book or go over to someone else's house. Sometimes the kid wouldn't even find the book and then he or she would have to pay for it.

Sometimes dirty tricks can be dangerous. I remember once a boy in my class thought it was funny to trip another kid in the classroom.

Well the boy that was tripped fell down and banged his head against the desk. He hit his head right above his eye and his eye almost got knocked out. He got a big cut over his eye and it was bleeding terribly. I really felt sorry for him and everybody was angry at the kid who tripped him. That kid, of course, got into a lot of trouble. The kid who got hurt had to go to the hospital for stitches and for treatment of his eye. His parents threatened to sue the parents of the kid who tripped their son. However, the parents of the boy who tripped the kid agreed to pay for all the medical expenses. So at least they both didn't have to pay for lawyers. These are just some of the reasons why I don't like playing dirty tricks on anyone. How do you feel about playing dirty tricks on people?"

In the attempt to strengthen the antisocial child's superego I elaborate upon the pains that can be caused by those who hurt others. Children with superego deficiencies, who act out hostilely, generally do not think about the discomforts and pains they cause others.

EXAMPLES OF THERAPIST-PATIENT INTERCHANGES

The examples given above are sample responses to individual cards that I provide when playing *The Talking, Feeling, and Doing Game*. Patient responses have thus far not been provided. In this section I present therapist-patient interchanges in which both the patients' and my own responses are provided. In addition, I comment throughout the transcripts on many aspects of the therapy that emerge from the interchanges.

The Case of Frank [Dealing with a Psychopathic Partner]

Frank, an eleven-year-old boy, was brought to treatment because of moderately severe antisocial behavior. He was disruptive in the classroom, a constant thorn in his teacher's side, and had little appreciation of the fact that he was interfering with the education of his classmates. His general sensitivity to the feelings of those who suffered because of his psychopathic tendencies was practically nil. In addition, he suffered with a severe impulsivity problem. He bas-

ically lived by the dictum: "I'll do what I want when I want it."
Frank's parents were divorced. However, five years after the separation they were still litigating over a wide variety of issues. Often,
Frank was embroiled in the divorce conflicts. Some of his psychopathic behavior was derived from identification with his warring
parents, both of whom had little sympathy or respect for one another's feelings. In addition, the anger he felt toward them was
being displaced onto school authorities. During his third month of
treatment we had this interchange:

> *Therapist:* My question says, "If you could live your life all over
> again, what things would you do differently?" Well, one thing I would
> do differently was I made a big mistake about 12 or 13 years ago.
> You see this building we are in right now?
> *Patient:* Uh huh.
> *Therapist:* I like this office very much. This is an office building
> that my wife and I built with a third person. That person became
> our partner.
> *Patient:* You built this whole building?
> *Therapist:* Not myself. An architect built it, but I worked with the
> architect in planning it, and told him exactly what I wanted in the
> various parts of the building. I am not an architect and I don't know
> how to build a building, but I can tell him what kinds of things I
> want.
> *Patient:* Uh huh.
> *Therapist:* And he was the one who actually designed it, and, of
> course, builders then came and built it.
> *Patient:* What was the mistake?
> *Therapist:* The mistake was that the man I became a partner with
> was someone I hardly knew. I knew him a little bit. He was a psy-
> chiatrist, and that was a big mistake because he turned out to be the
> kind of person who had many qualities that I didn't like. He wasn't
> honest. He didn't want to do his share of the work. And he didn't
> pay his money when it was due. He wasn't a true partner. He didn't
> think he had to keep promises that he had made or do the things he
> promised to do in contracts he had signed. And because we had
> signed papers and because we were locked in here together in the
> ownership of this building, I couldn't get rid of him so easily. It was
> a very messy situation.
> And I was partly to blame—not that I was doing anything wrong,
> in my opinion, and nobody was critical of me—because I didn't get
> to know the man better before I became his partner. I didn't think
> in advance of the consequences of what I was doing, and I acted so

impulsively and quickly. Had I taken time and gotten to know the person better, I might have been able to avoid the trouble. I might have learned things about his personality which would have warned me that this would be a bad idea that he was a bad-news person.

And for seven years he was my partner, and it was a lot of grief until finally I gave him—it was worth it—and I gave him a lot of money and bought him out. We bought him out, and he left the building, and I was glad to get rid of him. Then my wife and I sold the building afterwards to other people and I am a tenant here now. But that is not the point. The main point is that I shouldn't have acted so quickly. I should have thought in advance about the consequences of what I was doing.

Patient: You were partners?

Therapist: Yeah, right. So then when the guy left, my wife and I were 50/50 partners. What's my main point in saying this? What's the main point I am trying . . .

Patient: Think before you act.

Therapist: Right! Think before you act. And the second point is: If a person is dishonest, if a person doesn't pull his share of the load, then he's disliked by everybody around him. My wife and I had no respect for him. We couldn't stand him, but we were kind of locked in for a number of years until it became possible for us to get up enough money to buy him out and get rid of him. And so that's the other . . .

Patient: You got all that money back?

Therapist: Well, we sold the building to another person, and now we just rent it like any other tenant. But no. It was a loss of money to buy him out, but it was worth it to us. Although it was painful to give him all that money, it was so bad being with him that it was worth it to buy him out. Understand?

Patient: Yeah.

Therapist: He was such an obnoxious individual, and people who do those things really turn others off and produce a lot of resentment in others. Do you want to say anything else about that?

Patient: Yes.

Therapist: Yeah. What do you want to say?

Patient: You made a mistake to take him as a partner in the first place, but you got rid of him so that's really what counts.

Therapist: Right. Let me tell you an interesting story. You've heard of Japan, haven't you?

Patient: Yeah.

Therapist: Well, let me tell you something.

Patient: Okay. (mumbles) . . .

Therapist: Pardon me?

Patient: The Wall of China.

Therapist: Well, Japan is not China. They are two different countries. They are both in Asia.

Patient: Oh, yeah. That's right.

Therapist: Japan is closer to us, but it's off the coast of Asia. It's part of Asia. Anyway, what I want to tell you is that different people have different customs, and the Japanese are very good businessmen, and Americans . . .

Patient: They are?

Therapist: Oh, yeah. Very good businessmen.

Patient: Wow!

Therapist: Yeah. They're one of the richest countries in the world. Even though they are small. They are very good businessmen, very smart. Anyway, uh, years ago when Americans first went to Japan, American businessmen did not know their customs, and they wanted to make business arrangements with them. They sent some Americans to Japan to talk to the Japanese about business, and the men would come there and they'd say to the Japanese, "Okay, let's start talking about this deal. We want to buy. You want to sell."

And they would say, "No. Let's hold off for a while." And they'd say, "Let's go to dinner." They would go out to dinner, and the next day the Japanese would say, "How about playing golf tomorrow?" And they'd play golf. And then the third day they'd say, "Oh, let's go sailing, or let's go boating, or let's go to some restaurants."

And the people back in the United States would call, or wire, or write to their friends, you know, their associates and say: "Hey, what are you guys doing over there? Why don't you start signing a contract there and working out business arrangements?"

And the Americans in Japan would say, "We can't talk to them about business. All they want to do is sit around and talk, relax, recreation, golf, and they won't talk business yet. They keep holding off." Anyway, this would go on for five, six, seven days, and the Americans would get upset. And finally one day the Japanese would sit down and they'd say one of two things. Are you listening?

Patient: Yeah.

Therapist: They would say, "Okay, let's talk business," and they would very quickly negotiate and very quickly come to a decision. Or they would say, "We're very sorry. We've decided we don't want to sell you anything, or buy anything from you or work out some business arrangement." And they would very politely say, "Goodbye."

Now the Americans couldn't understand that kind of a practice, this custom. And if they did make an arrangement, they'd have a very small contract. They wouldn't have a lot of lawyers, and it would only be a very small contract. In the United States contracts might be almost a book or two with many pages. Do you know why the Japanese did that?

Patient: Why?

Therapist: They felt that the most important thing in a business relationship is the people that you're working with—whether they are honest, whether they are friendly, whether they're nice, whether you can trust them. They felt if they were trustworthy, then they would enter into a business arrangement. And if they didn't like . . .

Patient: Why, weren't the Americans trustworthy?

Therapist: Sometimes they were. Sometimes they weren't. Some Japanese businessmen are trustworthy and some aren't. But you don't want to have a contract or a business arrangement with someone you don't like. Someone you can't trust. Someone who lies. Someone who is going to steal. You know?

Patient: Yeah.

Therapist: So they decided that since these people came from the United States, and they were in Japan, it was so far away, it was the other side of the earth, they figured let's get to know the person better, and let's see if we like him, if we can trust him, and if we can, then we will sign, and if we can't, we'll say goodbye. What's my main point?

Patient: American don't trust. I mean to trust people.

Therapist: Good try. You're on the right track.

Patient: To, uh, work with the people you know and trust.

Therapist: Yeah. And if you don't know them too well?

Patient: Forget it.

Therapist: Yeah. Or wait. Don't forget it so quickly. Give them a chance, you know. Get to know them well. See if they are trustworthy and honest, and if they are, then you become friendly with them and then you can become friends with them and then you can become business partners or something like that. Okay. Anything else you want to say?

Patient: No.

As the reader can see, I got a lot of mileage out of this card. I first focused on my own impulsivity in making what soon turned out to be an ill-conceived partnership arrangement. My purpose here was to demonstrate to the patient the untoward consequences of impulsivity. My hope was that it would help him become less impulsive. In addition, in the process I was revealing a deficit, and I have discussed the therapeutic benefits to be derived from such revelations. Then, I pointed out how psychopathic individuals invite the ridicule and scorn of those about them. My hope here was that the patient would consider this repercussion with regard to his own antisocial behavior. As mentioned, I do not consider it necessary to switch to a discussion of the patient's behavior in such circumstances. I believe that getting the principle across may be all that is necessary.

The patient was interested in the story and so I decided to get even further mileage out of the card. I then discussed the situation that American businessmen faced when they first started doing business with the Japanese after World War II. My main point, of course, was that honorable and ethical individuals are more likely to be successful in life than those who are dishonorable. Had this message been given in a straightforward manner, it is not likely that it would have "sunk in." However, presented in the format of the Japanese businessmen, the mesage was more likely to be palatable.

The patient was absorbed in what I was saying. I believe that he got the general gist of my message. I believe that relating stories and experiences in this way is one of the most efficacious mediums for transmitting important therapeutic messages. As mentioned, it is an ancient tradition and the therapist does well to utilize it whenever possible.

> *Therapist:* Okay. Okay. What does your card say?
>
> *Patient:* "Make believe you are giving a gift to someone. What's that gift?" Here. (Patient makes believe he is giving the therapist a gift.)
>
> *Therapist:* Uh huh. Thank you. What is the gift?
>
> *Patient:* It's a thing you put on your desk, and it says, it's your name, Dr. Richard A. Gardner, M.D.
>
> *Therapist:* What is it? Something for my desk? You mean a desk sign? It gives my name? Okay. Thank you very much. That's very nice. I'll put this on my desk, and when I see it, it will make me think of you. You know? It's not just something that's there. When you give someone a gift, and they like you, your gift will remind them of you when they look at the gift and it will give them a nice feeling. It makes you feel good about the person who gave you the gift. And it makes the giver feel good when he knows that the person who got the gift thinks of him nicely and likes him. Okay. Now your chip. You take a chip.

One of Frank's problems was that he did not put himself into the position of those who were victims of his antisocial behavior. My hope here was to help him appreciate other people's feelings via a description of my reactions to a benevolent act on his part. In addition, I hoped that the interchange might contribute to the strengthening of our relationship. It was a description of pleasant and benevolent feelings that can transpire between people, and my hope was that it would contribute to such benevolent feelings between him and me. My basic feeling at the end of the session was that it did contribute to a strengthening of our relationship.

The Case of Andy
[The Boy with Hypospadias]

Andy entered treatment at the age of nine when he was in the fourth grade. The presenting problems were temper outbursts in school, low frustration tolerance, and a significant degree of self-denigration. Andy was an extremely bright boy who was so advanced in mathematics that he was receiving special tutoring at the ninth- and tenth-grade levels in that subject. In spite of his advanced mathematical competence, he was getting B and C grades because of his temper outbursts in the classroom.

Andy was born with hypospadias, a congenital abnormality in which the urethral opening is to be found at some point along the ventral aspect of the penis, rather than at the tip of the glans. During the first five years of his life he was hospitalized on four occasions for operative repair of his congenital defect. During these hospitalizations it was necessary to tie his hands to the bed rails in order to prevent him from tampering with the dressings. Accordingly, Andy not only suffered with the physical pain associated with his operations but with the psychological stress related to his lack of understanding as to why he was suffering.

Andy had an identical twin brother who was completely normal physically. Furthermore, the brother was also extremely bright and the two of them took their math tutoring together. The brother, however, did not exhibit any of the psychological problems with which Andy suffered and was getting extremely high grades. Nor did he exhibit the self-denigration problem and feelings of low self-worth. The boys had a younger sister who did not manifest any difficulties either. The parents had an excellent relationship both between themselves and among the members of the family. I believed that Andy's symptoms were related to the traumas he had experienced in the first four years of his life and that had he been born physically normal he would not have needed psychiatric attention.

Andy's therapy went quite well. From the outset we had an excellent relationship. I was immediately attracted to him, mainly because of the warmth of his personality and his strong desire to be helped. His high intelligence, I believe, also contributed to his therapeutic progress. There are some who hold that brighter people do not necessarily do better in treatment. Although it is certainly true that there are many highly intelligent people who are also so sick that they cannot profit significantly from therapy, I believe it is also true that the more intelligent the person is the greater the likelihood he or she will be successful in whatever endeavor the person chooses to be involved in—and therapy is one such endeavor. In the course of his treatment Andy learned to handle his anger more effectively and to deal with issues very early, before he suffered significant frustrations and pent-up anger—that would ultimately result in temper outbursts. He learned to become more respectful of himself, and this was associated with a reduction in his tendency to berate himself for the most minor errors. The vignettes from *The Talking, Feeling, and Doing Game* that are presented here are from a session that occurred in his sixth month of treatment, about a month before it terminated.

Therapist: Good afternoon, boys and girls, ladies and gentlemen. Today is Tuesday, December 2nd, 1980, and I'm happy to welcome you once again to Dr. Gardner's program. Our guest and I are playing *The Talking, Feeling, and Doing Game* and we'll be back with you when it's time for someone to answer a question. Okay, you go.

Patient: My card says, "A girl was listening through the keyhole of the closed door of her parents bedroom. They didn't know she was listening. What did she hear them saying?" Now she heard them saying that she, she had a temper tantrum, and they were talking about how to punish her.

Therapist: What were they saying exactly?

Patient: The father said to cut off her allowance for a week, but her mother said not to go to the skating rink Saturday.

Therapist: Uh huh. So it was decided . . .

Patient: It was decided, uh, to cut off her allowance for a week.

Therapist: Uh huh. Did that help? Did that help her to remember not to have temper tantrums?

Patient: Yes.

Therapist: But the big question is what did she have a temper tantrum *about*?

Patient: Well, she, she wanted to ride her two-wheeler, but the fender was all broken up. And her father said, "Yeah, we'll have to fix it, but it will be at least a week."

Therapist: Oh, so she was . . .

Patient: She wanted, she wanted to ride it badly.

Therapist: So she was upset that she had to wait so long. Was that it?

Patient: Yes.

Therapist: What could she have done instead of having a temper tantrum?

Patient: She could just have accepted it.

Therapist: Okay. Any other things she could have done? I think that's part of it.

Patient: . . . (big sighs). . . . I don't know.

Therapist: Anything else? There she was. . . . She wanted to go bike riding . . . and her bike was broken . . . and it would take her father a week to fix it. . . . What else could she have done?

Patient: She could . . . she could have just forgot about it.

Therapist: Well, that's also accepting it. Another thing she could have done is to think about another way she could have some fun. For instance, maybe she could borrow a bicycle from somebody.

Patient: Yeah.

Therapist: Like a neighbor. Or if she had a brother or sister. Then let's say she couldn't borrow a bike from somebody. What else could she have done?

Patient: She could have roller skated.

Therapist: Roller skated. She could have done something else that would be fun. Right? Okay, you get a chip for that. Okay. Now I go.

When answering the card about what the girl heard through the closed door of her parent's bedroom, Andy immediately spoke about his temper tantrums. This is an excellent example of how the cards in *The Talking, Feeling, and Doing Game* will often result in the child's focusing on the basic symptoms for which he or she has come to therapy. The parents are arguing about how to punish a girl who had a temper tantrum. The father suggests cutting off her allowance and the mother prefers that she not be allowed to go to the skating rink the following Saturday. The parents are basically utilizing behavior therapy techniques, that is, negative reinforcement. Of course, there is a place for such disciplinary measures, but they do not get to the heart of the problem. As a therapist, I want to go beyond that and not merely foster a method of dealing with temper tantrums that involves suppression and conscious control of them because of the threat of negative reinforcement.

Accordingly, as a point of departure for more extensive psychotherapeutic inquiry, I asked the patient what the girl had the temper tantrums *about*. In this way, I hoped to obtain a specific example which would serve as a point of departure for a discussion into the causes of the temper tantrum. As mentioned earlier in this book, (especially in Chapter Three), the therapist does well to use *concrete examples* rather than *abstractions* when discussing therapeutic issues. In response, the patient gave as an example the girl's broken bike. She was not only upset that she could not ride it but that it would take a week to have it fixed. At this point, I ask the patient, "What could she have done instead of having a temper tantrum?" In this way I introduce an alternative mode of adaptation to the problem. As mentioned, one of the purposes of therapy is to expand the patient's repertoire of options available for utilization when dealing with life's problems. A broken bicycle presents most children with one of the basic problems of life. In this case, the girl was dealing with it with a temper tantrum—clearly an inappropriate and maladaptive way of responding to the situation. Rather than suggesting immediately to the patient what I would consider to be a preferable mode of adaptation, I tried to elicit his contribution to the solution of this problem.

His response, was "She could just have accepted it." This is certainly a mode of adaptation that can be useful. However, I would not consider it high on the hierarchy of solutions. Rather, I would only recommend such resignation after all others have failed. There are certainly times in life when we have to resign ourselves to the fact that there is nothing we can do about a problem. However, I do not generally recommend that solution as the first. Rather, it should be the last, after all others have failed. Accordingly, I asked the patient if there were any *other* things she could have done. The patient had difficulty coming up with another solution. Accordingly, in order to facilitate his coming up with another solution I slowly repeated the problem: "There she was. . . . She wanted to go bike riding . . . and her bike was broken. . . . and it would take her father a week to fix it. . . . What else could she have done?" My hope here was that my restatement of the problem might catalyze the formulation of another solution by the patient.

Finally, Andy said, "She could . . . she could have just forgot

about it." This response, although somewhat different from the resignation response, is still low on the hierarchy of optimal adaptations. Relegating a problem to the unconscious is certainly a way
of adjusting to it. However, it is not a solution that generally involves any gratification, and so the frustrations that generate the
forgetting reaction are likely still to be operative. At this point, I
considered the patient to have exhausted all of his possibilities and
therefore considered it proper for me to suggest an adaptation myself. And this, too, is an important therapeutic principle. As mentioned in Chapter Three, it is only after the therapist has given the
patient every opportunity to find solutions him- or herself that he
or she should suggest modes of adaptation. Accordingly, I suggested that the girl might *borrow* a bicycle from someone (introducing thereby the principle of *substitute gratification*). The patient
immediately responded well to this suggestion. However, I did not
stop there and again invited the patient to consider what options
the girl might have if she could not borrow a bike from someone.
He responded, "She could have roller skated." This is certainly a
reasonable alternative and allowed the patient himself to contribute
to a solution to the problem.

> *Patient:* "What's the best kind of job a person can have? Why?
> Make believe you are doing that job." I think the best job a person
> can have is working for a charity drive, like UNICEF, or The Amer-
> ican Cancer Society or something like that.
> *Therapist:* Okay. Why is that?
> *Patient:* Because it can help other people who need the help.
> *Therapist:* Uh huh. Right! Right! So you can help other people
> through the Cancer Society and UNICEF.
> *Patient:* Uh. Try to raise money for treatment for cancer.
> *Therapist:* Right. And UNICEF?
> *Patient:* To raise money for poor people around the world.
> *Therapist:* Uh huh.
> *Patient:* For people who don't have enough food.
> *Therapist:* Do you know what that answer tells me about you?
> *Patient:* What?
> *Therapist:* It tells me that you're the kind of person who's very
> sensitive to other people's suffering, and who cares a lot about peo-
> ple who are sick, or who are starving, and that's a fine quality to
> have. And that tells me something about you that's a very admirable
> trait. Do you know what an admirable trait is?
> *Patient:* No. I don't know what it is.

Therapist: Admirable is something you admire in somebody. You know?

Patient: Yeah.

Therapist: It shows me that you're a thoughtful person who thinks about other people and feels sorry for those who are sick or in pain, and those who are hungry. That's what it tells me about you. Anything you want to say about that?

Patient: I . . . Thank you.

Therapist: You're welcome. Okay. You get a chip for that.

The patient's response was clearly an unusual one for a child of nine and a half. In fact, I cannot recall having had a response to that card which demonstrated so much sensitivity to and sympathy for the sick and the starving. I considered the response to reflect very healthy values, values that can only enhance the self-esteem of the person who has them. Furthermore, I praised Andy for his sensitivity, and he was genuinely touched by my comment. I believe this was an esteem-enhancing experience for him also.

Therapist: My card says, "Say something about your mother that gets you angry." Well, I remember when I was a kid, about nine years old or so. Those were the days that we had radios, but no TV, if you can imagine such a world. There was absolutely no television, which they had invented already, but it wasn't around in everybody's house. And I used to listen to the radio.

My favorite program was *The Lone Ranger*. Have you ever heard of *The Lone Ranger*? (The patient nods affirmatively.) The Lone Ranger and his Indian friend, Tonto. And I used to love listening to that at night. And I remember on a few occasions that my mother would say to me that I couldn't listen to it until I had finished my job. I had some jobs to do around the house, and I had this home-work, and then after I finished that I'd be able to listen to *The Lone Ranger*, and I used to get angry at her for that because . . .

Patient (interrupting): because it was your favorite program.

Therapist: It was my favorite program. Right. And then once I got very angry and I remember, uh, screaming and yelling and using bad language at her, and really having a fit, and then she punished me. She wouldn't let me watch it(sic) at all for a couple of days, and I really felt bad about that, and was very angry . . .

Patient: Did you have TV in your home?

Therapist: No, I said there was no TV in most people's homes then.

Patient: Then how come you said you "watch it"?

Therapist: Did I say "watch it"?
Patient: Yeah.
Therapist: Yeah? Did I say watch it?
Patient: Yeah.
Therapist: No, I *listened* to it.
Patient: Oh.
Therapist: That was my mistake. I guess I would have *wished* that I could have watched it, in my thinking back now as a kid, seeing it was really . . .
Patient: Did you have that when you finally got a TV? Or did you never get one?
Therapist: Oh, we have TVs now when I got older. But TV sets didn't come, weren't in people's homes, I believe, until the late 1940s, the early 1950s I think. It was after the Second World War. Then they had lots of TV sets around. At any rate, that was one of the things that I was angry at my mother about, her not letting me watch *The Lone Ranger.* But I guess it taught me some lessons about being angry about something. That you don't accomplish much by having a fit. That just makes it . . .
Patient: I know.
Therapist: That just makes it worse.
Patient: I know. I usually have a . . . before I came here, I usually had a lot of them.
Therapist: Uh huh. Do you . . .
Patient: And I got punished for them.
Therapist: Uh huh.
Patient: Usually I got sent up to my room, but I got really angry just for that.
Therapist: Uh huh.
Patient: I wanted to play with my brother and sister and I couldn't because I was upstairs.
Therapist: Oh, I see. You were being punished for a fit?
Patient: Uh huh.
Therapist: And what have you learned here about those fits?
Patient: They couldn't help anything!
Therapist: Uh huh. What's a better way? What's a better thing to do when you're angry?
Patient: Just to, just to . . .
Therapist: What's a better thing to do if you are angry about something?
Patient: Just to think about . . . . like . . . I could be angry. I could watch what I want to watch afterwards, after the punishment.
Therapist: Uh huh.
Patient: Besides, it would be on again.

Therapist: Uh huh. But what if you are angry about something, before you get the punishment, before you have the fit? What's a good way to handle something that bothers you?

Patient: Don't handle it in that way.

Therapist: Uh huh. What's a better way?

Patient: Uh . . . a better way is to talk about why you are angry.

Therapist: Right. Right! And by talking about it, what do you try to do?

Patient: You . . . you try to let out your anger but by not having any fits and talking about it.

Therapist: Right! And then what's the purpose in talking, besides letting out your anger? What else does it do?

Patient: It helps you understand . . .

Therapist: It helps you understand, and anything else?

Patient: Let's see . . .

Therapist: It helps you *solve* the problem. It helps you do something about the problem without having a fit.

Patient: That's right.

As mentioned, I always give an honest answer to the cards in *The Talking, Feeling, and Doing Game.* I usually have some ambivalence when I get a card that instructs me to make comments about members of my family. I believe that the therapist has an obligation to selectively and judiciously reveal things about him- or herself for the purposes of the therapy. However, one has an obligation to one's family members not to reveal things to others (patients or non-patients) that are private family matters. What one decides to reveal about oneself is a personal decision; what one reveals about one's family members must take into consideration their needs and right to privacy as well. I have also mentioned how useful I have found the response that relates to some childhood event of mine—an event that occurred when I was at approximately the age of my patient at the time of therapy. This helps strengthen the relationship and can enhance the likelihood that the child will become involved in the therapist's response.

Both of these principles were applied in response to the card. My "criticism" of my mother here really said nothing particularly critical about her. Rather, it describes a "deficiency" within me. In addition, I related an event that occurred during my childhood, an event that I suspected the patient could relate to. And he definitely did. He was interested in hearing about my childhood experience. Just as children's hearing about their parent's experiences strengthens the parent-child bond, a child's hearing about a therapist's childhood experiences (when appropriate) can strengthen the therapist-patient relationship.

Andy picked up my error regarding "watching" *The Lone Ranger* on radio and this in itself can be therapeutic. It makes me human and lessens the likelihood that the patient will idealize me. It can be ego-enhancing for him to benevolently correct an error of mine. It is important for the reader to appreciate that something very important happened here when the patient corrected me. My responding to it in a nonchalent manner provided the patient with a therapeutically beneficial experience. Were he to have been in my position he would have reacted with self-denigration ("How stupid can I be"). By my responding in a relaxed and nonself-deprecatory way, I served as a model for such behavior for the patient. He was also provided with the *living experience* that one can make a mistake and not necessarily castigate oneself for it.

The patient then spontaneously began talking about his *own* fits. This switch provided an opportunity to discuss what he learned about dealing with his anger. We spoke about the measures to take that would reduce the likelihood of his anger building up to such a level that he would have a temper outburst. We spoke about dealing with problems in the earliest phase by expressing one's resentment at the outset. As mentioned, the patient was very bright and was able to learn these lessons well. He clearly was able to use his intelligence therapeutically.

> *Patient:* My card says, "What is the worst thing a person can do? Show someone doing that thing." Waste their life away. That's what I think.
>
> *Therapist:* Uh huh. Give me an example, like somebody who would be wasting his or her life away.
>
> *Patient:* Let's say there were two boys. Their father died, and each got half the will. One boy . . .
>
> *Therapist (interrupts):* What's a will?
>
> *Patient:* The *will*.
>
> *Therapist:* The will . . . the will. Oh, the will when someone dies? Yeah. Yeah.
>
> *Patient (nods affirmatively):* Each got a thousand dollars.
>
> *Therapist:* This is a made-up story of yours?
>
> *Patient:* Yes.
>
> *Therapist:* Right.

Patient: One person, actually it's a different version of a story from the Bible.

Therapist: Okay.

Patient: The one that Jesus told.

Therapist: Okay.

Patient: Well, one person used it wisely and went and got a job, but the other one just wasted his life away with it, and wasted most of the money having a good time.

Therapist: Uh huh. Then what happened?

Patient: He did a lot of things. But when the money was gone, he lost his friends and had no more friends.

Therapist: Uh huh.

Patient: So he had to turn to be a bad guy.

Therapist: That was a real waste of his life.

Patient: But the other one continued, continued to prosper, and he still used his money wisely.

Therapist: Uh huh.

Patient: To get food . . .

Therapist: Uh huh.

Patient: Clothing.

Therapist: How did he get all that money?

Patient: Put it in a bank, and got interest on it.

Therapist: Is that how he . . . ? That was in the Bible?

Patient: No, it wasn't in the Bible.

Therapist (smiling): What was the interest rate in those days?

Patient (laughs): No, I said this is sort of like a modern-day fable.

Therapist: All right. I see. But besides putting the money in the bank and getting interest, did he do anything else?

Patient: Yes, he continued his job.

Therapist: Continued his job. That sounds more like the Bible to me. (therapist laughs)

Patient: Yes. (patient laughs)

Therapist: Uh, anyway, uh, now, so what do we learn from that story?

Patient: That you have only one life to live, and if you waste it, that's it!

Therapist: But some people would say that the second guy really had a great time. He just spent the money and really enjoyed himself while the first guy went to work. And what's so great about going to work? Some would say that this guy was the wise one. What would you say about that?

Patient: I think they're wrong.

Therapist: Why do you say they're wrong?

Patient: Because if you lose all your money, how can you have a good time when you lose all your money?

Therapist: Let's compare the two guys when they got older. See there was one guy, the first guy, he put his money in the bank—at a good interest we assume—and therefore didn't have much fun when he was young because he wanted to work and he put all his extra money in the bank. Then when he was old, he had a lot of money, but was too old to enjoy it. The second guy, the one who pissed all his money away when he was younger, ends up badly, but so does the first. What about those two guys? During that period of their lives?

Patient: They both were not living their lives wisely. Well, you put it that way I'm not really sure now.

Therapist: Uh huh.

Patient: Think it was about equal because . . .

Therapist: Why?

Patient: Because that person, the one who saved his money and stuff had a lot of fun when he retired and stuff.

Therapist: I see. So the one who worked was planning for the future. Was that it?

Patient: That's it.

Therapist: Okay. So that he was the smarter guy.

Patient: Uh huh.

Therapist: That's what you are saying?

Patient: Yes.

Therapist: Because he was taking care of his future. He just wasn't only thinking of the present. Is that what you are saying?

Patient: Yes.

Therapist: I would say that there is something else too. Depends upon the kind of job he had. Some people like their work, and some people don't. What about the guy in your story?

Patient: That guy liked his work.

Therapist: Uh huh. What kind of work did he do? What was he doing?

Patient: He was a founder for the ASPCA.

Therapist: A founder? What's a founder? Oh, you mean he started the organization?

Patient: Yes.

Therapist: I assume that this was not what happened in the Bible.

Patient: (patient laughs)

Therapist: Very good. So he was involved in an organization that took care of animals?

Patient: Yes.

Therapist: I see. Well, that's a very nice thing . . .

Patient: The American Society for the Prevention of Cruelty to Animals.

Therapist: Right. So he did a very noble thing.

Patient: Yes.

Therapist: Do you know what noble means?

Patient: I know what it means but I can't put it into words.

Therapist: Okay. It's very good and kind, and things like that.

Patient: That's what it usually means. Usually I know what it means, but I just can't put it into words.

Therapist: Yes. Sometimes it is hard to define the word that you know what it means. So, actually, though you are comparing the lives of these two guys in different phases of their lives. The guy who was working was still enjoying himself in a different way from the guy who was just splurging his money. Right? What happened to the guy who splurged his money?

Patient: He was dead in a couple of years.

Therapist: What about your guy who's working? Did he have any fun at all?

Patient: Yes he had fun.

Therapist: What did he do for fun?

Patient: Well, he had a pet of his own.

Therapist: Uh huh.

Patient: And, and he wanted a dog.

Therapist: Uh huh.

Patient: And since he took pretty good care of it, in the hunting season the dog returned his gratefulness.

Therapist: By?

Patient: Digging out rabbits out of his hole in the ground so he could shoot them.

Therapist: I see. So he was very helpful. But he had a good time with his dog? Is that what you are saying?

Patient: Yes.

Therapist: I see. So he wasn't just an all work kind of guy. He recognized that life required a balance of having fun and working at the same time. Is that right?

Patient: He was very smart.

Therapist: It sounds like that. Okay. Very good. You get a chip. That was a good one. Here's a chip for you.

The patient's response to the question about the worst thing a person could do revealed healthy values on the one hand and, in my opinion, a somewhat stringent value system on the other. His story, obviously based on biblical themes, revealed his appreciation that there is a price to be paid for the self-indulgent life. However, I considered his values to be somewhat rigid and self-abnegating. Accordingly, I introduced a little more flexibility in our conversation about his story. I helped the patient appreciate that a more balanced lifestyle might be the more judicious—a life style in which there was room for both work and play. I also reinforced the patient's selection of a benevolent career for the wise brother, namely, the ASPCA. This is another example of the patient's healthy values with regard to giving.

Therapist: Okay, now it's my turn. Mine says, "Make believe you're drinking a glass of water." Glugh, glugh, glugh, glugh. You know what?
Patient: What?
Therapist: I have to drink a lot of water.
Patient: How come?
Therapist: A couple of years ago, I had a very painful illness.
Patient: What is it?
Therapist: It's called a kidney stone. Do you know what a kidney is?
Patient: No.
Therapist: Well, I'll tell you. I was in the office here with a patient, with a boy and his mother really. In the middle of the session I started to get terrible cramps. And they were so bad that I had to interrupt the session, and I told the people that I can't go on, I had such pain. And we would have to stop the session, and I became . . .
Patient: Did they understand?
Therapist: Yes. They saw that I couldn't work. It was too painful for me. I was in such pain, and I didn't know what was going on. I had never had any pain like that before, and it was really terrible. And then finally, after about two hours, I thought about the various possibilities what it was. And I punched myself lightly over here (therapist points to his back over the kidney area) and I really leaped. And I knew *then* that I probably had a kidney stone.
Patient: How did you know?
Therapist: You see I'm a psychiatrist and I'm also a doctor. A regular doctor. And I figured when that happened . . . I remember from medical school that that means that I probably had a kidney stone. I didn't know. But certainly it sounded like it. Anyway, I called my doctor and went to the hospital and it was a very painful experience. Uh . . . but it finally passed out. And . . .
Patient: What is a kidney stone anyway?

Therapist: Well, you know the kidneys are up here? (Therapist points to kidney area on his back.)

Patient: Yes.

Therapist: Kidneys. And what the kidney does is take the waste from the blood.

Patient: What . . . it's all blocked up?

Therapist: It filters out waste. You know, your kidney makes your urine.

Patient: Yes.

Therapist: Urine is waste.

Patient: Yes.

Therapist: And waste goes out of your body in your urine when you urinate and go to the bathroom for a bowel movement. That's waste products. The things your body doesn't need.

Patient: Yes.

Therapist: Okay. Now the kidney manufactures the urine, and look what it does. It goes from here in the kidney, which is a round thing like that. (Therapist points to his fist.) And the urine goes down this tube called the ureter. (Therapist draws line with finger over anterior surface of his abdomen which follows the path of the ureter.) Then it goes into this thing called the bladder, which is like a ball or sac.

Patient: It's concentrated.

Therapist: Yes, it's concentrated. Very good! The kidney stores it there. It concentrates it and passes it down into the bladder.

Patient: You know what is done with it? When the bladder gets too full, you have to let it out.

Therapist: You let it out. Right! Now the kidney stone is from the kidney. The urine stagnates—it stands there—in certain little places in the kidney. And when that happens it forms stones, which are like little rocks. And then when that rock has to come out, it's very, very painful. It has to go down through the tube called the ureter. And that is very painful. Then the stone goes into the bladder.

Patient: Will I have to have those stones some day?

Therapist: I don't see any reason why.

Patient: Does everyone get them?

Therapist: No. No. I have a special problem with my kidney that makes my kidney make the stones. I mean it's more likely that I'm going to get them than other people. I have that problem. One of the things I have to do is to drink a lot of water; because if I drink a lot of water, then it will lessen the chances that I will get a stone.

Patient: Oh. That's why you have to drink a lot of water.

Therapist: Yeah. Right. That's for me. That's for my kidney. Now let's see. You had a problem too in that same area. Right?

Patient: Yes.
Therapist: Yep.
Patient: I know what it is.
Therapist: Well, what am I talking about?
Patient: Well, my kidneys . . .
Therapist: Not your kidney. Where was your problem?
Patient: In the bladder I think.
Therapist: No . . . no . . . what are you saying?
Patient: I am saying . . . ask my mom.
Therapist: You know. You know what you had.
Patient: No I don't.
Therapist: You had a problem in that your urine wouldn't come
out the right way?
Patient: Uhm.
Therapist: Do you remember that problem?
Patient: Yes.
Therapist: Uh huh. How do things stand with that problem now?
Patient: I didn't like it one bit!
Therapist: What happened with that problem?
Patient: Well, after the operation, they got it back to normal.
Therapist: How is it now?
Patient: Okay.
Therapist: Uh huh. What do you remember about those opera-
tions?
Patient (big sigh): The four of them I had in Englewood. The fifth
one, the last one, I was in New York.
Therapist: Uh hmm. And what do you remember about the op-
erations?
Patient: What do I remember of it?
Therapist: Uh huh.
Patient: Not much because they were four years ago.
Therapist: Uh huh. How old were you then?
Patient: Five.
Therapist: Uh huh. I see. Do you remember anything about them?
Patient: Uh . . . hmm.
Therapist: Do you remember anything about them?
Patient: Yes, it was really painful.
Therapist: Uh huh. Very upsetting, huh?
Patient: Yes.
Therapist: Do you still think you are upset about that now?
Patient: No.
Therapist: Do you think about it any more?
Patient: No.

Therapist: Did we talk about . . . did we talk about those operations here?

Patient: Yes.

Therapist: Did you learn anything here about them that was useful? Here? About those operations?

Patient: I don't really think so.

Therapist: You don't really think so. Uh huh. Did you feel worse about it before you came?

Patient: I felt worse about it before I came.

Therapist: Uh huh. Is there anything about anything that happened here to you that made you feel less worse about the operations?

Patient: Yes. When it was over.

Therapist: What?

Patient: When it was over.

Therapist: I don't know what you mean.

Patient: The operations were . . .

Therapist: No, no. I mean about coming here that made you feel less bad about the operations.

Patient: Yes. I remember everybody has to get sick once in a while, so I don't feel so bad about my operations.

Therapist: That's one thing. Right! Another thing is to talk about it. You know, not to be ashamed about it. It's no sin. It's no crime. You know?

Patient: I know.

Therapist: It's not . . . but you're right. I agree with you. Everybody has something. Everybody has some kind of sickness and things that happen to them, but it doesn't make you a terrible person or anything else. You know?

Patient: I know.

Therapist: Do you think less of me because I had this kidney stone. Do you think I was a terrible person for having it?

Patient: No.

Therapist: No? Anything to laugh about, or people to think it's funny or something?

Patient: No.

Therapist: Uh huh. Do you think I think less of you because you had that trouble?

Patient: No.

Therapist: No. Not at all. In fact, I admire you very much. I think you're a very fine young man.

Patient: Thank you.

Therapist: And I always think well of and respect you.

Patient (smiling): Thank you.
Therapist: Okay, I'll tell you. Our time is almost up. We want to watch a little bit of this. Okay?
Patient: Okay.
Therapist: So let's see who wins the game. Let's see. How many chips do you have?
Patient: Five.
Therapist: Five? I have three, so you are the winner. Congratulations. (Therapist and patient shake hands.) Okay. Let's watch this.

I used the relatively innocuous card "Make believe you're drinking a glass of water" as a point of departure for talking about a problem of mine that was similar to a problem of the patient's. I suspected that this was a good way of getting him to talk about his hypospadias, and my suspicion proved to be true. Talking about my kidney stone provided me with the opportunity to reveal a physical problem of my own and this, I believe, served the patient well. He and I had something in common. I too knew about pains in that area of the body. I had suffered as had he.

I believe that a factor in the patient's presenting complaint of self-denigration related to his feelings that he was less worthy an individual than others because of his hypospadias and the operative procedures he had suffered in association with its repair. The patient had the experience that I did not look upon him as less worthy a human being because of this problem. Furthermore, my telling him about my kidney stone provided him with the opportunity to see that he himself did not look down upon me for having had this disorder. And this added to my credibility when I said that I did not look down upon him and that others were not likely to disparage him because of his hypospadias.

Andy's treatment progressed quite well. The interchange transcribed here took place about one month prior to termination. He enjoyed a marked reduction of his temper outbursts as well as significant alleviation of his tendency to deprecate himself. His grades improved and he became much more acceptable to friends. I believe the primary factors in his therapeutic improvement were his high intelligence and his winning personality. These attracted me to him and this resulted in his liking me. I also admired his healthy values and I believe my reinforcement of them served to enhance his self-esteem. This enhancement of his feelings of self-worth was another significant factor in his improvement.

The Case of Morton
[Therapists Also Get Rejected]

Morton entered treatment at the age of nine because of disruptive behavior in the classroom. Although there was a mild neurological problem present (he was hyperactive, impulsive, and distractable), his primary problem centered on his relationship with his father. Morton's parents were separated and his father often did not show up for planned visits, or when he did he was often late. In addition, he was not the kind of man who basically enjoyed being with his children. Morton's anger was intense, but it was displaced onto his mother, teacher, and peers because he was fearful of revealing it to his father. While playing *The Talking, Feeling, and Doing Game*, the following conversation took place.

> *Therapist:* My question is "What's the worst thing that ever happened to you?"
> Well, I would say that one of the worst things that ever happened to me occurred when I was a teenager. There was a girl in my class in high school who I liked very much. I guess at that time I would say that I loved her. And I thought about nothing else but this girl, and I kept thinking about her and I stopped studying. All I could do was walk around and think about her and I don't think she cared for me too much. She wanted to be friendly with me, but she didn't like me anywhere near as much as I liked her. And I met her around June or so or May. I really got hooked on her and started thinking about her all the time, and she didn't treat me very nicely. And it wasn't until the end of August when she sent me a very painful letter in which she spoke about how much she didn't like me. And I discussed this with a friend of mine and he kind of knocked sense into my head and told me that I was crazy if I answered that letter. And after that, it was hard, but I didn't answer it and I stopped seeing her and I gradually got over it. But it was very painful to me and it was too bad that I didn't realize that it was a foolish thing . . .
> *Patient* (interrupting): I got the message.
> *Therapist:* What's the message?
> *Patient:* Like you loved the girl so much, but she didn't love you!
> *Therapist:* Right. And so what do you do in such a situation?
> *Patient:* Just ignore her. That's all I can think of. Other things? I don't know.
> *Therapist:* Well, what should you do?
> *Patient:* Don't let it bother you.

Therapist: Uh huh. Try to get wise, not trying to get something . . .
Patient: (interrupts): Yeah, yeah, yeah, yeah, yeah! (throws dice)
Therapist: Okay. Good.

I believe that my responding revelation about the incident that occurred when I was a teenager was of therapeutic benefit to the patient. While talking about my own experience, I was really encouraging him to take a more realistic attitude toward his father. By my relating the course of events that led to my own resolution to discontinue trying to get affection from someone who was not going to provide it, I was encouraging him to act similarly with his father. At the same time, I revealed to him that I too am susceptible to similar rejections and I hoped thereby to lessen the antitherapeutic idolization that so often occurs in treatment.

Some readers may have wondered at this point whether I was really being candid with the patient when I stated that being jilted by a teenage girl was the "worst thing that ever happened to me in my whole life." I can easily envision a reader saying, "Is that *really* true, Gardner? That was the *worst* thing that ever happened to you in your whole life?" My response is simply that 20 years ago, when this interchange took place, I still recalled the incident as one of the most painful of my life. It was selected because it lent itself well to therapeutic utilization. Had I to answer that question now, I would select from some more recent and certainly more formidable tragedies (such as the murder of my brother in 1985) that would more reasonably qualify for being considered the *worst*.

A subsequent interchange:

Therapist: Okay, my card says, "Make believe a piece of paper just blew in the window. Something is written on it. Make up what is said on the paper."
It says on the paper, "If at first you don't succeed, try, try again. If after that you still don't succeed, forget it. Don't make a big fool of yourself." That's what it says on the paper. What do you think of that?
Patient (laughing): That's a good one.
Therapist: Okay.

My response is a quote from W. C. Fields who is alleged to have made the statement. In my *The Boys and Girls Book About*

Divorce (1970, 1971b) I have elaborated on this message and made it into a chapter entitled "Fields' Rule." The message here is essentially a reiteration of my previously described experience with my teenage girlfriend. This time, however, the patient did not resist the message and stated with enthusiasm, "That's a good one."

The Case of Harry [Getting Therapeutic Mileage from an Auto Mechanic]

The interchange recorded below took place while playing *The Talking, Feeling, and Doing Game.*

> *Patient:* "What do you think about a boy who lets his dog make a mess in the house? What should his parents do?" His parents should not let him do what he wants and tell him that if he wants a dog, he's going to have to take care of his messes and everything.
> *Therapist:* And suppose he still doesn't listen?
> *Patient:* Then if he doesn't listen, he's not going to have a dog.
> *Therapist:* Right. And that would be a sad thing. Do you know any other way to do it?
> *Patient:* No.
> *Therapist:* I can't think of one. If he wants to have the fun of a dog, he has to have . . . what's the word?
> *Patient:* . . . the fun of the dog, then he has to take care of the dog.
> *Therapist:* Right!
> *Patient:* If he does not want the fun of the dog, then he is not going to get it.
> *Therapist:* Right! He has to have the responsibility, and he has to do things sometimes he doesn't like. That's how most things are in life. They're a mixture. If you want to get a certain amount of fun, you have to do certain things you don't like sometimes. Do you know anything that's not like that?
> *Patient:* (nods negatively)
> *Therapist:* Well, it's hard to think of something that isn't like that. There's always a mixture of these things.
> Okay, my card says, "Of all the things you learn in school, what do you like learning about least? Why?" Well, I don't go to school anymore, but I remember when I was in school the subject that I didn't like very much was economics. Do you know what economics is? What is economics?

Patient: Sort of like a job.

Therapist: Well, it's something like that. It's about money, and buying, and selling, and prices, and things like that. It didn't interest me very much, but I knew I had to take that subject if I wanted to pass in high school and in college. You know?

Patient: Yeah.

Therapist: They just required it. Because I wanted to get my diploma and finish up and because I wanted to take the other courses, I knew I had to take it. I had to take the bad with the good. Do you understand?

Patient: Yes.

Therapist: That's something like we were talking about before, that nothing is perfect and everything is a mixture. What do you think about that?

Patient: (nods negatively)

Therapist: You don't like that idea too much?

Patient (without much conviction): It's okay.

Therapist: It's okay. Is there anything like that in your life? Accepting the bad with the good? Do you know of anything in your life that's like that? I do. Do you have to accept bad things with the good things in any part of your life?

Patient: Yeah, I do.

Therapist: Can you give an example from your life of that?

Patient: No.

Therapist: I can think of one.

Patient: What?

Therapist: Your parent's divorce. There are things there where you have to accept the bad with the good. There are things with your parents' divorce that has to do with accepting the bad with the good.

Patient: No.

Therapist: Oh come on, you can think of something.

Patient: I don't want to say it.

Therapist: You don't want to say it. Well, okay. That's too bad. In this game you get chips for answering. Right? Do you feel like playing this game? Okay, because part of the game is to answer the questions. So if you want to get a chip, you have to say something about your parents'.

Patient (interrupts): Well, you've got to answer your questions, I don't.

Therapist: I answered already. I answered with economics. But I'm giving you a chance to get an extra chip if you can say something about your parents.

Patient: No, I don't want an extra chip.

Therapist: You don't want it. Okay.

One of Harry's problems was that he refused to accept responsibility. He did not want to suffer any discomfort or inconvenience. He fit well into the category of the boy whom I described earlier—the deprived child who lives by the pleasure principle because he was never rewarded with love and affection for self-restraint. I tried to use the examples of the dog and the subject of economics to get across the point that toleration of discomfort is often necessary if one is to enjoy certain benefits. On an intellectual basis the patient appeared to be somewhat receptive. I then tried to shift into a discussion of the advantages and disadvantages of parental divorce. However, Harry would have no part of the discussion. The lure of the chip reward did not serve as an incentive. Accordingly, I did not pressure him any further and we proceeded with the game.

The interchange with Harry here raises an important technical point in the treatment of patients. Some therapists take a very passive position regarding any pressures on the patient to speak about a specific subject. They consider this not only respectful of the patient's wishes, but believe that to do otherwise is to invite further resistance to the treatment. They also believe that such urging can be anxiety provoking and that it is per se antitherapeutic. I generally do not pull back so quickly when a patient exhibits manifestations of resistance and/or anxiety when discussing a "touchy subject." I believe to do so might deprive the patient of an important therapeutic experience. Some patients need a little urging and are better off afterwards for having experienced the thoughts and feelings attendant to dwelling on the sensitive subject. The therapist cannot know beforehand how much anxiety and resistance will be engendered by suggesting further inquiry into a given area. He or she should be exquisitely sensitive to whether or not the therapist's pressure is producing undue anxiety and/or resistance. If such appears to be the case, it is time to "pull back." Here, I believed that Harry was approaching that point when he adamantly refused to pursue this subject—even after being informed that he would thereby deprive himself of a further chip. He firmly stated, "No, I don't want an extra chip." I got the message, and we proceeded with the game.

>   *Therapist:* Let's go on then. (throws dice) My question is, "What do you think your life will be like 20 years from now?" Well, 20 years from now I will . . .

Patient (interrupts): You might be dead in 20 years.

Therapist: Well, how old do you think I am?

Patient: Forty-two.

Therapist: Thank you very much. I appreciate the compliment. No, I'm going to be 50 next month. What do you think of that?

Patient: I thought you were 40 something.

Therapist: I am 40 something. I am 49, I am 49 and 11/12. So twenty years from now I will be 50. (Therapist laughs as he immediately recognizes the slip and its obvious significance.) I really wish I would be fifty. Twenty years from now I will be 70. Do you think I'll be dead?

Patient: Yes.

Therapist: You think so?

Patient: Yes, because my uncle was in the hospital and he died.

Therapist: There are a lot of people who die before 70, and there are a lot of people who don't. I certainly hope that I'm still alive.

Patient (speaking with warmth and conviction): So do I.

Therapist: Anyway, if I am alive, and I think I probably will be, I can't be 100 percent sure, I will probably still be a psychiatrist and will be trying to help kids.

Patient: But you will not have me as a subject(sic) because I will be 30 years old.

Therapist: You will be 30 years old? What will you be doing then? I will be doing psychiatry.

Patient: I will be an auto mechanic.

Therapist: An auto mechanic.

Patient: Do I get a chip for that?

Therapist: Okay, you get a chip for that. I hope you will be a good auto mechanic, and I hope you have a very good business.

Patient: Yeah, so do I. Lots of money!

Therapist: But you have to work very hard at it you know. Whatever you do, if you're going to goof off, if you're an auto mechanic and you goof off, you're not going to have any customers. People are not going to come back. But if you do a good job, then you'll have many customers. Right?

Patient: (nods affirmatively)

Therapist: Okay. Very good.

One could argue that Harry's thinking I might be dead 20 years from now was definitely a manifestation of hostility. Although I admit this is certainly a possibility (especially because it was preceded by my strongly encouraging him to talk about the touchy subject of his parents' divorce), his comment may have had nothing to do with hostility. It is important to appreciate that Harry was 10 years old, and I was mid-to-late middle aged. Children's appreciation of adult's ages is often limited. Furthermore, his appreciation of the significance of a 20-year advance in my age is also likely to be somewhat distorted. I did not automatically assume that his interjected response reflected hostility. (I do not doubt the possibility either; I only consider it unlikely.)

I did, in the true analytic spirit, ask Harry to guess my age rather than blurt it out. However, in Harry's case, I did not consider it a fruitful area of inquiry to delve into his erroneous speculation any further. His guess that I was 42 instead of 49 was not, in my opinion, conclusive evidence for some kind of psychodynamically determined error. To have done so, in my opinion, could have been antitherapeutic in that it would have involved us in an inquiry into a subject that might or might not have had psychological significance. I was content to leave the issue alone and reveal my actual age. As mentioned, I believe there is often an important benefit to be derived in treatment from such revelations. They bring the patient and therapist closer, and this may be more important than an analytic inquiry. Even though the therapist may be depriving the patient of some important psychoanalytic insight, this may be more than compensated for by the strengthening of the therapist-patient relationship that such divulgences bring about.

I answered the question by informing Harry that I fully intended to be continuing to do psychiatry in 20 years. I wanted to get across the notion that I find my work interesting and enjoyable, and that the prospect of retiring completely is not only distasteful to me, but would be completely out of character for me. My hope was that some of this attitude toward productive endeavors might filter down to Harry.

Harry then answered the question and offered that he would be an auto mechanic. I generally follow through with such interruptions because they often provide useful therapeutic material. Unless the interruption is obviously a resistance maneuver, I "milk it for all it's worth." It would be completely outside of the philosophy of the game for me to say to the patient: "Hey, wait a minute now. This is my question. You wait your turn." Such a response would totally defeat the purpose of the game—which is to elicit psychodynamically meaningful material from the patient.

The patient emphasized the material benefits to be derived from being an auto mechanic. I took this opportunity to introduce a comment about the work ethic and the importance of doing a good job and establishing a good reputation. I do not believe at that point that the statement "hit him in the guts." However, it behooves the therapist to transmit his or her therapeutically important messages and hope that they will ultimately be received. In no way did I consider Harry's switching the subject to his future life as an auto mechanic to be a resistance maneuver. Rather, I welcomed it from the realization that school and work are analogous and that anything I could say about his work as an auto mechanic would be likely to have applicability to his school work. Furthermore, because Harry was extremely unreceptive to discussing his school work directly, I viewed discussions about the principles of being an auto mechanic to be a potential vehicle for talking symbolically about Harry's school difficulties in a way that Harry would welcome.

> *Patient:* My card says, "What would you do if you found $10,000?" If I found $10,000, first I would return it to the police station to see if it is anybody's. Then, if it is not anybody's, I would know in 30 days that I would get to keep it. If I get to keep it, then I am going to buy my own auto mechanic shop.
>
> *Therapist:* That's a good purpose.
>
> *Patient:* So my store will be nice, and many people will come. So it will be a nice clean place to get your car fixed, and washed, and everything, and take every bit of advice to make people's cars look nice. It will be a real, nice, clean place.
>
> *Therapist:* To create a good impression. Right?
>
> *Patient:* Yeah, to create a good impression.
>
> *Therapist:* That's important. It's important to create a good impression. It shows you have pride in your place; but it's also important that you do good work, you know. There are some places that look flashy and nice, but the work is no good.
>
> *Patient:* Mine is going to look flashy and do the best work.
>
> *Therapist:* Okay. I think that the important thing is the work. The second important thing is how it looks.

Here, the patient again focused on external appearances and made no mention of the quality of work that his auto mechanic shop would provide. I praised him on his interest in a clean shop that made a good appearance. But, I also emphasized the importance of high-quality work. This was especially important for this boy whose commitment to the work ethic in school left much to be desired.

These interchanges on the subject of the auto mechanic shop represent what I consider to be among the most efficacious forms of child psychotherapeutic interchange. To the casual observer the patient and I are involved in a relaxed discussion on the somewhat neutral and even banal subject of auto mechanic shops. There is almost a "folksy" quality to the conversation. However, from the patient's point of view it is probably just that: simply a conversation. From my point of view, however, much more is going on. At every point I am actively concerned with two processes: 1) the ostensible conversation and 2) the underlying psychodynamic meaning of what is going on. What may appear to be a relaxed conversation is, for me, almost a façade. The wheels are ever going around in my head. I am ever concerned with both of these processes simultaneously. I am ever trying to relate my comments to the patient's basic difficulties and how they are reflecting themselves in what he is saying. This is the way I transmit my most important therapeutic communications. I cannot emphasize this point strongly enough.

Freud referred to dreams as "the royal road to the unconscious." I am in full agreement. And I would consider stories and conversations of this kind to be the royal road to therapeutic change in children. And even with adults the process has merit. Quite often I will in the course of the session with an adult patient relate an anecdote or an event that has relevance to his or her problems. It is a way of getting home a point with a vehicle that is extremely powerful; far more powerful, I believe, than a therapeutic approach that relies upon gaining insight into unconscious processes. Lastly, it is an approach that has history to recommend it. It is an ancient method that has survived to the present day because of the universal recognition of its efficacy.

Therapist: "Of all the things you own what do you enjoy the most? Make believe you are doing something with that thing." I would say that one of the most important things I own is my typewriter. (therapist imitates typing)

Patient (interrupts): Isn't that your favorite thing? What about that? (patient points to mounted video camera)

Therapist: You like that too?

Patient: Yeah!

Therapist: Why do you think I would choose that?

Patient: Because you could make movies.

Therapist: That is a lot of fun. I think that's a good answer too. That is also one of my favorite things. I like the TV because I can see myself on television anytime I want.

Patient: You can say "hello," and you can look at the television, and see yourself say hello.

Therapist: Yes, but more important than that it helps me be a better psychiatrist.

Patient: It does?

Therapist: Yeah, because we are playing this game here and people see themselves on television, and it helps them see themselves better, and it helps me be a better psychiatrist in this way.

Patient: Uh-oh!

Therapist: What is uh-oh?

Patient: You're supposed to have two of these chips.

Therapist: Oh, did I forget? Okay, I guess I forgot. (therapist takes chip) Okay. Let's get back to the question. You were close when you guessed the TV camera, but I was not going to say that. I was going to say *typewriter* because with the typewriter I write books, and stories, and things like that. It makes me feel very good because when I write a book—and especially when it comes out—it makes me feel good that I created something.

I began responding to the question about my favorite possession by mentioning the typewriter. I planned to use it as a point of departure for discussing the gratifications I enjoy from writing. My hope was that this would engender in Harry greater motivation in his academic pursuits. However, he interrupted me and pointed to the video camera that was recording the program that we were making. As mentioned, I generally welcome such interruptions because they usually relate to issues that may be more relevant to the child than those that I may be focusing on at that point. (Of course, when the interruption is a reflection of resistance, then I do not permit it and insist upon my right to return to my card and answer my question.)

I allowed the digression and got as much mileage as I could out of a discussion of the video camera and the closed-circuit television system. I got in the message that it was useful for helping people see themselves and this, of course, is a crucial aspect of treatment. I did not get very far with this explanation when the patient noted that I had failed to collect one of my reward chips. When the game is being played at its best, both the therapist and the patient may forget whose turn it is and may forget to collect the reward chips. Following the rectification of this error, I returned to the typewriter theme and focused on the good feeling I have when a book of mine comes out. At that point Harry interrupted me, and the following interchange took place.

> *Patient* (interrupts): What's that over there? (Patient points to a pile of just-published books, *Dr. Gardner's Fables for Our Times* [1981].)
> *Therapist:* That's my new book. It just came out.
> *Patient:* When?
> *Therapist:* The book came out yesterday. Would you like to borrow a copy?
> *Patient* (very enthusiastically): Yeah!

The psychological significance of this interchange concerning the new book as well as the subsequent conversation, will be more meaningful with the following background information. I routinely give a complimentary copy of my book *Stories About the Real World* (1972a) to every new patient. These stories cover a wide variety of conflict situations of childhood, and it is a rare patient who does not relate to at least one of the stories. I use the child's reactions as a point of departure for therapeutic interchanges. Accordingly, Harry had been given a copy of this book during my initial consultation. Subsequently, I lent him a copy of my *Dorothy and the Lizard of Oz* (1980c). Unfortunately, he lost the book. When he told me of the loss, it was with a complete absence of embarrassment, guilt, remorse, or a desire to make restitution. Because of this I told him that I would lend him another book with the understanding that if he lost this one, he would have to pay for it. I considered this requirement to provide Harry with a useful therapeutic experience. Not to have made some attempt to require responsibility on his part would have been, in my opinion, antitherapeutic. This is just the kind of *living experience* that I consider important in therapy. The therapist should seize upon every opportunity he or she can to provide patients with such experiences. The interchange over the lost book is an excellent example. Harry absolutely refused to accept the book with that proviso. We discussed it for a few minutes at that time, and I tried to impress upon him that I felt bad that the book was lost and that I wanted to protect myself from further losses. I also tried to help him appreciate his own lack of remorse over the loss, but this fell on deaf ears. In the conversation I knew that he wished to borrow the book, but I knew also that he did not wish to assume responsibility for its loss. I believed that my refusal to lend him the book without "protecting myself" might have been a more valuable therapeutic experience than any discussions we did have or might have had on the subject.

This is what I was thinking when Harry pointed to the new book. It was not placed there to attract his attention. (I do not set up artificial situations like this in therapy. No matter what items are present in the therapist's office, the pressure of the unconscious is going to invest them with special meaning in accordance with the psychological processes of the patient.) Harry immediately expressed interest in the book, and I thought this would be a wonderful opportunity to offer to lend him a copy. He responded with enthusiasm.

Therapist: I'll let you borrow a copy, but let me ask you something. If you were in my place, would you be hesitant to lend the book? Should I be hesitant to lend you a book?

Patient: I think you should give me the book just like you gave the *The Real World Stories.*

Therapist: Okay, but what about lending you a book? You don't think I should lend you the book?

Patient: No.

Therapist: Why not?

Patient: I don't know.

Therapist: I had an experience with you that made me hesitate to lend you a book. Do you remember that experience? What was the experience?

Patient: The last . . . book you lent me I lost.

Therapist: Yeah, I lent you a book and you lost it.

Patient (angrily): So don't give me the book; I don't really care.

Therapist: But if I just give it to you, that won't help you remember not to lose things.

Patient: Ah, I don't want your book . . . just forget it!

Therapist: It's a new book of fables called *Dr. Gardner's Fables for Our Times.*

Patient: I don't really care about it; you can keep it for yourself.

Therapist: I just want to say something. If I lend it to you now . . . I would like to lend it to you and give you a second chance. I never condemn a person for one mistake. Do you know what I mean? You're entitled to a mistake; everybody makes mistakes. But it makes me hesitant; it makes me a little concerned. How about this? I'll lend you the book?

Patient (interrupts): No, I don't want it!

Therapist: Let me tell you what I'm suggesting.

Patient: I don't want it!

Therapist: I'll tell you what. I'll lend you the book, but if you lose it, you have to pay for it.

Patient: No, I'm not going to do it.

Therapist: Why not?

Patient: Because I don't *need* the book.

Therapist: Okay, that's up to you, but I would have liked you to have borrowed it, but I'm not going to lend it to you just like that, because I'm afraid you might lose it or not take good care of it. But maybe you'll change your mind. If you change your mind, let me know.

Patient: Okay. Did you answer your question?

Therapist: I think I did.

Patient: Wait . . . what was that question?

Therapist: "What are my favorite things?" I said my typewriter because it makes me feel good when I write books and the books help other people. Books help other people with their problems. They teach them things and lots of people say they learn a lot from them. And that makes me feel good too. You feel good when you do something that helps other people. Do you do things that make you feel good? What do you do that makes you feel good?

Patient: I'm nice to people.

Therapist: That's right, it makes you feel good when you're nice to people, right?

Patient: Yeah.

Therapist: Right. You get a chip for that answer, because it was a very good answer. And I get a chip for my answer.

It was quite clear that Harry really wanted to borrow the book. However, he absolutely refused to assume any responsibility for its loss. I tried to seduce him into making a commitment by continuing the conversation in the hope that it would intensify his craving for the book. Although I was unsuccessful in getting him to make the commitment to provide restitution if the book were lost, I do believe that he had a therapeutic experience. There were indeed repercussions for his casual attitude over the loss of my book, and he had the living experience that book owners under such circumstances are likely to be reluctant to lend him additional books. He suffered the frustration of not being able to borrow the book. This, I hoped, would be a useful therapeutic experience. There was no analytic inquiry here; there was little if any insight gained by Harry. However, something therapeutic was accomplished—the lack of insight on Harry's part notwithstanding.

Many therapists are far less enthusiastic than I about interchanges such as these. They are deeply committed to the notion that without insight there cannot be therapeutic change. They subscribe deeply to Freud's dictum: "Where there was unconscious, there let conscious be." I am not as enthusiastic as Freud was over the therapeutic benefit of insight. I am much more impressed with the therapeutic changes that occur from experiences as well as messages that are imparted at the symbolic level. For therapists who are deeply committed to the insight route to change, I often provide the analogy of my scuba-diving experience. My instructor repeatedly advised the class that it was vital for all of us to learn ways of dealing with emergency situations while under water. The worst thing that one can do in such situations is to hold one's breath and get to the top as rapidly as possible. It is one of the quickest ways of killing oneself. It is one of the quickest ways of bursting one's lungs. Accordingly, we were repeatedly advised to fight the impulse to rise to the top when we were in trouble. We were meticulously taught the various ways of dealing with underwater emergencies. I can tell the reader from personal experience that the urge to hold one's breath and rise to the top under such circumstances is immense. It seemed that every force and reflex in my body was dictating such a course of action. It was only with formidable self-control that I fought these urges on two occasions when I had difficulty. Of course, my knowledge of the consequences of submitting to them was of help in my suppressing them.

I mention the scuba experience because it relates directly to those therapists who are deeply committed to insight as the primary mode for helping their patients. Just as my scuba instructor urged me to fight my impulse to hold my breath and rise to the top, I suggest that therapists fight their impulses to pursue the insight route. I suggest that they consider the alternatives discussed in this book. I do not view insight as totally meaningless in the therapeutic process, but I generally view it as less significant for children than it is for adults, and even for adults it is a low-priority therapeutic modality. It is frosting on the cake. I am in agreement with Frieda Fromm-Reichmann who said, "The patient needs an experience **far** more than an insight."

CONCLUDING COMMENTS

The popularity of The Talking, Feeling, and Doing Game has been a great source of gratification. It has become standard equipment for the child psychotherapist, and many therapists consider it vital in their work with children. Over the years I have received many letters in which the therapist has expressed gratitude for my introduction of the game. I have even had the dubious compliment on a few occasions of plagiarized versions being introduced. These, to the best of my knowledge, have never enjoyed similar popularity. (One such plagiarizer lost motivation to continue marketing the game after a letter from my attorney "reminding him" of the consequences if he did not cease and desist.)

Although the game was originally devised in an attempt to engage children who were not free enough to provide self-created stories when utilizing the mutual storytelling technique and its derivative games, it has proven useful for more cooperative and insightful children as well. In fact, I would say that it is a rare child who will not get involved in the game.

I have also found it useful in the therapy of small groups of children in the five to twelve age range. Children in this age bracket are traditionally poor candidates for group therapy because of their age-appropriate rambunctiousness. Often, the therapist finds him- or herself serving more as a disciplinarian than a therapist. The Talking, Feeling, and Doing Game provides an organization and a structure that is often so powerful that children of this age are diverted from the horseplay that often compromises significantly the group therapy. One can use it for this purpose in a number of ways. One way I have found useful is to have the first child respond to a card and then get input from each of the other players on the first player's response. Each of the other participants, of course, receives a chip for his or her contribution. The second child may now answer the same question or choose one of his or her own. In this way I go around the board, engaging each child in the responses of the others. When utilizing the game in this manner the therapist can choose whether to participate as a player or merely as an organizer. I generally prefer to play as one who takes the card myself for the sake of "egalitarianism" and the desire to gain the therapeutic benefits to be derived by the patients from my revelations.

The game can also be useful in selected family therapy situations. Generally, unsophisticated and/or uneducated parents may welcome the game as a catalyst for family discussion; more sophisticated and/or educated parents will generally not need such assistance in their family therapy work.

The Talking, Feeling, and Doing Game is not without its disadvantages. All good drugs have their side effects. In fact, it is often the case that the more powerful the drug the greater the side effects. One of the main drawbacks of *The Talking, Feeling, and Doing Game* is that it may be *too* enticing to both the patient and the therapist. It is seemingly an easy therapeutic modality. Many therapists, I am certain, play it without fully appreciating its complexities and how difficult it can often be to utilize it properly for therapeutic purposes. The child, too, may find it attractive because it seemingly protects him or her from talking about more painful subjects directly. It should not be used as the only therapeutic modality because it will deprive the therapist of some of the deeper unconscious material that can more readily be obtained from projective play and storytelling. In short, therapists should not be tempted into using the game throughout every session; they should do their utmost to balance the therapeutic activities with other modalities.

I have also found the game particularly useful in the treatment of children with neurologically based learning disabilities. Its utilization for this purpose is described elsewhere (1973e; 1974; 1975a,b,c; 1979; 1980a,b). For further articles on the game's general utilization I refer the reader to book chapters of mine on the subject (1983b, 1986d).

SIX

Psychoanalytically Oriented Child Psychotherapy

Psychoanalysis is a field in which one man's fantasy becomes another man's reality.

Author of this wisdom unknown to the author of this book

THE SO-CALLED DISCIPLINE OF CHILD PSYCHOANALYSIS

There is no chapter on child psychoanalysis in this book. My main reason for excluding such a chapter is that I do not believe that a field with this name is justifiable. The number of children who are bona fide candidates for this kind of treatment is so small that I do not believe a whole discipline is justified for their treatment. To me, having a field called child psychoanalysis is like having a field called pediatric gerontology. What kind of child would a pediatric gerontologist treat? It would have to be a person who is chonologically very young but who is physically very old. Now, what kind of a disease could a child have that should warrant treatment by such a specialist? I recall from medical school learning about a disease called *progeria*, an endocrinological disorder that is seen in children. Here, the endocrine glands so malfunction that signs and symptoms develop that result in the child's looking like a little old person. If there are other such diseases I do not know of them. Do we start a field called pediatric gerontology for the treatment of the rare case of progeria? I say no. Similarly, I do not believe that we should have a field called child psychoanalysis for the small fraction of child patients who are candidates for such therapy.

I basically view child psychoanalysis to be a field in which attempts have been made to apply adult psychoanalytic treatment to children. The attempt on the part of those who do this is so strong that they often lose sight of the fact that only a small percentage of the children whom they are treating are basically truly candidates for this kind of treatment. They have to deny the obvious fact that the vast majority of the patients they are treating are not cognitively capable of availing themselves of the kind of therapy they are offering. As mentioned, I do not believe that most children are capable of involving themselves in meaningful psychoanalytic inquiry until the age of ten or eleven, when they reach what Piaget referred to as the level of *formal operations*. It is at this phase that the child of average intelligence first exhibits the capacity to separate an entity from the symbol used to denote it and cognitively move back and forth between the entity and the symbol. Under proper training and exposure, some children of average intelligence may be taught to do this earlier. Of course, by two or three years of age children will dream, and the creation of dreams involves the formation of symbols (manifest content) to denote specific unconscious entities (latent content). But the unconscious *formation* of dream symbols is not the same as the conscious cognitive capacity to appreciate the relationship between the dream's manifest and latent contents. I am not claiming that *no* capacity for such analysis is possible before the age of ten or eleven. I am only claiming that the average child has limited capacity for such prior to that time, and the younger the child is, the less the likelihood that a significant amount of time spent in such endeavors is possible. Of course, a seven year old with an extremely high IQ might be able to function intellectually as an eleven year old and then have the cognitive capacity for psychoanalytic inquiry.

Another factor that contributes to the paucity of child candidates for psychoanalytic treatment is the environmental one. There are some families in which the members routinely try to understand the underlying meaning of what they are doing. But these families are rare. Often, they are people who themselves have a strong commitment to psychoanalytic treatment. In the vast majority of families, however, people are not thinking much about the underlying reasons for the things they are doing. The child who grows up in an atmosphere where such inquiry is routine is more likely to be a candidate for psychoanalytic treatment.

Over the years I have had colleagues who have gone beyond their psychoanalytic training into the so-called subspecialty of child psychoanalysis. Quite often, I have been approached by such trainees with the request that I refer them patients who might be suitable candidates for child psychoanalytic treatment. Frequently, I am told that the ability to pay will not be a consideration in that the child will be treated at a minimal fee, and even for nothing, if found suitable for psychoanalytic therapy. The offer to treat at such low cost comes not generally from the altruistic desire to aid the needy; rather, it derives from the fact that candidates in these programs routinely have significant difficulty finding suitable child patients. The main reason for this is that the vast majority of parents absolutely refuse to involve their children in a treatment program four times a week over a span of three, four, or even more years. The typical child analytic patient, then, would start at age five or six and end at ten or eleven, spanning thereby most of the so-called latency period.

There is something psychopathic about those who make such a recommendation. I am not claiming that all therapists who involve themselves in such programs are psychopaths, only that it requires some kind of superego deficiency to recommend such a treatment program to parents. The patient's childhood has to be compromised significantly if a parent is stupid or gullible enough to involve a child in such a treatment program. To go to an analyst four times a week involves giving up four days a week of after-school activities. Playing with friends, recreational activities, sports, after-school extra-curricular activities, homework, television viewing (not necessarily 100 percent detrimental), and even relaxing and doing nothing must all be compromised for the allegedly higher purpose of the psychoanalytic treatment. The theory here is that the losses that result from such privations are more than counterbalanced by the benefits derived from the therapy. Although I believe that the treatment I provide is efficacious for many of the children I see, I do not believe that any child would derive more benefit from seeing me four times a week than from engaging in the aforementioned activities. Once or twice a week, maybe; four times a week, never!

It is not only the frequency of the treatment that deprives candidates of suitable patients. It is also the criterion that the child be analyzable. I see an average of one such child every two or three years. These colleagues have a long and hard search. What ultimately happens, however, is that they rarely find their patients. Rather, they somehow convince the parents of children with severe psychiatric disturbances to involve their children in such a program. They are so pleased to have finally found a parent who is willing to make such a commitment that they look less carefully at the nature of the child's problems—especially with regard to whether he or she has the capacity for introspection, self-inquiry, and analytic thinking. My experience has been that many of the patients who are receiving such treatment under the aegis of a formal child psychoanalytic training program are children with significant learning disabilities who in addition have formidable superimposed psychogenic problems. And such children are among the least likely to have the cognitive capacity for psychoanalytic inquiry. Others are children who could justifiably be classified as borderline psychotic. Here too, the disorder is so severe that the parents are willing to commit the child to such extensive treatment in the hope (not likely to be realized) that this more intensive form of therapy will bring about improvement and even cure of the child's disorder. However, such children are least likely to be able to form the kind of deep relationship that serves as the foundation for psychotherapeutic treatment (psychoanalysis being one branch of psychotherapy). Accordingly, we have many therapists graduating from such programs who have never basically analyzed a child.

For these reasons I have never pursued an educational program that would involve, either immediately or ultimately, training in child psychoanalysis. I consider myself to be an *adult* psychoanalyst and a child psychiatrist, but not a child psychoanalyst. If I had control over the use of the term *child psychiatrist*, however, I would refer to myself as a *pediatric psychiatrist*. The term child psychiatrist can easily connote an individual who is a child and yet is also a psychiatrist.

REASONS WHY ADULT PSYCHOANALYTIC TECHNIQUES CANNOT GENERALLY BE APPLIED TO CHILDREN

The cognitive incapability of children to involve themselves in psychoanalysis is only one of a variety of reasons why I consider such treatment to be inappropriate and inapplicable for children under the age of eleven or so. Here I will discuss some of the technical aspects of the therapy per se that make it extremely difficult, if not impossible in many cases, to apply this treatment modality to children.

"Where There Is Unconscious, There Shall Conscious Be"

Psychoanalytic treatment is based on the theory that certain psychogenic problems are the result of attempts on the part of the individual to deal with suppressed and repressed unconscious material. The primary way in which analytic treatment helps individuals with such problems is to assist in the process of bringing into conscious awareness those unconscious processes that have contributed to the development of the symptoms. In fact, most psychoanalysts would hold that a psychotherapeutic program that does not have this as one of its primary goals cannot justifiably be called psychoanalysis. Most such analysts would not say that the alternative treatment modality cannot possibly be useful; rather, they would hold that it cannot justifiably be called psychoanalysis. However, the same individuals also generally believe that psychoanalysis is the most definitive, "deep," and thorough treatment for psychogenic disorders in which the suppression and repression of unconscious processes are playing an important etiological role.

There are literally thousands of articles written describing how the process of bringing unconscious material into conscious awareness has resulted in significant alleviation and even cure of psychogenic symptoms. Many of these articles describe rapid alleviation of symptoms immediately after the patient has gained such awareness. After reading these articles I often refer to the treatment success as one in which there has been a "great leap forward into mental health." Other factors that may have been operative in bringing about the described change are often not described. The assumption is made that merely by bringing unconscious material into conscious awareness, the patient has improved markedly and has even been cured. I suspect that many of these reports are fabrications. I suspect that others are genuine, but that the patient has provided the therapist what he or she wanted to hear and the therapist has been quick to report the "cure" before the patient had the opportunity once again to exhibit the same symptoms or possibly others. These therapists are so desirous of confirming their theory and obtaining cures by their methods, and so eager to get their happy results into print, that they must selectively blind themselves to certain realities that are taking place with their patients and/or themselves.

Basically, then, I do not believe that this aspect of treatment, whether it be for adults or children, is the central therapeutic modality. I am not denying that such insights can often be helpful. However, as far back as my residency days I came to appreciate that much more had to happen in treatment—things unrelated to the gaining of insight—before therapeutic change could be brought about. I am not claiming that insight into unconscious processes is of no value. In fact, I routinely encourage such inquiry with my adult patients. I am only claiming that it is a small part of the therapeutic process and that other factors, many more important (see Chapter Two), are operative. Even if I am wrong here and insight into unconscious processes is indeed the central factor in the alleviation of certain types of psychogenic problems, I do not believe that the vast majority of children have the cognitive capacity to avail themselves of this route to the alleviation of their difficulties.

The Denial Mechanism

There is another factor that also makes it extremely difficult, if not impossible, to engage children in analytic treatment. I am referring here to the utilization of denial mechanisms. Denial may very well be the most commonly used defense mechanism. And children use it so frequently that it can be considered normal. Most if not all child therapists see boys who have behavioral problems in school. Typically, they tease, scapegoat, provoke, and involve themselves in a wide variety of alienating behaviors with peers. Invariably, the boy denies that he is the initiator and insists that it is always the other children who are the provocateurs. Generally, the patient describes himself as having been minding his own business when some wise guy came over and tried to knock the halo off his head. When the child is confronted with reports from his teacher in which the patient is described as having been observed to be the initiator dozens of times, the teacher is described as a "liar." Or, the child will describe *himself* as the one who was being scapegoated. If the examiner incredulously asks such a youngster, "Are you telling me that you have *never* once—in your whole life—started the fight," the child may sheepishly admit that he might have. When, however, the examiner asks the child to provide a specific example of such a time, the child will usually respond, "I can't remember" or "I forgot." The child described here is *normal*. If this is abnormal, then 99.9 percent of all children are abnormal. Has a boy been born who says, "I started it" when mother reprimands siblings for fighting? What mother ever says to her children, "Raise your hand if you stole the cookie?"

I recognize that the denial described here in children has both conscious and unconscious contributions. In some cases, I believe that unconscious processes are primarily operative, in other children conscious elements predominate. However, I do not believe it really matters what the balance is between these two factors. Whatever their balance, the net result is that the denial mechanism interferes significantly with the capacity of children to analyze meaningfully their behavior. In order to involve oneself in an analysis one must first view the behavior as undesirable. Then one must be motivated to remove it. And then one must be capable of analyzing the unconscious contributing factors if one believes that such a procedure is the best way to remove the symptoms. Denial mechanisms interfere with the child's reaching the first step. One could use the metaphor of the baseball diamond here. The denying child is still on home plate and has not progressed one millimeter toward first base.

Transference and the Resolution of the Transference Neurosis

In Chapter Two I discussed the classical psychoanalytic theory of the transference and the resolution of the transference neurosis. I describe there how these factors are considered central in analytic cure. Specifically, in psychoanalytic theory the term *transference* refers to the transfer of thoughts and feelings from significant figures in one's life (especially people who were influential in early childhood) onto the analyst. As a result of such transfer the patient attempts to involve the analyst in the same kinds of psychopathological interactions that were utilized when relating to parents and other significant figures. Such a pathological reaction is referred to as the *transference neurosis*. When the term *transference neurosis* is used, however, it refers to a compulsive and repetitious pattern. It refers to a situation in which the patient consistently attempts to involve the therapist in the neurotic relationship. The resolution of the transference neurosis involves not only the development of insight into what is occurring but experiences over time that the interactions that worked successfully with others will not succeed with the analyst. One factor (among many) that motivates the patient to give up the pathological mode of interaction is the fear of loss of the therapist's affection if the patient persists in the attempts to so involve the therapist. Implicit in this theory is that children will develop a transference neurosis, that is, they will attempt to involve the analyst in the same pathological patterns that they have utilized with parents and/or parental surrogates.

Anna Freud and Melanie Klein differed with regard to their views on whether or not a child could develop a transference neurosis. Melanie Klein held that the child could do so and believed also that the analysis of such a neurotic pattern was central to successful psychoanalytic treatment. Anna Freud was more cautious and most often took the position that children's transferential reactions were weaker than adults'. My own experience has been that the vast majority of children do not develop strong transferential reactions with their therapists. I believe that this relates primarily to the fact that their investment in their parents is so great that there is little "left over" for the analyst. Children are deeply wrapped up in their home lives and the most of their emotional commitment is to their parents. When one thinks about it, it cannot be otherwise. The parents are the providers of food, clothing, shelter, protection, guidance, and a wide variety of other services. So enmeshed are children in their home lives, they are not likely to develop significant involvement with others. The younger the child the more this principle holds. Of course, children can become involved with their teachers, but rarely does such involvement come close to that which exists with a parent. Even when a child's involvement with a teacher is unusually strong, it does not generally last significantly into the summer vaction. A child may have spent five to seven hours a day with a teacher, more than 180 days of a year. And such involvement is far greater than that which any child has with an analyst, even a child who sees an analyst four sessions a week. Yet even the strongest involvements with teachers do not generally result in deep attachments.

In the therapeutic situation children rarely develop the depth of involvement that can serve, I believe, as a foundation for the development of a bona fide transference neurosis. I could envision an extremely deprived child developing such involvement, but this is rare. Such deprived children are rarely brought for intensive on-going treatment. The same disinterest and neglect results in the parents not being willing to take the time, trouble, and most often incur the expense to bring the child for therapy. The deprived child embraces strangers who come to the door; the child who has a good relationship with a parent is likely to be cautious and only slowly gets involved. One could compare these two children with two women of 28, both of whom are patients of the same 35-year-old male analyst. One is married, has three young children, and comes to treatment because of marital difficulties. The other is single, lives alone, and comes for therapy because she is approaching 30, suspects that she may have difficulties relating to men, and fears she may not marry and have children (things she wishes very much to do). The first woman may view the analytic sessions as an intrusion that just stretches her out more and adds to her already formidable burden of taking care of her house and children and involving herself with her husband. The second may live from session to session and may become deeply absorbed with strong thoughts and feelings about the analyst. The first may have never thought about whether or not he is married. The second may be obsessed with the question. The first may welcome the therapist's vacations as a respite from the hassles of her daily living. The second may dread their occurrence and may become obsessed with where he is vacationing and what he is doing. And now I ask the reader: "Which woman will develop a stronger transferential reaction to the analyst?" The answer is obvious.

Accordingly, I do not believe then that the vast majority of children develop the strong kind of transferential reaction that classical analysts consider to be crucial for the development of the transference neurosis. This is not to say that the therapist should not refrain from involving him- or herself in attempts on the child's part to involve the therapist in psychopathological interactions. I am only saying that the restraints that the therapist makes in this area are not likely to cause as much frustration as they would in an adult who has a strong transferential reaction. The reason here is basically that the child doesn't care very much about whether the therapist withdraws affection in response to alienating behavior: there was little love in the first place and so there is little love lost.

Free Association and the Blank Screen

Another central element in the psychoanalytic process is based on the theory that the analyst obtains the best information about the unconscious processes that underly the patient's symptoms by encouraging the patient to free associate, that is to verbalize his or her thoughts as they enter conscious awareness without any censoring, altering, or placement in logical sequence. One of the best atmospheres for facilitating free association is said to be the one in which the patient lies on a couch in order to remove him- or herself from environmental stimuli that might "contaminate" the free associations and direct them into particular channels. And the most important of these potentially contaminating stimuli are those that may emanate directly from the therapist via facial expressions, gestures, comments, and even his or her existence. The method came to be described as one in which the patient talks to a "blank screen." This procedure stemmed from Freud's original work with hypnotherapy. Although he abandoned the technique from the recognition that it had significant limitations in bringing about the alleviation and cure of psychoneurotic problems, he retained the basic practice of the patient's remaining in the supine postion, removed from the ability to visualize the therapist. Freud stated that one of his reasons for retaining this aspect of hypnotherapy was that he felt uncomfortable with a face-to-face relationship with a patient seven days a week. (Originally, psychoanalytic treatment was given seven days a week. When Freud's wife complained that she and the children hardly ever saw him, he dropped the frequency down to six times a week. Efficiencies necessitated during World War II dropped the frequency down to five.) This pathological reason for Freud's retaining the couch, after recognizing that hypnotherapy had serious limitations, is not given the attention it deserves by classical analysts. I believe that many of them have the same reason for retaining the couch, that is, they too are uncomfortable with ongoing face-to-face involvement with their patients. Of course, other reasons are given for retaining the couch, such as the fact that it lessens the likelihood that the patient's associations will be contaminated. As mentioned earlier in this book, I believe that this advantage of the couch is far outweighed by the disadvantages associated with the unreal interactions and often pathological relationship it produces between the patient and the therapist.

Even Freud did not believe that it was appropriate to put children on the couch and have them free associate to a "blank screen." But he did believe that the child's bringing unconscious processes into conscious awareness was extremely important if one were to psychoanalyze a child. As mentioned earlier in this book, H. Von Hug-Hellmuth, A. Freud, and M. Klein all held that the child's self-created stories were analogous to the free associations of the adult and could provide similar information for psychoanalytic utilization. Just as the adult analyst helps a patient analyze his or her free associations, the child analyst is supposed to help the child analyze self-created stories. I am in agreement that self-created stories are often a rich source of information about unconscious processes and can justifiably be compared to (but are not identical with) the free associations of an adult. I am somewhat dubious, however, about the ease with which child analysts claim they are able to get children to analyze their stories. I have had far less success than they, and I do not believe that it relates to any particular therapeutic impairments on my part; rather, I believe it relates more to the child's cognitive immaturity and other factors discussed in this chapter.

Another disadvantage of the blank screen—and this may be its most important—is that it lessens the likelihood that an optimally beneficial therapist-patient relationship will emerge. Rather, it tends to produce idealization of the therapist, that is, a view that the therapist is perfect or close to it. It also contributes to idolization of the therapist, that is, a view that the therapist is somewhat God-like. These thoughts and feelings about the therapist are definitely antitherapeutic. Many therapists welcome such reactions by their patients. I believe the most likely cause of this desire to be aggrandized is that it helps them compensate for feelings of inadequacy. The optimum kind of therapist-patient relationship is one in which the patient comes to see the therapist as a *real* human being, with both assets and liabilities. Viewing the therapist as perfect is going to make it difficult for the patient to relate to others who are merely human and who will inevitably reveal qualities that will be alienating to the patient. Just as viewing one's parents as perfect can interfere with the ultimate development of healthy human relationships, viewing one's therapist as perfect can also have this detrimental effect.

Analysis of the Childhood Roots
of the Symptoms

Psychoanalytic treatment is also based on the theory that if patients are to enjoy permanent alleviation of symptoms, then they must go back and understand their childhood roots. Most analysts hold that such understanding is best arrived at via free association and analytic inquiry. Such insight, they believe, is an important factor in psychoanalytic cure. Others believe that simple understanding is not enough and that patients must reexperience certain early childhood experiences (especially psychological deprivations and traumas), particularly if such reliving is followed by movement along healthier paths. Others hold that important contributing factors to the development of symptoms are suppressed and repressed feelings that were not exhibited at the time of early traumas and that the belated expression of these pent-up feelings is central to psychoanalytic cure. I have significant reservations about both of these theories.

First, with regard to the issue of going back to childhood roots, the child patient is already back there. Accordingly, child analysts would say that when one treats children one has the opportunity to deal with the problem *before* or *at the time* it originates and can thereby "nip the problem in the bud." Others would say that the fact that the child exhibits a symptom indicates that there have been *earlier* traumas which must be understood if there is to be a cure. Accordingly, if a six- or seven-year-old child comes for treatment, one tries to go back to earlier ages, perhaps two and three, when the problems began. Although a child might be able to recall a few events from that earlier period, I cannot imagine the overwhelming majority of children utilizing such fragmentary recollections in a meaningful way over time. I certainly have never seen a child who is interested in or capable of doing this. Of course, it could be argued that my own lack of conviction for the approach might be sensed by the child and I would thereby be squelching a procedure that might be useful. I cannot deny that this might be the case, but I consider it unlikely.

With regard to the theory that the patient must go back and relive past experiences and thereby channel them into new directions, I also have little conviction for this approach. My general view is that one's past experiences certainly contribute to the development of present behavior, both normal and pathological. However, I also consider past experiences to be like "water under the bridge." One can remember the past, one can learn from it, but one cannot relive it. Reliving is artificial and is not, in my opinion, going to bring about therapeutic change.

With regard to the theory that expressing past, buried emotions that were previously unexpressed is important in the therapeutic process, the notion here is that these pent-up feelings are like a well-encased pocket of pus in an abscess. The analogy goes further and compares the analyst to the surgeon who lances the abscess in order to release the pus. This too I consider extremely unlikely. Although I believe that there may be some therapeutic value derived from belated reactions of this kind ("better late then never"), I believe that the longer the time between the trauma and the analytic treatment, the more diffuse the "abscess" is going to become and the more enmeshed the unresolved feelings will become fused and entwined with other unconscious material. Simple expression ("lancing") then is not likely to work. To alleviate problems related to longstanding supression and repression, one must deal with the factors that produced the original suppressions and repressions and which may still be operative at the present time. Accordingly, one avoids a repetition of the same suppression in the future by learning from the past and present.

The Freudian Stages
of Psychosexual Development

Classical psychoanalytic treatment is not simply based on the theory that neurotic problems have their roots in childhood. The theory gets more specific and relates the childhood difficulties to problems related to Freudian stages of psychosexual development: oral, anal, phallic, and genital. Freud's theory of the childhood stages of psychosexual development was based on the analysis of adults many years after these events allegedly took place. Freud never treated a child. Little Hans' treatment was conducted by his father under Freud's supervision. What to me is amazing about the theory is that so many people have believed it, although it is becoming less popular these days. As I have discussed in detail elsewhere (Gardner, 1973b) I have little conviction for Freud's theory of childhood development. Accordingly, I am not likely to explain symptoms in accordance with its prescriptions and so would not be providing children with an important element in their psychoanalysis, namely, relating their difficulties to fixations, regressions, and so forth, at the oedipal and the so-called pre-oedipal levels of development.

The Superego and Intrapsychic Conflict

Psychoanalytic treatment was designed to alleviate and cure neurotic problems. Neurotic problems, according to classical theory, are considered to be the result of intrapsychic conflicts. Specifically, there may be conflicts between the *id* (unconscious primitive impulses) and the *superego* (the conscience and the ego-ideal). Or there may be conflicts between the superego and the *ego* (a variety of ideas that are either in or readily accessible to conscious awareness). I will not discuss here my areas of agreement and disagreement about this fundamental concept. What I wish to focus on here is the issue of superego development. To have a neurosis one must have a superego. Furthermore, one must have a strongly developed superego to have a neurotic conflict. All would agree that there are stages in superego development and that the progression goes from a very weak to almost nonexistant superego in infancy to the potential for very strong superego functioning as one gets older. And this progression develops from birth to death. All would agree, as well, that children have more poorly developed superegos than adults. Psychoanalysis is designed primarily for psychoneurotic problems, those in which there is some kind of intrapsychic conflict, especially one that involves the superego.

Classical Freudians generally consider children's superegos to be more developed than I view them to be. Most children below the age of 11 or 12 do not have such strong superego development that intrapsychic conflicts are set up. And when I do see such children they are generally in the upper age levels of childhood, 10 to

12. The paucity of children with intrapsychic conflicts at younger ages reduces even further the potential population of children who are candidates for psychoanalysis. Even Freud appreciated the fact that people who act out their impulses, rather than internalize and cogitate over them, are not likely to be candidates for psychoanalysis. Accordingly, he did not consider juvenile delinquents and those with psychopathic tendencies to be candidates for psychoanalytic treatment. The vast majority of children I see act out rather than dwell over and introspect about their thoughts, feelings, and impulses. They need more guilt, not less. Again, the rarity of intrapsychic conflict in children (especially younger ones) is another reason why they are generally poor candidates for psychoanalysis.

PSYCHOANALYTICALLY ORIENTED CHILD PSYCHOTHERAPY

My criticisms of psychoanalysis notwithstanding, I still consider myself a psychoanalyst. I still believe that unconscious processes play an important role in the development of the majority of psychogenic problems. I believe that the defense mechanisms described by S. Freud and A. Freud are for the most part valid and that they play an important role in the development of symptoms. They help us understand the linkages (discussed in Chapter Two) between the fundamental problems of life and the symptoms that are derived in an attempt to deal with them. In short, they help us understand *psychodynamics*. I believe that dream analysis (discussed later in this chapter) is a therapeutically useful procedure. And even free association—in selected situations—can be a valuable therapeutic tool.

Accordingly, I have not discarded entirely psychoanalytic theory. Rather, I believe that we do well to take from the theory and the techniques that have been devised to utilize it those elements that appear to be useful and to discard those that we suspect will be of little value. Here I describe how I use those aspects of the theory and technique that I have found useful in my work, specifically those techniques that are derived from and are modifications of traditional psychoanalytic procedure. For the purposes of this discussion, I refer to this approach as *psychoanalytically oriented child psychotherapy*.

The Development and Utilization of Insight

First, as mentioned, the approach here is based on the theory that unconscious processes play a role in symptom formation. However, I do not believe that it is necessary (and certainly not crucial) for patients to gain conscious awareness of their unconscious processes in order to derive therapeutic benefit. This not only holds true for adults (who are often resistant to doing so, even though they may profess receptivity to the process), but to children who, as mentioned, are often cognitively incapable of such an endeavor. If the patient does gain such insight, I am certainly pleased. In fact, I welcome such insight but I do not pressure patients, especially children, into deriving it. I do not consider insight to be a crucial factor in bringing about therapeutic change. Rather, I view it as "frosting on the cake." It is an additional and potentially useful therapeutic modality which is nice to have when one can get it, but I do not pressure patients into deriving it. What is crucial is that the *therapist* make every attempt to learn as much as possible about the child's unconscious processes. If the therapist doesn't learn about these factors, then no one is equipped to help the child (at least by psychotherapeutic methods). The therapist utilizes such knowledge in the child's treatment. And the therapist's knowledge is gained by the analysis of the child's stories, pictures, verbal productions, etc.

The next question relates to what the therapist does with such information. If the therapist uses the information to provide a responding story, then the technique cannot justifiably be called analytically oriented therapy because basic issues are *not* being brought into conscious awareness. Rather, I would call the procedure *utilization of the mutual storytelling technique.* If the therapist uses the information to involve the child in a discussion at the symbolic level ("Why did the cat bite the dog?"), this also cannot justifiably be called analytically oriented child psychotherapy. I would refer to this procedure as *discussion at the symbolic level.* Here again, nothing is being brought to conscious awareness. It is when the therapist attempts to use the information so gained in the attempt to help the child gain insight that the procedure might justifiably be called analytically oriented psychotherapy. In pure psychoanalysis every reasonable attempt is made to get the patient him- or herself to derive the insight, with only catalytic comments by the analyst. In the form of treatment I am discussing here *the analyst surmises the psychodynamic meaning of the patient's productions and then attempts to impart information to the patient and/ or the parents.* The purpose here is for them to utilize this information in bringing about symptom alleviation.

One can say that there is a continuum between pure psychoanalysis and analytically oriented therapy. To the degree that the patient him-or herself derives the insights, to that degree could the procedure justifiably be called psychoanalysis. In contrast, to the degree that the therapist provides back the information learned from the child's unconscious, to that degree should the procedure be referred to as analytically oriented child psychotherapy. Of course, the patient's own guesses, hunches, and "associations" could also be useful for the therapist in helping him or her surmise the underlying meaning of the presented material. To the degree that the child's contribution to the understanding of the underlying psychodynamics have been operative, to that degree can the procedure be justifiably called psychoanalysis. And to the degree that the therapist's contribution to insight has been operative, to that degree can the procedure be considered analytically oriented psychotherapy.

What Psychoanalytically Oriented Child Therapy Is, and What It Is Not

When I use this term *analytically oriented psychotherapy*, I am referring to a procedure that does not rely upon the analysis of resistances in order to remove them. I do not expect the child to do so. This is not only the result of the ubiquitous use of the denial mechanism by children, but the wide variety of other mechanisms that children might utilize to protect themselves from conscious awareness of their unconscious processes, for example, reaction formation, compensation, and projection. It does not rely upon the development of the transferential reaction or transference neurosis. It utilizes free association of the type to be found when the child is asked to provide a self-created story. It does not rely upon insight into earlier childhood roots of the symptoms; rather, it focuses on the immediate past and the present to provide guidelines for future behavior. It is not based on Freud's theory of childhood psychosexual development. In fact, it is not based on any single particular theory of development. Rather, it is based on the specific developmental issues that are applicable to that particular child at that time. Accordingly, there might be children who are having trouble with toilet training and others who are masturbating excessively. In both cases, I would address myself to individual and family factors that might be causing trouble. Others exhibit age-appropriate sibling rivalry problems, difficulties in adjusting to new situations, separation fears, and so on, and each of these is dealt with with some understanding of the developmental norm but without any need to fit the behavioral manifestation into a particular developmental theory or therapeutic approach. I am not claiming here that developmental theories have no validity. Nor am I claiming that one cannot learn some useful things from them (some more than others, however, and one of the very least being the Freudian theory of psychosexual development). I am only stating that one should avoid the trap of trying to put a particular child into a particular theoretical Procrustean bed.

Some Common Ways in Which the Therapist Uses Psychodynamic Information

The information that the therapist gains can be used for a wide variety of psychotherapeutic purposes. It can be used to help the patient assert him- or herself more appropriately (at the age-appropriate level). It can be used to increase or decrease guilt, depending upon what is appropriate for the patient. S. Freud considered it necessary to attempt to reduce the guilt of his hysterical women who were too inhibited in the expression of their sexual feelings. This has resulted in many therapists' believing that they should uniformly try to reduce patients' guilt and *never* do anything to increase it. This is an error. Some patients need *more* guilt and some *less*. Most of the children I see need more guilt, not less. They have behavior disorders, they act out, and many exhibit manifestations of the ever-increasing psychopathy of our society.

The therapist may use the information to help patients express their resentment in appropriate ways. It can be used to help people with low self-esteem involve themselves in maneuvers that are likely to enhance feelings of self-worth. The information can be used to help the child correct cognitive distortions, for example: "It's wrong to have angry thoughts toward a parent," "If someone calls me a bad name that person must be right," and "It's okay to cheat on tests." It can be used to help a child gain a more accurate

view of his or her parents—both their assets and their liabilities—
and to respond more appropriately to this knowledge. It can be
used to help a child alter pathological emulation and identification.
It can help to reduce overdemanding ego-ideals, for example, " A
grade of B is a perfectly acceptable grade. As long as you think that
you're a failure if you don't get an A, you're going to be miserable."
And it can be used to help a child expose him- or herself to anxiety-
provoking situations in order to facilitate the desensitization process. In short, the information obtained from the child by the therapist can be used for a wide variety of therapeutic procedures. The
case of Tara, described in Chapter Four, is an excellent example of
how the therapist's insight into the unconscious factors that were
causing symptoms proved useful in bringing about therapeutic
alleviation. In fact, this is one case in which the term "cure" might
be applicable.

THE USE OF THE TALKING, FEELING, AND DOING GAME IN FACILITATING PSYCHOANALYTIC INQUIRY

As mentioned, there are rare children who can make use of analytic
inquiry. I am not against children's doing so. I am only against the
attempt to apply the technique to the vast majority of children. In
this section I will discuss the value of *The Talking, Feeling, and
Doing Game* in facilitating inquiry in children who are possible candidates for such an introspective approach to the alleviation of their
problems.

* * *

Question: Of all the things you own, what do you enjoy the most?
Make believe you're doing something with that thing.
Response: Of all the things I own, one of the things I enjoy the
most is my video cassette recorder and camera. I like making television programs of myself and the children whom I treat. It's even
better now since I bought a color TV system, because now we can
see it in color rather than black and white. It not only helps me learn
things about the children who come to see me, but it helps me learn
things about myself. The TV system gives people a chance to see
themselves the way others see them. It's very hard for most people
to look at themselves clearly. The TV system helps people do this.

Even though some of the things that people learn from it may not be pleasant, the information can be useful. I'm very interested in understanding why people do the things they do, and the television system helps me learn these things. This is a subject that interests me very much. I'm very curious about how the human mind works and why people do the things they do. I find it an interesting and fascinating subject to learn about. And that information can help me be of help to other people, and the television set helps me to learn these things.

My hope here is that some of my own enthusiasm for psychological inquiry will engender a similar interest in the child.

* * *

Question: What is one of the stupidest things a person can do? Show someone doing that thing.
Response: One of the stupidest things a person can do is to make believe there is no problem when there really is. The person who does that is not going to do anything to solve the problem. So it's going to continue to exist and may even get worse.

At this point I might ask the child if he or she can think of an example of someone who does this, that is, someone who has a problem and makes believe that there is no problem. It is hoped that the child will provide an example that relates to his or her own situation. If not, I might provide the following example for the child who is unmotivated in school and denies the problem.

Response: Well, one example would be of a girl who is doing very poorly in school and is making believe that she has no problem. She just thinks about other things. When others try to tell her that she's having a problem in school, she doesn't want to listen. Then she doesn't do anything to correct the problem or to solve it. Then things will probably just get worse and at the end of the year she may find that she'll have to repeat the grade. Or, even if she gets promoted, she may find that she gets very embarrassed in school because most of the other children know the answers and she doesn't.

I might at this point discuss with the child my story "Oliver and the Ostrich" from *Dr. Gardner's Stories About the Real World* (1972a). The story deals with the issue of the denial mechanism in the context of a discussion of the ostrich. In the story it becomes apparent that the ostrich does *not* hide its head in the sand in times of danger ("The ostrich wouldn't do such a foolish thing"). It focuses on the adaptive mechanisms (primarily involved in flight or fight) that ostriches utilize in dangerous situations. (They do not differ from the rest of the animal kingdom in this regard.) This story has proven popular among my patients, and it can contribute, I believe, to a reduction in the utilization of the denial mechanisms.

* * *

Question: What is the worst problem a person can have?

Response: I think one of the worst problems a person can have is to make believe that there are no problems when there really are. Such people don't do anything about the problems they have. By making believe there are no problems, they continue to ignore them; but problems don't go away. Because they make believe there are no problems, they don't do anything to solve their problems.

A boy, for example, might be doing very poorly in school, but might not wish to think about it. When his parents try to tell him about the trouble, he might stick his fingers in his ears so that he can't hear them, or he might close his eyes so that he can't see them waving his poor report card at him. This may make him feel better at the time because he then doesn't have to think about his terrible report card. However, he might end up with having to repeat the grade. By then it would have been too late to do anything about the problem. Perhaps then he'll learn his lesson. That's why I say that making believe there's no problem when there really is can be one of the worst problems a person can have.

* * *

Question: Who was the best teacher you ever had? Why?

Response: The best teacher I ever had was a man named Dr. Geoffrey Osler. He was a neurologist. A neurologist is a kind of doctor who specializes in diseases of the nerves. He really loved being a teacher. He was very excited about what he taught. When he taught, everybody in the class got excited about the subject matter as well. Enthusiasm spread throughout the whole class. In his class, learning was fun. In addition, he had a tremendous amount of knowledge and everyone respected him for it. Although it's been over twenty years since I took his course, I still remember many of the things he said. In addition, he started me thinking about a lot of things I hadn't thought about before and I still find myself trying to learn more about those things. He increased my curiosity. He increased my desire to find out the answers to interesting questions. I feel very lucky to have had such a teacher.

Dr. Osler was also interested in understanding how the human mind worked. He was also a psychiatrist, but he was primarily a neurologist. He liked to understand why people did the things they did. I, of course, am a psychiatrist, and I want to learn even more about the reasons why people do the things they do. And I try to get my patients to be curious about that as well. It's sometimes amazing to find out the reasons why a person does what he or she does. Often, people don't understand why they do something and, when they come to understand why they do things, they are really amazed. Also, when they do understand these things, it can often help them prevent or avoid trouble.

My aim here, clearly, is to sweep the child up in the same enthusiasm that I had, and still have, about Dr. Geoffrey Osler. My hope here also is that the child may develop some curiosity about finding out about the inner workings of his or her own mind.

* * *

Question: What turns you on, that is, what excites you?

Response: One of the things that excites me is puzzles and games in which you have to try to figure out answers. I remember when I was a kid I used to love playing checkers and chess. I also used to like doing puzzles in children's books. Later on I used to like doing crossword puzzles in newspapers. When I was in Junior High School, and started to learn algebra, I used to love to figure out mathematical problems, especially those that were very hard to figure out the answer. I remember when I was a teenager there was a program on the radio called "The Quiz Kids." They used to take the best students from the various high schools and ask them very hard questions. I wasn't smart enough to be a quiz kid, but I used to love listening to that program. I used to love trying to figure out the answers to the questions and once or twice I even got an answer when none of the quiz kids did. I really felt good about myself then. But, more important, I found it a lot of fun to try to figure out the answers to difficult questions. That's the kind of thing that really turns me on. It also turns me on to understand why people do the things they do. That can help people stop doing those things.

My hope here, obviously, is to engender in the child the same kind of excitement I have about learning. Perhaps, by getting a feeling for such gratification, there may be some enhancement of the child's curiosity and motivation to learn as well, both about things in general and about his or her own inner mental processes.

* * *

Question: Make believe you've just opened a letter you've received from someone. What does this letter say?

Response: Let's say it's a letter from a former patient. I'll read the letter:

Dear Dr. Gardner:

I am writing you from this college where I'm now going. I appreciate very much your therapy. Before I came to treatment I was not doing very well in school, and I learned some of the reasons why I was having trouble in school and I solved some of those problems so that I now have been able to go to college. I didn't want to think about the reasons why I was doing certain things at first. But after I started thinking about them I realized that I could learn some important things about myself.

Your friend,

Bob

Anything you want to say about that?

My hope here is that the child might be motivated for self-inquiry in order to enjoy the benefits derived by Bob.

DREAM PSYCHOANALYSIS

The best way to demonstrate psychoanalytic technique is via the analysis of dreams. I am in full agreement with Freud who held that the dream is the "royal road to the unconscious." Accordingly, I present here dream analyses of a few child patients (as stated, they are relatively rare) who were interested in and receptive to the analysis of their dreams. Because the same principles are applicable to the analysis of other material as well, I will use dream analysis to present my views on this treatment modality. Before proceeding to the clinical vignettes, I will present my views (not unique) regarding the meaning of dreams and then some basic principles applicable to helping children analyze their dreams. The same principles that I utilize with adults are applicable to children; however, as will be seen, I must modify these when working with children.

The Purposes of Dreams

It is reasonable to speculate that human beings have wondered about the meaning of dreams as far back as there were people dreaming. Wise men and seers have often been viewed as particularly astute in ascertaining the meaning of dreams. Joseph's dreams in the Bible are well known. Although I have many criticisms of psychoanalytic theory and technique, I still consider certain elements in psychoanalysis to be extremely useful. One of these is its contribution to dream analysis. Although I am not in agreement with the reflex way in which many analysts see oral, anal, and oedipal themes in them, I am in agreement with some of the basic theories of Sigmund Freud regarding the meaning of dreams. Particularly, I believe that the emergence of unconscious material is more likely to take place at night. During the day the necessary involvements and distractions of real living do not allow us much time to attend to unconscious material that may be pressuring for eruption into conscious awareness. At night, when these external stimuli are reduced significantly, unconscious material becomes freer to pass into conscious awareness. However, because of guilt and/or anxiety attendant to the emergence of such material, the individual disguises the material. The dream is a product of such emerged material. I consider it to be one of the richest (if not the most rich) source of information about unconscious processes. It is also a testimony to the creativity of the human being (even that of a child) because of the ingenuity that is sometimes utilized in its formation. I present here what I consider to be some of the most reasonable theories regarding the meaning of dreams. I do not claim that this is an exhaustive statement, only that these theories appear most reasonable to me. Our paucity of knowledge about the meaning of dreams also compromises our ability to provide a comprehensive statement about their meaning at this point.

The Dream as a Vehicle for Wish Fulfillment   The theory that the dream serves the purpose of wish fulfillment is ancient. Many dreams are obvious examples of this mechanism. The hungry person dreams of food. The thirsty individual dreams of drink. The sexually frustrated person dreams of sexual gratification. And the angry person dreams of wreaking vengeance. Freud too considered wish fulfillment to be one of the dream's primary purposes. Freud went further, however. He described dreams to have a *latent* and a *manifest* content. The latent material resides within the unconscious because its emergence into conscious awareness produces guilt and/or anxiety. However, so strong are the forces pressing for release of unconscious material that its emergence into conscious awareness cannot be long prevented. Accordingly, an internal psychological compromise is devised in which the repressed material is permitted access to conscious awareness, but in a disguised form. By using such disguise mechanisms as *symbolization* and *condensation*, the individual essentially fools him- or herself into not recognizing the true nature of the material that has now entered conscious awareness. It is as if the right hand has fooled the left hand. In addition, the individual utilizes the mechanism of *secondary elaboration* in which the dream is given an organization that it does not intrinsically possess. Such organization enables the individual to feel more comfortable with the dream because it now follows some traditional sequence. Secondary elaboration also serves the purposes of self-deception, in that the reorganization process disguises the dream even more.

Freud believed that one of the dream's primary purposes was to preserve sleep. For example, a hungry person might be awakened by hunger pangs that threaten to interrupt the vital sleep process. By dreaming of eating, the individual again "fools" the hunger pangs, fantasizes satiety, and thereby preserves sleep. Another example provided by Freud of the dream's sleep-preserving function is that of the person who, while dreaming, hears loud environmental noise. In order to prevent the noise from awakening the dreamer, the fracas is incorporated into the dream. In this way, the dream satisfies its sleep-preservation function. However, Freud had difficulty fitting the nightmare into this theory, in that this kind of dream usually ends with the person's awakening. This exception did not cause him to abandon the general theory of sleep preservation; rather, he concluded that the nightmare was an exception to this principle and when an individual had a nightmare the dream process was considered to have broken down and failed in its primary function of sleep preservation. Although I am in agreement with Freud that *one* of the purposes of the dream is to provide wish fulfillment, I believe Freud put too much emphasis on this dream function, to the neglect of others. I consider the wish-fulfillment function to apply only to one possible category of dream. As I will discuss, I consider there to be other functions unrelated to wish fulfillment. And the nightmare, which I will discuss below, is an example of one of these functions.

Freud ascribed many sexual meanings to dreams, meanings that I would be less prone to consider sexual. In particular, many of the symbols found in dreams were considered by him to be phallic or vaginal. However, Freud also emphasized the importance of utilizing the patient's own free associations in order to ascertain what the symbols meant for that particular patient. He presents, thereby, a somewhat contradictory theory about the symbols. He considered certain symbols to be universal, especially in the phallic/vaginal realm. Yet he viewed other symbols to be idiosyncratic and devised by the patient. I have little conviction for the notion of universal symbols that are somehow inherited from the unconscious minds of one's parents and ancestors. (Carl Jung was especially committed to this notion.) Rather, I believe that environmental influences (familial, social, and cultural) are the most important (if not exclusive) determinants of what a symbol (dream or otherwise) will mean. In addition, I am far less likely to ascribe sexual meanings to many of the symbols that Freud and his followers so quickly assumed to have such significance. These criticisms notwithstanding, I consider Freud's *The Interpretation of Dreams* (1900) to be a monumental contribution and recommend it to all those who are interested in learning about the classical psychoanalytic theory of dreams.

There are some dreams in which there is simple release of pent-up thoughts and feelings which might also be considered a kind of wish-fulfillment dream. I am referring here to sexual dreams in which the individual gains sexual gratification as a way of providing release for pent-up and frustrated sexual feelings. The adolescent boy's "wet dream" would be an example of this kind of dream. As the youngster grows older, and has greater opportunities for sexual fulfillment, he experiences a diminution in the frequency of such dreams. The association of the dream with ejaculation raises some interesting questions. Does the dream fantasy precede the sexual excitation and resultant ejaculation, or does the hormonally induced genital arousal stimulate the production of the dream fantasy? Another type of simple release dream would be one in which an individual fantasizes harm befalling some individual toward whom intense angry feelings are felt. In these simple release types of wish-fulfillment dreams, there is little if any disguise. The individual is generally quite clear about the basic function of the dream. However, if there is guilt and/or anxiety over the release of these feelings, then some disguise elements may be introduced, such as substituting the identity of the object of the sexual or hostile feelings.

The Dream as a Vehicle for Alerting the Individual to Danger
This is an extremely important function of the dream which I believe was not given proper attention by Freud. In fact, I believe that the dream may more commonly serve the alerting role than the role of simple wish-fulfillment. Most dangers are not repressed. The individual looks at them squarely and then reacts appropriately, generally either by fight or flight. However, there are certain situations in which an individual may wish to ignore the fact that a danger exists because to appreciate it might result in guilt, anxiety, or other untoward reactions. Under such circumstances the information about the danger is relegated to unconscious awareness. An internal psychological conflict then arises. On the one hand, thoughts of the danger press for release into conscious awareness in order to alert the individual to its existence. On the other hand, such appreciation may result in a variety of unpleasant and even painful psychological reactions. Again, the dream compromise is brought into play. The danger emerges into conscious awareness in disguised form, satisfying thereby both arms of the conflict.

Let us take as a theoretical example of this kind of dream a situation in which a personnel manager in a large corporation has an appointment with a prospective employee. About an hour prior to the interview with the job candidate he receives a call from a senior official in his organization telling him that the interviewee is a relative of his wife's and that he should be given special consideration. During the interview the personnel manager scans briefly the man's application, but does not give it the detailed perusal that he normally does. Following the interview the personnel manager decides that he is going to recommend the applicant for a position and hopes that this decision will place him in a favorable position with the senior official who recommended that he give the man every opportunity. That night the personnel manager has a dream in which the applicant that he saw that day, now an employee in the company, stealthily enters the company vault and successfully absconds with a huge sum of money. Then, after the theft is discovered, the personnel manager finds himself under serious criticism—even to the point where his job is in jeopardy—because he has hired the man. He wakes up, horrified over the prospect of losing his job.

Let us carry the example further and place this man in psychoanalytic treatment. The analyst encourages the patient to think about any possible clues he was given that the man might have had criminal tendencies, or even a record. The patient states that he had absolutely no awareness of such. However, when reviewing carefully the details of the interview, the analyst learns that the patient rapidly looked over the application. Recognizing this as atypical behavior, the analyst suggests that the patient review again—but this time very carefully—the applicant's application. The patient then returns to his office, reviews the application very carefully, and notes that there was a two-year period which appears to be completely unaccounted for. This occurred when the interviewee was between 19 and 21 years of age. Immediately he calls back the applicant and, in the course of the interview, asks him about the gap in his school and work history. At this point, the applicant, somewhat apologetically, states that he was in jail during that period, but dismisses it as the result of a series of "adolescent indiscretions" that were not even worth mentioning. He goes on to reassure the personnel manager that these incidents are "water under the bridge," that he has learned his lesson, "paid his debt to society," and can be relied upon to be a "solid citizen." The personnel manager returns to his next analytic session and, in the discussion of what has transpired, comes to the realization that the applicant is *still* somewhat psychopathic, in that he withheld the information from the application rather than disclose it, and that such deceptive tendencies not only existed in the past but exist at the present time as well.

He now finds himself presented with a new problem. Does he hire the man in order to keep himself in favor with the senior company official or does he reject the applicant and risk thereby the disfavor of his superior? As a result of further analytic work he decides that this dilemma is not a burden he need assume himself; rather, he can present the information to the senior official and let *him* decide what to do. This is not an option that he had previously considered, but it emerged from the analytic interchange. It is an example of the way in which therapy opens up new options, options that may not have previously been considered by the patient, options that are often preferable to those already operating in the patient's repertoire. If he follows this course, he need not feel responsible for any untoward consequences of hiring this individual. Now it becomes the senior official's responsibility if the applicant does not prove trustworthy.

This example has been presented because it demonstrates well how the dream can serve to alert an individual to a danger that he or she might not previously have been aware of. In this case, the man had to repress from conscious awareness his recognition of the gap in the application to avoid risking the displeasure of a senior company official. There was a danger, however, and it pressed for release into conscious awareness. A dream compromise was made, one that satisfied both unconscious and conscious processes. Had the man not been in treatment he might not have appreciated the significance of the dream and might thereby have suffered significant untoward repercussions of his oversight. Furthermore, and unrelated to this discussion of dreams, the vignette demonstrates how therapy, by opening up new options, can help individuals deal better with the fundamental problems of life in ways that they might not have previously considered.

At this point, I will present a dream that I myself had about a patient. It serves as an excellent example of the dream's value as an alerting mechanism. Many years ago a man of 25 requested treatment for homosexual difficulties. He considered his homosexuality to be psychogenic and hoped that therapy would help him achieve a heterosexual life pattern. The patient was born and raised in New England and had attended a prestigious boarding school and Ivy League college. His father had died when he was three and he had absolutely no recollection of him. He was raised with his mother and three older sisters, all of whom doted over him. His mother often undressed in front of him, even into the teen period. He first began having homosexual experiences in boarding school, but did describe some successful heterosexual experiences as well. However, his homosexual experiences were much more gratifying to him. In his early twenties he married in the hope that this might bring about a heterosexual orientation. He had not told his wife about his homosexuality at the time of his marriage. After about a year she became aware of his activities and at first hoped that she might be able to salvage the marriage. When I saw him, she had decided upon divorce and he went into therapy, hoping that he could avoid future similar consequences of his homosexuality. At the time he entered treatment, he was also in difficulty in the firm where he worked. He was employed by an investment banking firm, and it was becoming increasingly clear to him that he was being passed over for promotions because of suspicions of his homosexual lifestyle.

During the first two months of treatment, the patient appeared to be involving himself well in the therapy. He was a mild-mannered man who was quite polite and formal. His relationships, however, were invariably tempestuous, especially his homosexual relationships, in which there was significant jealous rivalry. In association with the stresses of these relationships, he would often drink heavily and sometimes became quite depressed. Consciously, I did not consider the patient to be significantly different from other patients I was seeing with regard to any particular thoughts and/ or emotional reactions that I might be having about them. One night, however, after about two months of treatment, I had a dream in which the patient was pursuing me with a knife in an attempt to murder me. Although I fled in terror, he was gaining on me and I awakened just at the point where he was about to stab me. When I awakened, it was with a sigh of relief that I appreciated that it was only a dream. I was in analytic training at the time and so I began to think seriously about what the possible meaning of the dream could be. I had to consider the most obvious explanation, namely, that my dream was a reflection of unconscious homosexual desires toward my patient. Because I had never previously had any particular inclinations in this direction (and none since, I might say), I found it difficult to accept this as a possible explanation. However, I also had to accept reluctantly the latent homosexual explanation because of the way unconscious processes operate. I was also taught in analytic training that when a therapist has a dream about a patient, it invariably indicates inappropriate countertransferential reactions. I was not too comfortable with this unflattering explanation either. I could not recall having had any dreams previously about my patients (nor have I had any since), but I did, on occasion, exhibit what I had to accept were inappropriate countertransferential reactions. Accordingly, I was left with the feeling that the dream was important but without any particular explanation for its meaning. (At that time, I was not appreciative of the alerting value of dreams.)

About two weeks after the dream, the patient entered the session in an agitated state. Although I do not have verbatim notes on the interchange that ensued during that session, the following is essentially what took place:

Patient (quite tense):   I'm very upset. I can't take it any longer. I can't continue this way.

Therapist: Tell me.

Patient: This is very difficult to talk about.

Therapist: I suspect that it will be, but I know you appreciate that it's important for you to discuss those things here that you are hesitant to speak about.

Patient: Yes, I know I have to tell you but it's difficult.

Therapist: I'm listening.

Patient: I can't stand it any longer. I've got to tell you. I'm in love with you. And I've been in love with you since the first session. I can't stand it any longer. While I'm talking to you about my problems, I keep thinking about how much I love you.

Therapist: You know, the word *love* can mean many things. It would be helpful to us if you could tell me the *exact* kinds of thoughts and feelings you've been having when you say that you love me.

Patient: That's even harder.

Therapist: I can appreciate that; however, if we're to fully understand what's happening, it's important that you try to tell me.

Patient: If you really want to know, I want to have sex with you.

Therapist: Even there, having sex with someone is a statement that covers a lot of ground. I'd like you to try to be more specific about the particular kinds of thoughts and feelings you're having when you say that you want to have sex with me.

Patient: Well, I just wouldn't want to start having sex right away. I'd want there to be some overtures on your part, some advances by you.

Therapist: I'm starting to get the picture. Now what specifically would you want me to say and do?

Patient: Well, I just wouldn't want you to simply ask me. I'd want you to plead.

Therapist: What would you want me to say specifically?

Patient: I'd want you to beg me. I'd want you to get down on your knees and beg me to have sex with you. (Patient now becoming agitated.) I'd want you to be extremely frustrated, to be very horny. I'd want you to be on the floor kissing my feet, begging me over and over again to have sex with you.

Therapist: What then?

Patient: Well, I wouldn't just have sex with you then. I'd want you to beg more. I'd want you to kiss my feet. I'd want you to promise to do anything at all to get me to have sex with you. You'd be on the floor crying and pleading. But I still wouldn't gratify you. I'd let you squirm. I'd let you plead. (Patient now becoming enraged.)

Therapist: What then?

Patient: Finally, when I felt you had enough punishment, I'd make you get undressed and then I'd make you lie down on the ground on your belly. Then I'd fuck you in the asshole and reduce you to my level. I'd humiliate you and gratify you at the same time.

Therapist: Is that the end of the fantasy or is there more?

Patient: Oh, there's more; I just wouldn't stop at that. First, I'd call your wife. I know you're married; you have that ring on your finger. And I saw those pictures on your desk; I assume those are your kids. Anyway, what I'd do then would be to call your wife. I'd tell her that you're a fag. And I'd tell her that you have sex with your patients.

Therapist: What do you think would happen then?

Patient: Then she'd divorce you. What woman would want to live with a fag?

Therapist: Anything else?

Patient: Yeah, I wouldn't stop there. I'd call the people who are in charge at the Columbia Medical School, the dean or whoever it is. I'd tell him that they have someone on the faculty there who fucks his patients. I'd also tell them you're gay. And I'd tell them that you had sex with me. Then they'd kick you off the faculty.

Therapist: Anything else?

Patient: Yeah, one more thing. I'd call the medical society and tell them what you really are, a fag, a gay doctor who fucks with patients. And they'd take away your license.

Therapist: Anything else?

Patient: No, that's it.

Therapist: You know, you started this session by telling me that you "love" me. Is this your concept of love?

Patient: Well, maybe it's not love, but it's the way I feel. Maybe it's the way I feel because I know that you don't love me the way I love you.

Therapist: Here you tell me you love me and then you tell me how you want to humiliate me, expose me as a doctor who has sex with patients. Then you tell me that you would like to have my wife divorce me and then I'd be kicked off the faculty at the medical school and then lose my medical license. It sounds to me like you want to destroy me. It doesn't sound very much like love to me. It sounds to me like the opposite, like hate.

In the ensuing discussion, the patient was too upset to

be able to gain any insight into what was going on. His treatment did not last much longer. He left about two weeks later, claiming that I really did not have very much affection for him. If I really wanted to show my affection, I would have sex with him. Although the vignette demonstrates well an important psychodynamic mechanism operative in some patients with male homosexuality, namely, the use of love as a reaction formation to hate, it is not presented here for that purpose. Rather, it is presented as an example of an alerting dream. It is reasonable to speculate that at the time of the dream I was already receiving subtle signals of the patient's hostility. I was not aware of these consciously and may have been threatened by them. However, the awareness of the hostility built up in my unconscious and finally erupted into conscious awareness via the alerting dream. Had the man continued in therapy I would have used the dream to help me make decisions regarding hospitalization. The dream suggested that this was indeed a dangerous man. Of course, one would not and should not use one's own dream as an important criterion for deciding whether or not to hospitalize a patient. The clinical behavior must be paramount; however, the dream should not be ignored either. As I hope the reader agrees, the dream can be a powerful source of information about dimly sensed but not overtly recognized dangers.

The Dream as a Method of Desensitization to a Trauma   This is another function of the dream that has nothing to do with wish fulfillment. Here the individual has been exposed to a severe psychological trauma and the dream serves the process of desensitization. Following the trauma the individual is not only consciously preoccupied with thoughts and feelings associated with the trauma but is so overwhelmed by it that many of the psychological reactions associated with it become relegated to unconscious awareness as well. This is not specifically related to the fact that the individual feels guilt and/or anxiety over thinking about the trauma; rather, the trauma is so overwhelming that sleep time must also be utililzed if one is to effectively accomplish the purposes of desensitization. The principle of desensitization is basically this: Each time the individual reexperiences the trauma it becomes a little more bearable. And, over time, with repeated reliving of the trauma, even though only in fantasy, the individual adjusts to it.

A situation in which desensitization dreams are common is the one in which a soldier has been exposed to uninterrupted battlefield conditions over an extended period. He may have been injured and observed friends to have been injured and even killed. Under these circumstances he may have suffered a severe enough stress reaction to the combat that hospitalization may prove necessary because he has become ineffective in his capacity to function adequately on the battlefield. In the hospital the soldier has repetitious dreams in which the battlefield conditions are being reexperienced. In the dream he may hear shells blasting around him and even may respond with the same fright reaction that was present during combat. So powerful may be the need to relive the experience that the dreams themselves may not appear to be enough and he may actually hallucinate the same experiences, again in the service of desensitization. Whereas the dreams occur at night, the hallucinations take place in the waking state. The dream and hallucination may not be the only vehicles for desensitization. The soldier becomes obsessed as well with thoughts of the battlefield conditions. And each time they are relived mentally, some adjustment takes place. Last, he is likely to be talking about his experiences frequently and such discussions serve as a desensitization mechanism as well.

The Nightmare   In the typical nightmare the child is fearful that some malevolent figure will cause him or her terrible harm. Typically, the figure is a monster, frightening creature, and sometimes even a nebulous blob or point that is approaching the child menacingly. Usually, the figure comes into the child's room from a window, or out of a closet, or out from under the child's bed. The closer the malevolent fantasy gets to the child, the more frightened the child becomes. And the child generally awakens just at the point when the malevolent creature is about to touch or envelop the child. At the point of awakening, the child is generally quite frightened, is often crying, and is usually consoled by parents who reassure the child that there are no such things as monsters, creatures, et cetera. The creatures in nightmares have a way of evaporating completely when lights are turned on and do not appear in broad daylight. Like vampires, they abhor the rays of the sun.

In my residency days I was taught that the malevolent figures in a child's nightmare represent one or both parents. In order to ascertain whether the creature is symbolic of mother or father, the examiner was advised to question the child in order to elicit information about the sex of the interloper. If male, then father was

viewed to be the hostile parent and, if female, then mother got accused. The child who dreamed of witches was to be viewed as one
whose mother was inordinately hostile to him or her, and the child
who dreamed of monsters (usually identified as male) had the mis-
fortune of being brought up in a home where father was hostile.
Even then, I was uncomfortable with this explanation and suspected that I was falsely accusing parents of being hostile when
there was no significant evidence for more than the normal amount
of irritation and impatience that any parent will exhibit from time
to time in the child-rearing process.

It was with these considerations that I began to formulate another concept of the meaning of the nightmare. Specifically, I believe that the interloper is better understood as the incarnation of
the child's own unacceptable angry impulses that have been relegated to the unconscious. Nightmares begin when children are
about two to three years of age. This is a time when they are continually being frustrated by parents who must—if they are worthy of
the name *parents*—inhibit and restrict the child continually
throughout the course of the day: "Don't go into that cabinet,"
"Don't stick your hand up on top of the stove," "Stay away from
the baby," "Big boys don't wet their pants," "Don't run out in the
street," et cetera. There is hardly a five-minute period when children of this age are not restrained, constricted, and warned about
some catastrophe that will befall them if they're allowed to go their
merry way. The resentments engendered by such frustrations are
enormous, yet they cannot be expressed overtly for fear the children may lose the affection of significant figures who are vital for
their well-being and even survival. Also, there are many other stimuli impinging upon the child during the day that distract him or
her from the pent-up anger. At night, when these other distracting
stimuli are removed, the pent-up hostilities of the day, which are
continually pressing for expression, are allowed release. Daytime
activities such as sports, sibling fights, and television—which have
provided some release of hostility—are no longer available. At night,
residual hostility from unresolved daytime frustrations is then
freer to press for release.

In the nightmare, the symbolic derivatives of the child's anger
(the robber, monster, terrible creature, etc.) press for expression into
the child's conscious awareness (symbolized, I believe, by the
child's room). The child disowns the angry feelings that are his or
her own by projecting them outward. They are viewed as coming

from outside the house, the closet, or from under the bed. Accordingly, the child utilizes two mechanisms for reducing guilt and/or anxiety over the expression of anger: symbolization and projection. Via symbolization, the anger is not viewed as anger; rather, it is viewed as some malevolent creature. And via projection, the anger is not viewed as the child's own; rather, it is projected outward in the form of a creature that comes toward the child from some distance. The child wakes when the anger is about to enter the child's own space, at the point where there is the risk that it will be recognized as coming from within. The malevolent figure may (as I was taught in residency) symbolize hostile elements within significant figures (such as parents). I believe, however, that this explanation should not be given first priority. When the frightening figures threaten to abduct or kidnap the child, then the dream may reflect separation anxieties.

With this theory of the meaning of a child's nightmares, I generally do not consider them to be an abnormal phenomenon between the ages of two and seven or eight, unless they occur with a frequency greater than three or four times a week. I consider them to be a normal way of dealing with the inevitable frustrations and resentments that arise during the course of the child's life in this phase of development. If they are occurring more frequently than a few times a week, then one must look for some problems in the child's life that may be contributing to their intensification. Generally, this would involve looking for abnormal degrees of anger-engendering experiences, such as harsh treatment by parents, neglect, and rigid, and/or punitive teachers.

Last, it is important that the examiner differentiate the nightmare from the *sleep terror disorder*. I generally view the former as a psychological phenomenon which may reach pathological proportions. Most psychiatrists today agree that the latter is a physiological disorder associated with very specific EEG changes. Phenomenologically the sleep terror disorder is quite different from the nightmare in that during the nightmare the child is lying in bed with eyes closed and some restlessness may be observed. In the sleep terror disorder the child's eyes are open and the child may even be running around the house—even though in an altered state of consciousness. In addition, when the nightmare is over the child generally remembers most if not all of what he or she has dreamt. When the child is awakened or wakes up spontaneously from the sleep terror disorder, there is generally amnesia for the event.

The Panic Dream   On occasion I have seen patients who have dreams in which there is no recollection at all of any cognitive material. They wake up panicky and, as hard as they try, they cannot think of any associated fantasies. Many psychoanalysts hold that such dreams are a manifestation of the threatened eruption into conscious awareness of unconscious thoughts and feelings over which the individual feels guilt and/or anxiety. Whereas some individuals are able to allow themselves release of such material via symbolization, condensation, projection, and a variety of other disguise mechanisms, these individuals are so fearful of release of these thoughts and feelings that even the disguised representations are not permitted eruption into conscious awareness.

A number of years ago I had such a patient, a young woman of about 21. She was clearly a very tense and inhibited individual who not only did not allow herself to enjoy sexual experiences, but even denied having sexual urges. I suspected that her panic dreams related to the threatened eruption into conscious awareness of sexual feelings over which she was so guilty that she could not even allow their expression through dreams at night. I theorized that her dreams produced awakening just at the point where some kind of symbolic release might materialize. A friend and colleague of mine at the time was actively involved in sleep research and we both agreed that she might be a good candidate for study. Specifically, the plan was that we would monitor her sleep in the sleep lab, awaken her immediately after she had dreamt, and then learn the nature of her dream fantasies.

Although this occurred over 20 years ago, I still remember the evening quite clearly. The patient went to sleep in one room and was wired up to my friend's equipment in the adjacent room where my colleague and I could observe her and review the recordings of her sleep patterns. Because of his sleep research, my friend had already adjusted well to being a night person. Because I was very much a traditional day person, it was decided that I would sleep as much as possible, only to be awakened when my patient showed evidence of dreaming. There being no bed in the monitoring room, I had to sleep on the floor. On five or six occasions throughout the course of the night my friend awakened me and whispered excitedly that my patient was now dreaming. However, after a few seconds, she would spontaneously awaken—at which point she denied any recall of any dreams. This was not surprising because there were only a few seconds of dream activity recorded. Finally, around six in the morning, my colleague informed me that she was now having what appeared to be a lengthy dream. At the end of this dream we awakened her to have her record her dream verbally on an audio tape recorder. Her response: "I dreamed that I was with these two men. I don't know who they were. They were strangers. They kept asking me to go on a picnic with them, but I wouldn't. They kept asking me to go on the picnic and I kept telling them no. That's all I can remember, but I know that I never went to a picnic with them." The only conclusion that one can definitely draw from this experience is that a patient's resistances can be so formidable that they can prevent the revelation of anything the patient really doesn't want to reveal, no matter how intrusive the examiner's tools of investigation. I cannot say whether the "picnic" the patient envisioned my friend and I to be taking her to involved sexual activities. I could only say that whatever its purpose, she was going to have no part of it.

In recent years, most psychiatrists would consider this kind of dream to be the nighttime equivalent of the panic attack. It would be interpreted simply as some kind of cerebral discharge, analogous to a seizure. I believe that this explanation has some merit. I believe that there are some people with very low threshholds for flight reactions with the result that such reactions may be triggered off by inconsequential stimuli. The panic attack, then, may be a manifestation of such a reaction. I would not, however, completely discount the psychoanalytic explanation as being totally inapplicable to all patients. I still hold that the aforementioned patient's attacks were more likely related to the threatened eruption into conscious awareness of unconscious material (in this case sexual) over which she felt guilty. She never had any similar attacks during the day. This, of course, does not disprove my explanation but it certainly may lend some support to it. At night, without the distracting stimuli of the day, the repressed sexual urges were more likely to pressure for release and attention and produce the panic (anxiety) attack (dream).

The Dream as a Mechanism for Providing Brain Cell Stimulation I do not believe that the aforementioned categories cover all the different types of dreams. They cover the main kinds of dreams that I have had experience with in my work with patients. There are many dreams that I do not understand. Even after eliciting the patient's associations, I am still left without the faintest idea about the dream's meaning. I suspect that for some of these dreams, there may not be a meaning and that they may simply be a manifestation of nocturnal cerebral activity. Just as muscle cells need to be constantly stimulated to remain strong and viable, so do nerve cells. Tonic contractions of muscle cells keep them "in shape"; perhaps nerve cells in the brain need cognitive stimulation to keep them in shape. Such nerve cell stimulation may be provided in the daytime by cognitive rambling and daydreams, and during the nighttime by dreams that may have no additional meaning other than to provide such stimulation. This notion, of course, is one that many psychoanalysts would have difficulty with in that they would argue that the contents of a dream are selected from a universe of possible combinations of thoughts, feelings, and imagery, and that it must be highly meaningful. Although I approach dream work with the goal of analyzing and with the belief that most are analyzable, I am still left with the lingering feeling that my failure to analyze some (but not all) of them has less to do with analyzing inadequacies on my part (certainly possible) and more to do with the fact that the dream may not be analyzable. And the reason it is not analyzable is that there is nothing to analyze. The dream is merely a manifestation of some kind of cognitive brain activity that is taking place throughout the course of the night. Last, I recognize that there may be other categories of dreams that I am not appreciative of, and so I do not consider these additional possible explanations when attempting to understand a patient's dream.

Teaching Children How to Psychoanalyze Dreams

Children Who Are Candidates for Dream Analysis   The older the child the greater the likelihood he or she will be able to profit from a psychoanalytic inquiry into a dream's meaning. Also, the more intelligent the child the more receptive will he or she be to the therapist's suggestion to try to understand the meaning of the dream. Introspective children are more likely to be receptive to such endeavors than those who tend to act out their thoughts and feelings. Children whose parents are introspective, especially if they have had psychoanalytic experiences themselves, are more likely to involve themselves in the endeavor of analyzing a dream. Another factor is intellectual curiosity. Children who are good students are more likely to be good dream analyzers. They are interested in expanding their horizons and learning new things. They enjoy learning for learning's sake. And learning about the meaning of a dream is just another example of an opportunity to satisfy one's intellectual curiosity.

If the therapist has had a successful dream experience with the child, then the likelihood of the child's involving him- or herself meaningfully and enthusiastically in further dream analysis is enhanced. Such a successful analytic experience would be one in which the child and the therapist together have successfully analyzed a dream with the result that the child has had the experience that such inquiries provide interesting and useful information. This experience is hard to define. It is one in which the patient essentially says "Ah ha, now it all fits together," or "That's right," or "What do you know?". There is a kind of "eureka" response. Not only is there an intellectual understanding in which everything seems to fall into place, but an associated emotional reaction of having made a wonderful discovery. This is an important goal to be worked toward. If this aim is realized, then one is more likely to have a patient who will be receptive to dream analysis (regardless of age); and if one does not reach this goal, then one is not likely to have a patient who will commit him- or herself in a meaningful way to dream analysis (again regardless of age). Obviously, the older the patient, the greater the possibility that the therapist will be successful in reaching this goal.

If, during my initial two-hour consultation, I consider a child to be a possible candidate for dream analysis, I will recommend that the child tell a parent each morning whether or not he or she has had a dream. If so, I recommend that the child tell the parent the dream and have the parent write it down at that point. I emphasize that there is no dream that is so short, silly, or embarrassing that it doesn't warrant my attention. I advise shy children, or those who show evidence for hesitation, to reveal their dreams to their parents; that if they don't wish to tell a parent the dream, then they should write it down themselves. My first suggestion, that the dream be told to the parents, is consistent with my general therapeutic philosophy that one should attempt to establish an open pool of communication among family members about the child's problems and that the parents should be working actively along with the child in the treatment. This does not preclude certain privacies.

It is only a statement that the general thrust of my approach is to "put things out on the table." The child whose mother asks each morning about a dream and who is attentive to writing it down is more likely to stimulate interest in and cooperation by the child in the dream analysis endeavor.

Fundamental Principles of Dream Analysis   As a foundation for my subsequent discussion on teaching children how to understand the formation of dreams and techniques for analyzing them, I present here what I consider to be the basic theory of dream formation by unconscious processes. I do not claim that I am presenting here a comprehensive theory of dream formation. As the reader can already appreciate, my discussion above of the various types of dreams can only lead one to the conclusion that they are quite complex and that there is still much that we have to learn. These qualifications notwithstanding, I believe that the principles outlined here can serve well to help children analyze their dreams. Children's dreams tend to be easier to analyze than those of adults. Their repertoire of knowledge is smaller than adults', and the information they can draw upon to form dreams is less comprehensive. In addition, the processes of symbolization, condensation, and projection tend to be less complex and sophisticated than those utilized by adults.

One does well to view the dream setting as a theatrical production. The dreamer not only writes the script, but is also the choreographer and dictates the movements, gestures, and behavior of all the protagonists. The dreamer also sets the stage and decides what props shall be brought in, where they shall be placed on the stage, and when they shall be utilized. The individuals who appear in the dream may be drawn from the whole gamut of humanity: real and fictional, past and present, well-known and unknown. The props can be selected from the infinite variety of things, scenes, and objects. Animals may be used and even composites of a wide variety of animate and inanimate objects. Traditional rules of logic, movement, and sequence need not be respected.

The protagonists of the dream generally represent the dreamer and/or individuals who are of significance to the dreamer at that time. An individual may divide him- or herself into two or more parts, with each part representing one or more aspects of the dreamer's personality. For example, a very religious adolescent girl, who is guilty over her emerging sexual feelings, may have a dream

in which she is observing the Virgin Mary reprimanding a prostitute. It is not unreasonable to conclude that the girl is symbolizing
herself here in three separate forms: 1) the Virgin Mary, a symbol
of her desire to be pure, 2) the prostitute, who symbolizes her
emerging sexual inclinations, and 3) the observer, the girl herself
who is witness to her conflict. The dream also is a demonstration
of her guilt over sex and her view that people who do not engage
in such activities are pure and innocent and those who do are no
better than whores.

Another rule that is useful to follow in understanding dreams
is that individuals who appear in the dream who are ostensibly of
trivial or inconseqential significance are generally not so. If, for
example, an adult women of 50 has a dream in which she is walking
with another woman whom she has not seen since childhood, then
one does well to conclude that the friend is being brought into the
dream as a symbol of some quality that exists in the dreamer herself. They were both childhood friends and therefore the two lend
themselves well to serving as alter egos of one another. The examiner does well to ask the woman what thoughts comes to mind
regarding the old friend whom she has not seen for many years.
With rare exception, the qualities that she recalls the friend to have
had during childhood are likely to be qualities of her own that are
of some concern to her (the dreamer) at the time of the dream. The
old friend is not being brought in for the friend's benefit. Rather,
she is being brought in for the dreamer's benefit. Our dreams are
very egotistical, and we do not waste our valuable dream time for
the benefit of others, especially people we haven't seen in 40 years.

It is also reasonable to assume that the dream is dealing with
issues that are related to events that occurred within the day or two
prior to the dream's occurrence. Each night, the dream deals with
the "unfinished business" of the day. Most people's lives are so
filled with various kinds of recent "unfinished business" that we
do not dip back in time to weeks or months before the dream to
work through older problems that may not have been resolved.
Generally, the unresolved problems of the day are dealt with the
same night or the next night. Then, even though older business may
be "unfinished," there are newer events that take priority over older
unresolved issues. The "old stuff" appears to pass into oblivion and
is superseded by material that now commands our attention. We
cannot go around endlessly nursing old wounds or continually
trying to resolve every problem that we are confronted with. Our

minds tend to work on the same principle as that used by the administrator who files away problems and never has the need to resolve them. The difference, however, is that the administrator may never deal with any problem and files them all away. We try to deal with each problem each day and try to deal, as well, with problems that may have taken place the day before, but we continually have to deal with new problems that confront us and command our more immediate attention. It is hoped that the dreams will at least solve some of these problems so that our minds do not end up like the administrator who routinely files away every problem without any resolution at all of any of them. It would be an error for the reader to conclude that the older material *never* is dealt with in dreams. If the older material relates to severe psychological traumas, especially those that have persisted over time, then the dream may be utilized in the service of dealing with these. An example of this would be the desensitization kind of dream that is used to deal with the psychological traumas attendant to prolonged exposure to military combat. Under these circumstances, the older material takes priority over newer; however, it does so because it has remained a present-day concern as well.

Consistent with this notion of the higher priority that dreams give recent material, the props that have been brought in are more likely to be related to recent events, especially the previous days' experiences. Whatever the object that the patient selects to put on the stage—and these are selected from a universe of possible objects—it generally has some relevance to things that were going on in the day or two prior to the dream's occurrence. Also, one must consider the general ambiance of the dream. Does it take place in the frozen snow or the warm jungle? Are there grey clouds or bright sunshine and a clear sky? Is it underground in a cave or above ground on top of a mountain? All these aspects of the environment are of meaning in the dream because they have been selected from the infinite variety of possible milieus.

As mentioned, I do not believe that a particular symbol necessarily has the same meaning for everyone. Freud was especially prone to ascribe sexual meaning to many dream symbols. A snake, for example, may very well symbolize a penis. But it can also symbolize feelings of low self-worth and surreptitiousness. Snakes crawl on the ground and are quite "sneaky" in the way they sneak up upon us. However, snakes are also poisonous and they may therefore symbolize hostility and murderous wishes. One cannot know what the snake means to any particular person unless one elicits that individual's free associations to it. There are individuals for whom a snake may have some special significance, unrelated to the aforementioned possible meanings. The examiner who starts off with the assumption that the snake has some particular meaning is likely to lead the patient into incorrect interpretations of the dream. Furthermore, even traditional sexual symbols may stand for other things. A phallic symbol may not simply stand for a penis but for power and strength—traditional associations to the penis in our society. A vaginal symbol may not simply stand for the vagina but for femininity, passivity, and child rearing. These, too, are traditional associations to the female in our society. (I am making no statements here as to whether or not these associations are "good" or "bad." I am merely stating that they are common associations in our society at this time, although things may be changing somewhat.) A common dream experience is the one in which the individual feels like he or she is being overwhelmed by bugs, insects, or other noxious vermin. These often represent threatened eruption into conscious awareness of a variety of unacceptable thoughts, feelings, and impulses. One must try to ascertain from the dreamer what these noxious intruders might symbolize for him or her.

Explaining the Theory of Dream Formation and Analysis to a Child   With the aforementioned principles as background, the examiner is in a better position to explain the principles of dream formation and interpretation to the child who is a potential candidate for dream analysis. I generally begin in the following way with the potentially receptive child: "Did you know that the mind has two parts, a conscious part and an unconscious part?" (The reader may wonder here whether I have forgotten about the superego. Of course, I have not. I simply use this oversimplified dichotomy for the purposes of helping a child learn the basic principles of dream analysis.) I then try to get the child to appreciate that in the *conscious mind* are facts that people are generally aware of, for example, age, address, name of school, name of teacher, favorite flavor ice cream, etc. I will then discuss the kinds of things that are to be found in the *unconscious mind*. Here are thoughts and feelings which the child may feel guilty about and may think are wrong. For example, a child may think that it is very bad to have an occasional wish that a brother or sister might get hit by a car. To such a child I might say, "That child doesn't realize that to have a thought like that *once in a while* is normal and that it doesn't really mean that the person wishes the brother or sister *really* to be hit by a car. It only means that the child is angry at that brother or sister at that point. Anyway, if the person feels very bad about such a thought and thinks that only the worst kinds of children have such a thought, then that person is going to push that thought out of his or her mind and push it into the unconscious part of the mind so that he or she doesn't have to think about it at all."

I then engage the child in a discussion of the kinds of thoughts and feelings that might be relegated to the unconscious and those that a person might comfortably accept as conscious. When the child provides examples of thoughts and feelings that might be relegated to the unconcious, I may learn something about the things that that particular child is guilty about.

Once the concept of conscious/unconscious has been understood, I proceed to a discussion of the process of dream symbolism. One technique that I have found useful in helping children understand this concept is that of the "secret code." I ask the child if he or she has ever seen a James Bond movie. I generally receive an answer in the affirmative. I try to help the child recall some secret agent therein who used a secret code. We then discuss the formation of secret codes, for example, a code in which the number 1 stands for A, 2 for B, 3 for C, etc. When one "cracks" the code, one merely tries to figure out which letter stands for which number. In this way the code is "decoded." I will generally use the terms "crack the code" or "decode the code" to refer to the process of analyzing the symbol. Once this concept is understood, I explain to the child that dreams also make up their own codes. I explain that the unconscious mind changes information into code form before it goes into the conscious mind. In this way the person may not feel so bad or ashamed about the stuff that comes out of the unconscious mind into the conscious mind.

I will then ask the child to see if he or she can decode or crack the code of a dream that I will now present. I have found this example to be useful:

> A little girl is walking down the street. She sees a boy her own age making wee-wee. In her home she was taught that it's naughty to look at a little boy doing that. She wanted to look at the boy, but she felt very bad and guilty because she wanted to look at him. So

she turned away and didn't look. But she was still *very* curious to see what his penis looked like. That night she had a dream. In that dream she saw that *very same* little boy watering the grass with a hose. He was holding the hose in his hands and a stream of water was coming out of the hose. The water curved out from the hose down to the grass. What do you think the hose stands for? What do you think the water stands for? Do you think that dream had anything to do with what happened that afternoon when she saw the boy making wee-wee and wished that she could see his penis?

The overwhelming majority of children will generally "figure out" the meaning of this dream. When they do, I try to emphasize the point that the dream satisfies a wish: "The little girl wished that she could see the boy make wee-wee, but felt that it was wrong or bad and so could not satisfy her wish. At night, she gratified the wish to see his penis. However, because she felt this was the wrong thing to do she had to put it into a code form."

I also try to emphasize the wish-fulfillment function of the dream. In order to do this I will generally provide other questions to the child that provide practice with the use of the dream for this purpose. For example, I might give this question:

A boy's father comes home one day and tells him that he has tickets for the circus that weekend. He is very happy. He is very excited about the fact that he will be going to the circus in a few days. In fact, he tells all his friends about the fact that that Saturday he's going to the circus. Unfortunately, on Friday the boy gets sick. He is so sick that he has to stay in bed and he can't go to school. He has high fever and a headache and he's nauseated and he vomits. The doctor says that he'll have to stay home and will have to remain in bed for at least three days. The boy is very sad. He wishes that he could go to the circus. What do you think he dreams of that night?

Again, it is a rare child who does not get the correct answer to this question. I then take the wish fulfillment issue further. I may discuss the kinds of dreams a poor boy may have, a boy who has no money. Or the kinds of dreams a very hungry girl might have, a girl who hasn't eaten or drunk anything for many days. I will then follow these relatively simple dreams with dreams in which there is a combination of both wish fulfillment and symbol formation. For example:

A boy named Tom started a fight with his younger brother Bill, and Bill went crying to their father and told him what Tom had done. The father got very angry and punished Tom. He told him that he could not watch his favorite television program that night. Tom was *very sad* that he couldn't watch his television program. He was also *very angry*, so angry that he felt like doing something very mean and cruel to his father. But he quickly put that thought out of his mind because he realized that if he were to do something mean or cruel to his father that he might even get a worse punishment. That night Tom had a dream about his father in which the angry feelings came out. Can you make up a dream showing how the angry feelings came out?

If the child tells a dream in which the anger is acted out overtly, I may accept that as an answer. However, I may also say, "Well, that's one possible dream. However, this particular boy felt very bad about such angry thoughts. He felt so bad and guilty about having such thoughts that he could not let them into his conscious mind. He had to make up a code. He had to disguise the angry thoughts before he could let them come into his conscious mind." I will then ask the child to make up a dream in which the anger is released in coded form. If the child cannot do so I may suggest a dream in which the boy's *friend* hits the father with a baseball bat. Or, the child might have a dream in which he is hitting a policeman. Or the father, while driving his car, has an accident. In this way I help the child appreciate the concept of wish fulfillment by symbolic processes.

With this introduction into the theory of dream formation and analysis, I may then turn to the child's dream and ask him or her to try to figure out what it means. A good principle to follow is that the element that is most likely to produce useful information is the idiosyncratic or atypical one. These are the more highly individualized symbols and are more likely to provide useful leads regarding the dream's meaning. The therapist must keep in mind the fact that his or her suggestions regarding the meaning of a particular element in the dream are always speculations. The therapist should do everything to get the patient to present his or her guesses and hunches regarding a symbol's meaning before offering his or her speculations. Even the patient's "wild guesses" may be more on point than the therapist's carefully considered explanations. The patient's guesses are more likely to be related to the issues that have brought about the dream's formation.

One device that I have found useful in getting children to free associate to a dream entity is to utilize what I call the "foreign boy" question. Let us say, for example, a child has a dream in which a shoe appears. One could simply ask the child what comes to mind in association with the word *shoe*. If a child appears to have difficulty providing associations I might ask this question: "Suppose a foreign boy moved into your neighborhood and he didn't know very much English. Suppose he asked you what the word *shoe* means. What would you say?" I have found this question provides a much higher percentage of useful associations than the more general question "What comes to mind about the word *shoe*?"

It is only after the patient has exhausted all possible associations and explanations that the therapist should offer his or her interpretations or hunches for the patient's consideration. The hope here is that the patient will latch on to the explanation and have the aforementioned feeling that "It fits," "You're right," or "That's it." When the therapist observes this response, then he or she knows that the interpretation is likely to be valid. But if the patient just merely says, "yes, that sounds right," without the feeling that the explanation "clicks" or is on target, then one cannot be sure that the interpretation was indeed valid. Last, one does not merely analyze dreams as an intellectual game. The purpose is to utilize what is learned in the service of the therapeutic goals. Here I will present some sample dream analyses of patients who were unusually gifted in this regard.

Clinical Examples

The Case of Sean (The Monks, the Spanish Inquisitors, and the Lions)   Sean, a ten-year-old boy, was referred because of marked anxiety, feelings of inadequacy, and poor school performance in spite of high intelligence. He was an extremely "uptight" and tense youngster. He sucked his thumb and his tension interfered with his falling asleep. His massive feelings of inadequacy and insecurity interfered with his properly asserting himself. He spoke in a low voice, to the point where he was sometimes almost inaudible. He was easily scapegoated by peers because of his fear of self-assertion. His mother's overprotectiveness played an important role in bringing about these symptoms. Her indulgence did not provide him with the opportunities to gain the feelings of self-confidence that come with competence. She was particularly fearful of exposing him to any unpleasant experiences and this played a role in his having a "thin skin." Furthermore, she was afraid to do anything that might evoke anger in Sean, fearing that such expressions on his part would be a reflection of parental deficiency in her. Sean's father was a busy businessman who left much of the care of the children to the mother. Even on weekends, he was so engrossed in his business that there was little time left for Sean and his older sister. Sean was basically quite angry over his father's withdrawal, but was afraid to express it.

During his third month in therapy, Sean's mother informed me at the beginning of the session that he was not doing his homework. In subsequent discussion it became apparent that my previous advice to the mother that Sean not be permitted to watch television until he had completed his homework assignments was not being implemented. Although the mother stated that she thought my recommendation was a good one, she claimed that she was hesitant to follow through with it. It became apparent that the mother was hesitant to implement my recommendation because the patient would consider her "mean." This was just another example of the mother's intolerance of any resentment on Sean's part toward her. In the ensuing discussion I learned that, from an early age, Sean had found that he could manipulate his mother into not instituting appropriate restrictions and punishments by accusing her of being mean to him. As a result of our discussion, the mother stated that she was going to be firmer in her determination not to allow herself to be so manipulated. Then I asked the patient how he felt about his mother's new determination. He stated that he was pleased with the outcome of the discussion because now he would probably get more homework done. Recognizing that Sean might be suppressing and repressing the inevitable anger I suspected he felt over his mother's resolution, I tried to encourage his expression of such. I expressed incredulity that he was reacting in such a calm way with comments such as "Are you sure that this doesn't bother you at all?" and "I can't believe, that somewhere deep down, there aren't at least some thoughts and feelings of resentment over your mother's saying that she's going to come down harder on you from now on."

In the next session the patient stated that he was more diligent in doing his homework and was pleased about the discussion of the previous session. He then presented the following dream:

> There was a group of men. They were old and they had beards. The beards were long and hung way down. They wore grey robes which covered their whole bodies. They looked like Monks from the Spanish Inquisition. They were in a dark castle and they were chasing me around the castle.
>
> Then they chased me to a trap where there were lions. I managed to escape through a trap door and I got out of there. I got away from the lions and the men in the grey robes. I was in the bright sun.

When analyzing this dream the patient was first asked what an inquisitor was. He said they were judges from the Middle Ages who had torture chambers and dungeons, and they would put prisoners in there. On further inquiry he stated that they asked prisoners lots of questions. He was then asked who these inquisitors could stand for—a person who is a judge, who asks a lot of questions, and who is capable of punishing. He responded in a surprised fashion that they might stand for the therapist whom he saw as a judge and as someone who asked him many questions. He denied, however, that he felt that my recommendation to his mother that she firmly uphold the homework-television policy was seen by him as punishment.

Following this I asked him who the lions might represent and he replied that they were probably his parents who were also pressuring him to fulfill his obligations, but against whom he denied any anger.

I pointed out to him that although he professed compliance with my recommendation and pleasure with its implementation, his dream suggested that he looked upon both his parents and me as being punitive and that we were people to be avoided and escaped from. I therefore informed him that I was somewhat dubious about his commitment to the new homework program because his dream reflected his view that it was oppressive and his desire to avoid its implementation.

The analysis of this dream enabled me to avoid unwittingly supporting the patient's resistances. To have praised the patient for his compliance would have gone along with him in his denial of his anger and his devious avoidance of his responsibilities. The session ended with the attitude on my part that he would really have to show me his good intentions and that I, at the present time, was somewhat incredulous that he would follow through with conviction. Having been overprotected so long and having so skillfully manipulated his mother into being extremely "soft" with him, this boy needed a "hard line," and the dream offered me good justification for such.

About three months later, by which time there had been moderate diminution of Sean's tension and anxiety, there was little change in his school performance. Because of the improvement in his anxiety symptoms, Sean began to talk about leaving treatment. He was no longer feeling much discomfort over his tension and, as far as he was concerned, he could live quite well without doing much homework. His request to stop came near the end of the session and so it was decided to discuss the matter further in the next session.

When he arrived for his next session, Sean told me that he had a dream. For the purposes of understanding this dream, the reader should appreciate that the patient's treatment took place in 1964 and 1965, a few years after President Kennedy's assassination. This was the dream:

> We were on a class trip to the junior high school. It was Kennedy's birthday and there were exhibits on Kennedy's life. First, we went to the Kennedy exhibit. Then we went to the gym and we were playing basketball. Then we saw some drunken janitor stumbling about in the gym. Then I was at Kevin's house and I was playing the organ. Then I woke up.

When analyzing the dream, the patient was first asked about John Kennedy. He said that Kennedy was an Irish Catholic just like himself. He was then asked what Kennedy could stand for in his own life and he replied,"studying, school, and success." He was then asked what the drunken janitor could stand for and he replied, "failure." He was then asked to tell me about his friend, Kevin. He said that Kevin was a "smart kid who does well without doing very much work." He then described how he would like to be like Kevin and also be able to get good grades without working very hard. He interpreted his being at Kevin's house as implying that he would like to be like Kevin. When asked about the organ he said, "That stands for playing games just like the gymnasium period." The patient was then asked what the whole dream meant. He responded that it stood for the three choices he had regarding what he could do with his life. First, he could work hard and try to be like John

Kennedy. Or he could spend his time playing and end up a drunken bum. His third option was to be like his friend Kevin who does well without working too hard.

I then asked him what the dream meant in view of the fact that the was considering leaving treatment. He replied that it was probably telling him that his leaving treatment was dangerous in that he might end up a drunken bum if he did. I then asked him if the dream might lead him to change his mind and he replied that it did not. I asked him if he had an emotional reaction to the dream, if it "grabbed him," and he said no.

This dream is a good example of how a patient can provide an accurate intellectual analysis of a dream without a resulting effect on the patient's clinical behavior. One reason for the failure of such linkage in Sean's case was that the forces encouraging him to leave treatment were strong. His mother, at the time of this dream, was exhibiting marked resistance to Sean's therapy, and he was no doubt responding to and complying with her attitudes toward the treatment.

Sean's treatment could not justifiably be called psychoanalysis. Most of the sessions were spent playing the mutual storytelling and derivative games. There was, of course, some discussion. There were times, however, when Sean actively participated in dream analysis and the dreams just presented are representative samples. Accordingly there were times when his therapy could justifiably be called *psychoanalytically oriented psychotherapy*. Timothy, the next patient to be presented, spent much more time involved in analytic work. Accordingly, his treatment could more justifiably be considered closer to pure *psychoanalytic therapy*. However, I would not even consider Timothy's treatment to justify the label *psychoanalysis* because much of the time was still spent in nonanalytic work because he was disinclined to involve himself in such inquiry on an ongoing basis.

The Case of Timothy ("A Boy Eats His Belt and His Mother Gets Angry")   Timothy entered treatment at the age of eight because of generalized tension. He was an extremely "uptight" boy who was best described as a "worry wart." Although very serious minded, he was not attending properly to his studies. It was obvious from the first interview that he was identifying strongly with his mother who had similar characteristics. She was an English teacher who constantly had a sad look on her face and always appeared as if the weight of the world was on her shoulders. Timothy's father was a successful businessman. Timothy and his older brother were both in classes for the intellectually gifted, even though Timothy was doing poorly in school. Both parents had had extensive psychoanalytic treatment, and both were continually talking about the underlying meaning of many of the things that were said and done in the household. It was not surprising, then, that Timothy approached the world from that vantage point, and his high intelligence enabled him to profit from psychoanalytic inquiry. I would not consider his treatment to be justifiably called psychoanalysis because he was still unreceptive to spending most of his sessions talking directly about the underlying meaning of what he was doing and saying. Furthermore, when the topic got difficult for him he preferred to play the mutual storytelling game. But even there, at times, he would try to analyze directly his stories.

From the first weeks in treatment it became quite apparent that Timothy suffered with an anger inhibition problem and this, I believed, was a factor in his chronic state of tension and seriousness. During his sixth month of treatment Timothy reported this dream:

A boy eats his belt and his mother gets angry.

Timothy's mother wrote down every dream and the slip of paper on which this dream was written had nothing else recorded. When I asked Timothy if there was anything more in the dream he replied that there wasn't. The following interchange then took place:

Therapist: What do you think this dream means?
Patient: I don't know.
Therapist: I'd like you to try to guess what you think the dream means.
Patient: I'm trying to guess, Dr. Gardner, but I really don't know.
Therapist: Okay, let's try to do it this way. Suppose a foreign boy moved into your neighborhood and he didn't know too much English. Suppose he asked you what the word *belt* means, what would you say?
Patient: It's something that holds up your pants.
Therapist: So if you eat your belt what happens?
Patient: My pants would fall down.
Therapist: And what would happen then?

Patient (somewhat ashamed): Everybody could see my underwear.

Therapist: Okay, so now what do you think the dream means?

Patient: I don't know.

Therapist: Well, your mother is in the dream too. Isn't she?

Patient: Yes.

Therapist: What did you say happened with her in the dream?

Patient: Well, she got angry.

Therapist: So, what could that mean that your mother gets angry if you pull down your pants.

Patient: She'd get angry if I pull down my pants and she saw my underwear.

Therapist: Okay, but what does all that stand for? What could all that mean?

Patient: It means that if I show her my underwear she'll get angry.

Therapist: Yeah, but as you know, things in dreams stand for other things. What could her being angry when you show her your underpants mean? What could that stand for? How would you decode that?

Patient: Well, maybe it means that if I take off the outside clothing and show her what's inside me I think she'll be angry.

Therapist: What do you mean when you say that if you show her what's inside you?

Patient: Well, maybe it means that I think she'll get angry at me if I tell her about the thoughts and feelings that I have that are underneath. Maybe my angry feelings.

Therapist: So what you are saying, then, is if you show her your angry feelings you think she'll get angry at you? Is that it?

Patient: Yes, that's it. I'm always scared that she'll get angry at me.

Therapist: Well, what kinds of things might you say that would get her angry at you, especially things that you're afraid to talk about?

Patient: She's always on my back all the time. She's always asking me a lot of questions. When I tell her that she bothers me too much, she gets even angrier at me.

Therapist: Well, I think that we should talk about that with your mother and father in our next family meeting.

Patient: Okay. But I still think she'll get angry at me.

Therapist: Well, we'll see.

I believe that many classical psychoanalysts would consider me to have missed entirely the purpose of this dream. They would have considered it an excellent example of an oedipal dream. They would consider the boy's exposing his underpants to his mother to be the first step toward his exposing his penis for the purposes of oedipal gratification. There are two possibilities here, namely, that the oedipal explanation is valid or it is not. The patient's associations certainly did not suggest directly sexual-oedipal themes. Rather, his associations suggested fear of revealing his underlying thoughts and feelings. The argument that these are merely cover-ups for underlying sexual-oedipal thoughts and feelings may very well be valid, but they are not substantiated directly by the patient's associations. Furthermore, one of the most humiliating things that can happen to a boy in the latency period is that his genital area be seen by the girls in his class. This has nothing to do with sex, but more to do with embarrassment. Accordingly, I consider embarrassment over genital exposure to be a far more likely explanation for this dream than the oedipal-sexual theory.

When a child has difficulty expressing anger to parents, one cannot simply recommend that the anger be expressed. After all, the child is a child and the parent is an adult and has much more power than the child. We are not dealing here with an egalitarian situation. Accordingly, the therapist must be somewhat cautious when encouraging children to express their anger toward their parents. One has to have a thorough knowledge of the parents, especially with regard to how reasonable they will be about accepting benevolently the child's civilized expression of resentment. If the therapist believes that the child can handle the situation him- or herself, and if the parents can be relied upon to listen with receptivity to the child's complaints (especially when presented in a civilized way), then it is in the best interests of the child's treatment for him or her to express the resentment *without* the therapist being present. However, when one expects irrational and/or inappropriate responses from the parents—especially excessively punitive ones—then it is best that the anger be expressed in a family session. In the office setting there is an implied protection by the therapist because he or she is in a position to monitor the parents' responses. And this was my decision in Timothy's case because of his parents' (especially his mother's) difficulty in handling his angry expressions in a completely rational way.

One month later, Timothy came in with this dream:

My grandfather said that he was going to take me and my brother to the circus. At one o'clock we asked him to take us and he said he was too busy. At two o'clock he said he was busy. At three o'clock he said he was going to kill me. I was scared and then I woke up.

As mentioned, the patient's father was a businessman. He was deeply involved in his business and often came home quite late. On weekends, as well, he was so often engrossed in his work that he had little meaningful time for his children. At times he would interrupt his weekend work to be with his sons; at other times he was unreceptive to their requests. This is the interchange that took place in association with the analysis of this dream.

> *Therapist:* So, Timothy, what do you think this dream means?
> *Patient:* I don't know. This isn't circus season. Nothing was said about the circus in my house.
> *Therapist:* Well, what could *circus* stand for? See if you can figure out the meaning of circus. What comes to mind about the circus?
> *Patient:* Well, the circus is a lot of fun. I really have a good time when I go.
> *Therapist:* Well, maybe then the circus means fun things. What do you think?
> *Patient:* Okay, maybe it means fun things. But my grandfather's never taken me to the circus.
> *Therapist:* Yeah, but also your grandfather doesn't live here. Doesn't he live in San Francisco?
> *Patient:* Yeah, he does. I hardly ever see him.
> *Therapist:* So maybe it's not your grandfather in the dream. Remember what we said about people sometimes standing for other people in dreams?
> *Patient:* Yes. Maybe he stands for my father because my father took us to the circus last year and the year before that.
> *Therapist:* That seems reasonable to me. So what is the dream saying when it talks about your grandfather and the circus?
> *Patient:* It's something about doing fun things with my father.
> *Therapist:* I agree. So, now what could the dream mean? What's all the rest of it about?
> *Patient:* Well, it says that I keep asking my father to do fun things with me and he keeps saying that he's too busy. He's always busy with his work. He works in his den at home. And he's always up there working.
> *Therapist:* Is he always up there? Doesn't he come down at all?
> *Patient:* Yeah, he comes down.
> *Therapist:* Will he come down if you ask him?
> *Patient:* Sometimes he will and sometimes he won't.

Therapist: Does he get very angry at you when you ask him?
Patient: Sometimes he gets angry, and sometimes he doesn't.
Therapist: What does the dream say about how angry he'll get?
Patient: The dream says that he'll kill me.
Therapist: Do you think he'll *really* kill you?
Patient: No, he wouldn't do that.
Therapist: Do you think maybe you're seeing it as worse than it really is? Do you think he would really be as angry at you as the dream says?
Patient: No, I guess not. I guess I'm worrying too much about that, like you always say that I worry too much about things.
Therapist: So what can you do about this now?
Patient: I think I should talk to him more.
Therapist: I think so too. I don't think he'll be as mean as you expect him to be.

In the first dream, I recommended a family session when Timothy expressed his fears of telling his mother how angry he was. In the second, I suggested that he tell his father directly. My reasons for this were that, as mentioned, I did not believe that Timothy's *mother* would respond properly to his expressions of resentment. However, I did anticipate that his *father* would be more receptive to such expression and that Timothy did not need my help on this issue. This is an extremely important point therapeutically and one that some family therapists do not fully appreciate. Routinely conducting family therapy may deprive patients of independent self-assertion because every session involves a certain amount of implied protection by the therapist.

In his ninth month of treatment Timothy related this dream:

I was telling jokes and trying to make some people laugh. Then Alfred E. Newman, the guy from *Mad* comics, came in. He was funny and made everyone laugh. He chased me for fun until they got to my house where there was very good cake and jam that was very bitter. I poured the jam on Alfred's cake. My mother scolded me and gave Alfred a fresh piece of cake. Then I woke up.

The following interchange took place in association with the analysis of this dream:

Therapist: So, lets hear. What do you think about this dream?
Patient: I love *Mad* comics. It's my favorite magazine. It's really very funny.

Therapist: Okay, but who does Alfred E. Newman stand for? Do you remember what I said about the people in a dream and how strangers usually stand for other people or parts of yourself?

Patient: Alfred E. Newman's ears stick out, just like my brother's. Sometimes I tease him and I call him Alfred E. Newman.

Therapist: So do you think Alfred E. Newman in the dream stands for your brother?

Patient: Yeah, I guess so. I can't think of anybody else who he might stand for.

Therapist: So what's happening there in the dream between you and your brother?

Patient: Well I'm starting to tell jokes and then he comes in and tells better jokes. He knows more jokes than I do. That gets me angry when he tells better jokes.

Therapist: But you know, he's older than you and I'm sure that when you're as old as he is you'll be able to tell as many good jokes as he can. What do you think about that?

Patient: Well maybe. I hope so.

Therapist: Okay, let's go on with the dream. So what else is it saying?

Patient: I guess I'm getting back at him by pouring that lousy jam on his cake. And then my mother gets angry at me because I did that. She's always getting angry at me when I fight with him.

Therapist: But it sounds like here you're starting up. In the dream he wasn't doing anything to you and you just poured that bitter jam on his cake. Isn't that right?

Patient: Yeah.

Therapist: So what this dream tells me is that one way of getting your mother to be less angry at you is for you not to start up with your brother so much. Wouldn't you agree?

Patient: Yes.

I considered this dream to be a normal sibling rivalry dream. My advice that Timothy not start up with his brother was not likely to be complied with to a significant degree. I consider sibling rivalry normally to be fierce and advice by parents and therapists that siblings squelch the expression of their rivalrous feelings are not likely to be complied with to a significant degree. In fact, if they did comply with such advice I would suspect one or both children to have anger inhibition problems. The predictable failure of such advice notwithstanding, it still behooves therapists and parents to recommend that the children "cool it."

One month later, during his tenth month of treatment, Timothy related this dream:

My friend Robert had a contest. The winner was to get his house. The family that won moved into the house. After the family moved in Robert sent me to the house to remind them about some lights in the basement. I went into the basement. There I got a needle in my eye. A voice told me that I would have to catch a lion in order to get the needle out.

As mentioned, the therapist does well to focus on the most idiosyncratic element in a dream. It is the most highly individualized aspect of the dream and is generally going to provide the richest amount of information about the dream's meaning. I am not recommending, however, that the therapist automatically encourage the patient to focus on that element first. One must still sit back and let the patient select those elements that he or she considers important to focus on. However, at some point the therapist must direct attention to that element in the dream if the patient has not. Otherwise, the most meaningful and revealing part of the dream may be bypassed. This is the interchange that took place in association with the analysis of this dream:

> *Therapist:*   That sounds like a very good dream, Timothy. Let's hear what you think about it.
> *Patient:*   I think that's a hard dream to figure out. I don't know what it means.
> *Therapist:*   Did anything happen in your life in the last day or two that's anything like anything in the dream?
> *Patient:*   I can't remember anything.
> *Therapist:*   Are you sure? Was there anything that happened that was like in the dream?
> *Patient:*   Well, Michael (the patient's brother) is scared to go down into the basement of my house. He's going to be 11 and he's still scared to go down in the basement. Yesterday my mother asked him to get some light bulbs that we have down there, and he didn't want to go. He was scared. So they asked me to go and I went.
> *Therapist:*   Are you scared at all to go down into the basement?
> *Patient:*   Well, sometimes a little bit, especially at night. But I'm not as scared as he is. He's *really* scared and won't even go.
> *Therapist:*   Do you think any of this has to do with the dream?
> *Patient:*   Maybe it does, but I don't know how.
> *Therapist:*   Well, the house is divided into two parts. The light part and the dark part. Isn't that so?
> *Patient:*   I guess it is that way. There's the part that you see and the part that you can't see.

Therapist: Does that sound like anything we've been talking about?

Patient: Do you think it has something to do with the two parts of the mind, the conscious part that we know about and the unconscious part that we don't know about?

Therapist: That's *right!* That's *very good!* You really remembered that very well. I'm very proud of you. You're really a smart boy. I've told you that before, and I'm telling you that again. Most kids wouldn't have been able to figure that out.

Patient: Thank you.

Therapist: You're welcome. Now let's go on and see if we can figure out more about the dream. Now what are you doing in the basement?

Patient: Well, I'm taking the lights out of the basement.

Therapist: What could that mean?

Patient: If you take the lights out of a place then you can't light it up. Then it stays dark.

Therapist: Right. So what does that mean in your dream?

Patient: I guess I don't want to see what's in the dark place, in my unconscious mind.

Therapist: I would agree. I think that's what that means. You'd rather not look at certain things. Now let's try to figure out more about the dream. What happens in the basement?

Patient: While I was down there I got a needle in my eye, and a voice said that I would have to catch a lion in order to get the needle out.

Therapist: What do you think that's all about?

Patient: I don't know. That's a funny thing.

Therapist: That sure is. I never heard of anything like that in a dream before. I think it's a very important thing to try to understand. Let's take one part at a time. I think it might be a good idea to start with the needle. What do you think that needle stands for? What did the needle look like?

Patient: It looked like one of those needles that doctors use when they give you an injection.

Therapist: I think that's giving us very important information. You say it's a doctor's needle. What could that mean?

Patient: Well, maybe it has something to do with you. You're a doctor.

Therapist: I agree. I think it probably does have something to do with me. What could it mean that I'm putting a needle in your eye?

Patient: I don't know.

Therapist: Well, why does a doctor put a needle in you. Why do doctors give shots?

Patient: To make you better. When you're sick they give you shots to make you better.

Therapist: So what does that mean in your dream?

Patient: It means that you're putting a needle in my eye to make me better.

Therapist: But why in your eye?

Patient: The eye is where I see. Maybe you're trying to make my eyes better. Maybe you're trying to help me see better.

Therapist: Very good! I thought that too. Here I try to help you see things more clearly. So the needle in your eye has something to do with your therapy. Is that right?

Patient: Yes. That's right.

Therapist: Now what else is happening there?

Patient: Well the dream says that in order to get the needle out I would have to catch a lion.

Therapist: That's an interesting thought. I wonder what that means? Do you have any idea?

Patient: I don't know.

Therapist: Well, it says something about the needle staying in there and then something has to happen before it comes out. If putting the needle in and keeping it there stands for your treatment, what does taking the needle out stand for?

Patient: The end of treatment. It has something to with the time I can stop treatment.

Therapist: That's the thought that I had, that is has something to do with your stopping treatment. Then the needle would come out. But it says something else. It says something about your having to catch a lion before you can stop treatment. What could that be all about?

Patient: It's about a lion. I don't know.

Therapist: Well, what does a lion stand for? What comes to mind about a lion?

Patient: They roar. They're the king of the beasts. They're the strongest animal in the jungle. Lots of people are scared of them. They can eat a lot of other animals.

Therapist: Okay, so what does the lion stand for?

Patient: The lion is scary. It's something that I'm scared of. I think the lion stands for my anger.

Therapist: I agree with you. It sounds to me like a good guess. Now let's go further with that. The dream says you have to catch a lion before the needle can come out of your eye. Is that right?

Patient: Yes. Maybe catching a lion means looking at my anger.

Therapist: Tell me more about that. I think you're on the right track.

Patient: Well, maybe it means that I have to talk more about my anger and do more things with my anger before I can stop treatment.

Therapist: I *agree!* I *agree 100 percent.* I want to congratulate you on your figuring out the meaning of this dream. I think you did a great job. I'm really *proud* of you. We really did it together. Without your ideas, we could never have figured out the meaning of the dream. Most kids your age could never have done such a good job with a dream.

Patient: Thank you.

Therapist: You're welcome.

There is nothing else to say here; I believe everything in the interchange is self-explanatory. The vignette certainly demonstrates well the power of the analytic inquiry for those rare patients who can avail themselves of this form of treatment. However, it is important for the reader to appreciate that, as I have said so many times in this book, insight is only one step toward alleviation of psychopathology. Unless it is translated into experience and ongoing changes in thinking it is not likely to be effective.

During his tenth month in treatment the patient related this dream:

I was playing with my chemistry set and I was going to light a candle with a match. I looked down and I saw a wasp's nest on the floor. It was very big. My mother asked me to do something and I stepped on the wasp's nest and I was stung. I didn't step on it on purpose; I stepped on it by mistake.

The following interchange then took place:

Therapist: So, Timothy, what do you think about this dream?

Patient (providing his usual first response):   I don't know. I don't know what to think.

Therapist: Is there anything in this dream that's like anything that happened in any of the other dreams we talked about recently?

Patient: Well, it has something to do with lighting up a place or a room. And I had that other dream in which I took the light bulbs out of the basement.

Therapist: Yes, I had that thought too. What did it mean in the other dream, about the lights?

Patient: Well in that dream I was taking the bulbs out of the cellar, which meant that I didn't want to look at the things in my unconscious mind.

Therapist: Yes, that's right. You have a good memory for such things. And that's very useful. It helps us figure out the meaning of dreams when you have a good memory. You're lucky to have such a good memory. Okay now, that's what it meant in the other dream. Now what's happening here?

Patient: Well, here I'm lighting a candle. I'm making it light.

Therapist: So what does that mean?

Patient: It means that I want to look at things. In the other dream I didn't.

Therapist: But do you actually look at things here? Did you actually light the candle with the match in this dream?

Patient: No, I was going to but I didn't because I saw the wasp's nest on the floor.

Therapist: Let's hold off with the wasp's nest for just a minute. What is this dream telling us then about your desire to light up your unconscious mind?

Patient: It tells me that I'm not sure, that I have mixed feelings about it.

Therapist: Right! That's right. I like to use those words *mixed feelings*. So a part of you wants to light it up and a part of you doesn't. Is that right?

Patient: Yes.

Therapist: This also tells me that you're getting closer to doing it, to putting on the lights in your unconscious mind. In the other dream you just took the bulbs out of the cellar. In this dream you're thinking about lighting the candle, but you don't get to do it. You have mixed feelings about it. I guess you're still scared.

Patient: I guess so. But I was going to, but then I saw the wasp's nest on the floor.

Therapist: Okay, let's talk about that. What could the wasp's nest stand for?

Patient: I think that's like my anger again. Wasps sting and they're mean and they can hurt you.

Therapist: Okay, that sounds reasonable. That sounds like a good explanation. Then what?

Patient: Well I stepped on them.

Therapist: So what does that mean?

Patient: Maybe it's like catching a lion from the other dream. I'm less scared of touching angry things.

Therapist: I think that's a good explanation.

Patient: That was a good dream.

Therapist: Yes, you did a very good job so far, but there's still another part that we have to try to figure out.

Patient: What's that? I thought we're all finished with this dream.

Therapist: No, I think there's one other part that may be hard for you to understand, but I think it's important for us to discuss it.

Patient: What's that?

Therapist: Well, at first you said that you stepped on the wasp's nest and then you said that you did it by mistake.

Patient: Is that important?

Therapist: Yes, it's important. Why do you think I think it is important?

Patient: I don't know.

Therapist: Can you try to figure out why I think that's important?

Patient: I can't think of the reason. I just said that I did it and then I said it was a mistake.

Therapist: Well, I think that shows me that you had mixed feelings about stepping on the wasp's nest. It may also mean that you felt bad or guilty about it, and that's why you had to say that you did it by mistake. When somebody does something by mistake you can't blame them for it. It says to me that maybe you thought you might get punished or something if you stepped on the wasp's nest on purpose, that is, if you touched your anger or let your anger come out.

Patient: I don't understand what you're saying.

Therapist: Let me try it again. When you say that you did something by mistake, you hope that you won't get punished. Isn't that right?

Patient: Right.

Therapist: You just could have dreamed that you stepped on the wasp's nest, but then you had to tell me that you did it by mistake. I think from that that you probably feel that there's something wrong about doing it and you had to apologize in advance. Saying you made a mistake is a way of protecting yourself from getting punished for doing something.

Patient: Do you mean that I was scared that something would happen to me if I did it on purpose and that saying it was a mistake was an excuse so I wouldn't get punished?

Therapist: Yes, that's it. I'm glad you understand that.

Patient: I think I do.

Therapist: Why don't you tell it to me again so I'm sure you understand?

Patient: It means that I don't want to say that I wanted to do it but that I am scared to say I want to do it so I said it was a mistake so I wouldn't get punished!

Therapist: That's right! You certainly are a smart boy. Most kids your age would not have been able to understand that. Now, the important question is what do you think would happen if you were to show your anger?

Patient: I guess my mother and father would get very angry at me.

Therapist: Have you learned anythng here about that?

Patient: Yes, I learned that they won't get as angry as I think they will. I make them mean sometimes when they aren't. But my mother is pretty mean sometimes.

Therapist: Yes, but not all the time. And you make her worse than she really is. I think the more practice you have talking about your anger, the easier it will be for you to let it out and the more practice you have letting it out in a nice good way with your mother and father the less scared you'll be about it.

Again, little need be said about the analysis of this dream. It shows therapeutic progress with regard to the patient's comfort with gaining insight into his unconscious processes as well as increasing comfort with the expression of anger. However, in both cases there was ambivalence, but this was still a step forward. Timothy had some difficulty understanding the significance of his statement that he had stepped on the wasp's nest "by mistake." I believe he finally did come to understand the meaning of this statement. However, I did not stop there and tried to relate his understanding to the reality of his situation with his parents. There is no point to gaining a psychoanalytic insight if it is not translated into clinical behavior.

Timothy's treatment lasted about a year and a half. By the time we discontinued therapy he had enjoyed significant improvement in his ability to assert himself and express resentment in appropriate ways. He was far less tense and worrisome. His relationships with his parents had improved significantly, and he was generally a much happier boy. However, there was still residua of his serious attitude, and at times he would become inhibited in expressing himself.

A follow-up. Timothy and I lived in the same community. Our families were members of the same community swim club. One day, as I was basking in the sun, Timothy came over to me and said, "Excuse me Dr. Gardner, I know you're not on duty now, but I had a dream last night and I was wondering if you could help me analyze it. I don't have much money, but I can pay you fifty cents." I informed Timothy that post-treatment dream analyses were free and I would be happy to discuss the dream with him. I cannot recall at this point what the dream was, but I do know that he handled himself with amazing facility regarding its analysis. I mention this here for two reasons. First, it is a demonstration of how the patient's facility with analysis remained with him following the therapy and probably has held him in good stead ever since. In addition, it is a statement of the good relationship that I had with him that he was able to approach me a year later in the way he did.

CONCLUDING COMMENTS

Throughout this book I have been critical of many aspects of psychoanalytic theory and its application to treatment. It would have been an error for the reader to conclude that I am completely critical of *all* aspects of psychoanalysis. Rather, I consider myself to have been selective and have retained and utilized what I consider to be valuable contributions and have rejected that which I consider to be of little or no value. It is also important for the reader to appreciate that my criticisms of psychoanalysis (both as a theory and as a method of treatment) do not stem from a book I once read on the subject. Rather, I went through a full six-year program of psychoanalytic training at the William A. White Psychoanalytic Institute in New York City. There I was schooled not only in the classical Freudian tradition but in the modifications introduced by others, especially Harry Stack Sullivan, Erich Fromm, and Frieda Fromm-Reichmann.

In addition, in medical school, in residency, and again during my psychoanalytic training I underwent personal psychoanalysis with analysts of three different persuasions (one classical and two culturally oriented). Furthermore, I believe that most of the techniques described in this book are within the psychoanalytic tradition. They are based on the belief that there does exist a mental compartment that is justifiably referred to as *the unconscious part of the mind*. Also, I believe that unconscious processes play an important role in the development of psychogenic symptoms. I believe also that knowledge of these processes is an important factor in bringing about therapeutic change. However, my approach does not rely heavily on the patient's (especially children's) conscious awareness of these unconscious processes. Rather, I believe that the therapist's awareness is crucial, as is the therapist's utilization of such information in bringing about therapeutic change for the patient.

It is my hope that, after reading this chapter, the reader will come away with the conclusion that I do indeed have some talents in understanding and utilizing psychoanalytic techniques and that this will lend greater credibility to my criticisms for those who are dubious about my areas of disagreement with the traditional psychoanalytic model, both as a theory and as a treatment modality.

SEVEN

The Home Video
Cassette Recorder

In 1786, in his poem *To a Louse*, Robert Burns wrote:

> Oh wad some power the giftie gie (give) us
> To see oursels as others see us!
> It wad frae (from) monie (many) a blunder free us
>   An' foolish notion.

We can only wonder whether Robert Burns would have guessed that in less than 200 years his wish would be realized. The "power" is SONY, Panasonic, and other manufacturers. The gift (not so small) they have given us is the home video cassette recorder (VCR), which enables us "to see oursels as others see us." And, when used in psychotherapy, it can contribute in a unique way to freeing our patients from the "blunders" and "foolish notions" that cause and perpetuate their psychopathology. I have been using the video recorder in my office since 1970. For the first eleven years I used a somewhat bulky, allegedly portable, SONY reel-to-reel videotape recorder. It allowed playback in my office, but my patients did not have equipment that enabled them to review the tape at home. Since 1981 I have used the standard home video cassette recorder (VHS, the more common size) in such a way that two tapes can be made simultaneously (one VCR connected to another). Patients bring their tapes to the office; two tapes are made simultaneously, and the patients take their tapes home to use as desired. On the basis of these experiences I am convinced that the home video cassette recorder has the potential to be a powerful psychotherapeutic tool.

One of the most important goals of the psychotherapeutic process is that of enabling patients to gain a clearer view of themselves. Whether the new information comes from within (the unconscious) or from without (the therapist, other patients in group therapy, other family members in family therapy), the ultimate aim is enhanced self-awareness. Our primary mode of therapeutic communication, however, is verbal. Our patients (especially children) call us "talking doctors," and psychotherapy is sometimes referred to as "talk therapy." Our gestures may provide some visual communication, but the patient's visual observation is of another person (the therapist), not of himself or herself. It would be an extremely rare situation in which a therapist would provide a patient with direct visual observation of himself or herself by, for example, placing a mirror in front of the patient. The videotape provides the patient with an opportunity for such visual observation. In traditional psychotherapy the therapist's communications are designed to help patients form a more accurate mental picture (sometimes visual) of themselves. The capacity of the patient to distort such communications is enormous. And therapists' accuracy when providing such feedback is certainly compromised, at times, by their own biases, "blind spots," and counter-transferential reactions. The videotape provides patients with self-confrontations that are essentially free from distortion. It does not misrepresent. It does not deceive. It does not miss a thing: Every word, every intonation, every gesture, every movement is captured. It is not selective. It has no guilt that suppresses and represses. It has no fears of what may be revealed—fears that bring into operation a wide variety of defense mechanisms and symptoms. Our narcissism draws us to it. And children, especially, are attracted to it because of the ubiquity of this medium in their lives. Although the VCR's inventors were probably not thinking about psychotherapists when they developed the instrument, they have provided us with an extremely powerful therapeutic modality.

TECHNICAL CONSIDERATIONS

The camera is mounted on a permanent bracket in one corner of my consultation room, and the child and I sit at the play table at the opposite end of the room. Below the camera, on a table, are two video cassette recorders. One records the original tape and the second makes the copy. Because of the inevitable decline in quality that one gets with each successive generation of copies, I have found it useful to use an instrument that is referred to as an *enhancer*. This is connected between the original and copying machines and reduces the degradation of the visual image. Also connected to the video cassette recorder is a television monitor to ensure that all are seated properly in the camera's view. The monitor also provides subsequent playback that may be desired or warranted. The more recent and better model cameras automatically focus on the subjects and adjust to the lighting in the room. At this point I have found that halogen lamps provide the best lighting. I have two, which point toward the ceiling on each side of the room. The light then reflects onto the participants, bathing them in light that is bright enough to provide excellent tapes, but not so bright as to produce eye discomfort. Last, I have two microphones joined by a Y connector into the audio input of the master video cassette recorder. One microphone is placed on the play table, and the other off to the side for use by other parties who may be involved in the session. I would not recommend that the powerful omni-directional microphone on the camera be used because it is likely to pick up extraneous sounds such as traffic and loud voices in adjacent rooms.

At 1990 prices one should be able to purchase all of the aforementioned equipment (plus connecting wires) for about $2,000-$2,500. This price may initially appear quite high; yet, these are the lowest prices ever. For therapeutic purposes one need not purchase a video cassette recorder with many complex functions such as daily fourteen-day recording capacity. All one needs is a basic instrument for simple recording and playback. I am convinced that therapists who go to the expense of purchasing such equipment and the trouble of installing it will ultimately conclude that it was one of the best investments of their professional careers.

In the course of my psychotherapeutic work with children, I engage parents (especially mothers) to a significant degree. I generally refer to my approach as *individual child psychotherapy with parental observation and intermittent participation* (Gardner 1975, 1986a). Accordingly, when the mother and child arrive, the mother brings the child's videotape (which is placed in the copy machine) and my own is then placed in the machine recording on the original tape. The ten to twelve steps necessary for turning everything on generally take about 1-2 minutes—after one has become familiar with the procedure. When conducting child psychotherapy without the video cassette recorders, I generally sit face to face with my patients. When positioned in front of the camera, we do not sit face to face; rather, the chairs are positioned halfway between frontal and lateral camera views. Accordingly, we are free to look directly at each other, turn our heads toward the camera, reposition our bodies, and so forth. The child's mother usually sits off to the side, in front of the second microphone. However, on occasion she may join us in view of the camera if this is therapeutically warranted. Although the monitor is initially turned on to ensure that we are positioned properly in front of the camera's field, I generally turn off the monitor during the actual recording because of its potential distraction. My experience has been that the presence of the video equipment has not interfered with my patients' freedom to speak or to involve themselves unselfconsciously in the treatment. Although some may have transient initial hesitation, most quickly involve themselves in the work at hand.

The reader may have been wondering why I make two tapes instead of one. I usually save only a small fraction of the tapes that I make for myself. I use these, with patients' permission, for teaching purposes. I assure the patients that I will take every reasonable step to ensure their confidentiality. With regard to the patients' copies, I advise them to save their tapes for a few weeks, if not longer. One reason for making this recommendation is that it will enable us to look at a segment of a past tape if warranted. I impress upon both the child and parent the importance of viewing each tape soon after the session during which it has been made. This is the optimum time for therapeutic utilization. The efficacy of such use of tapes is markedly reduced if the parents allow them to "stack up" and then try to "catch up" by reviewing a series in quick succession.

BENEFITS TO THE PATIENT WITHIN THE SESSION

When compared to the benefits derived *after* the session, the benefits of using the video cassette recorder *during* the session are small. However, there are situations, admittedly infrequent, when the videotape proves useful in the course of a meeting. For example, a patient and I may have a difference of opinion regarding what was said at an earlier point in the session. As every therapist knows, patients distort significantly—especially in areas relating to their psychopathology. At times, the patient will agree that he or she did distort and/or misinterpret what the therapist said. At such times an inquiry into the reasons for the distortion may prove useful. Of course, such inquiry is much more likely to take place in the treatment of adults than it is in child therapy. In the situation in which the patient denies that any distortion has taken place—and insists that he or she recollects more clearly than the therapist what was said— most therapists agree that little therapeutic benefit can be derived from such an impasse. It would be antitherapeutic to get into an argument with the patient over whose memory is correct. A patient cannot analyze meaningfully a distortion without first having the conviction that the distortion did indeed take place.

Accordingly, before the days when I used a video cassette recorder, I would generally say something like this to the patient: "It's clear that you and I have very different opinions regarding what was said. We've gone around two or three times trying to refresh each other's memory and we're each firmly of the belief that our own rendition is the correct one. I think the best thing to do at this point is to go on to something else, and hope that future experiences will shed light on this point." Although such a comment is more likely to take place in the treatment of adults, I have certainly spoken in this way to children, especially older ones. However, since using the video cassette recorder, I am able to say, "Let's get the tape's opinion regarding what was said." We then roll back the tape to the specific point, and the difference of opinion is usually resolved instantaneously. If there are numerous such disagreements in the treatment, and if the video cassette tape's opinion most often favors the patient, then the question must be raised about the therapist's unhealthy counter-transferential reactions.

And now to a benefit related to Robert Burns's wish. Sometimes, during the course of a session, I will point out to patients that although they were saying one thing, their gestures and facial expressions were communicating an entirely different message. Or, I may just confront patients with certain gestures and/or expressions, which they may not have been aware of, and that are of importance to our interchanges. The patient may accept my statement and then we can discuss it meaningfully. However, there are situations in which the patient denies that any such gestures or expressions manifested themselves. In such cases, there is no need for an argument or a decision to shelve the issue. We can go to the video cassette recorder and see what its "opinion" is of my perception. Its opinion is generally quite convincing.

BENEFITS TO THE PATIENT BETWEEN SESSIONS

Patients Viewing Tapes Alone

As mentioned, the benefits to be derived from videotape observation within sessions are small (in quantity but not necessarily in quality) compared to those derived from viewing tapes *between* sessions. In this section I will confine myself to the patients' reviewing the tapes alone. In the next section I will discuss the use of the tapes with and by third parties.

Many patients basically view the therapeutic process as one in which they will "check in" X number of times a week for Y number of months or years and then, at the end of the treatment, will enjoy alleviation and even cure of their problems. Although advised by the therapist that this is not the way it works, and although told that therapy involves an implementation in life—outside the consultation room—of what has been learned in the office, most patients (especially children) still operate in accordance with the aforementioned view of the procedure. When discussing the therapeutic process with patients and parents, I have often used the analogy of a course in which there is a lecture and a laboratory section. The therapeutic sessions are like the lectures, and life beyond the confines of the consultation room is analogous to the laboratory. Both together are necessary if one is to truly learn the lessons of treatment. Watching a videotape of the session, between sessions, provides the patient and parents with an experience—outside of the consultation room—that is likely to bring to mind the therapeutic messages to and increase involvement in the treatment. It is like a psychotherapeutic booster shot.

Review of the tape between sessions also provides the patient with the opportunity for reiteration. All therapists know that patients do not get better after being told something once. The same messages may have to be transmitted dozens of times, and even then the message may not sink in. And this is even more the case for child patients—as every parent and teacher well knows. I recall many years ago seeing a cartoon in which a patient is lying on a couch and the analyst, sitting behind, is hammering the patient on the head with a mallet. The caption: "Well, maybe *that* will help you remember what I've said." The video cassette recorder provides the patient with an opportunity for reiteration of the therapist's messages with no extra cost to the patient. In fact, the patient does not even have to travel to the therapist's office to derive this therapeutic benefit; one can repeat the session in one's own home. It is *really* free therapy. When I do save a tape for teaching purposes, I have found that it takes five to ten showings to students and conference participants before I myself am convinced that I have extracted as much as I could from the therapeutic interchanges. And this relates to things I learn not only about the patient, but about myself as well.

All therapists have had the experience of a patient's coming in quite upset and saying something along these lines: "You ruined my weekend. That was a terrible thing you said to me last Thursday. I had trouble sleeping for three nights. You can't imagine how upset I was." Then, when the patient tells the therapist what was said, the therapist may be convinced with 100 percent certainty that just the opposite was said and the patient had completely misinterpreted the remarks. Under such circumstances I will often say: "If you had called me up Thursday and said to me on the phone, 'Tell me, yes or no, did you say this?' and I responded, 'No, I did *not* say that,' would you then have had a better weekend? Could just one word have made the difference?" Usually, the patient will respond in the affirmative. I will then ask why he or she did not make such a call. Aside from the psychoanalytic significance of the failure to make the call, I get in the message that knowledge is power, and the more information one has about a situation, the greater the likelihood one is going to be able to deal with it. I try to impress upon the patient that for many conflicts and crises in life, getting vital information about an important aspect may decompress significantly strong emotional reactions and even prevent a variety of painful feelings like fear, anger, and grief. Sometimes only *one* word, or one fact, can accomplish this. Although children in treatment are much less likely to have such experiences, the parent who brings them may very well have. Having a videotape available may save the person the telephone call or the time expended in making contact with the therapist if he or she is not available. More importantly, if there is still some question in the patient's mind about what the therapist really said, the videotape leaves no doubt.

It is in the viewing between sessions that patients have the greatest opportunity to avail themselves of the benefits of Robert Burns's "giftie" of "seeing oursels as others see us." In the privacy of their homes, when relaxed and alone, they can scrutinize the videotape and look carefully at themselves over the course of the session. For many patients it is far more interesting than their favorite television program. In the session my confrontations and observations relate to what *I* am observing about them. With the video cassette recording *they* are seeing themselves. They (not I) are seeing themselves. It is not *my* opinion about what is being observed, but rather their own opinions about what they are observing. Because the observer is observing himself or herself, self-awareness becomes enhanced immeasurably. Conviction, then, for the accuracy and validity of the observations becomes enhanced formidably. Many patients have said to me that they had heard me say something about themselves previously, but that they never really believed me until they saw the videotapes. It is much harder to deny ego-alien personality traits when one is confronted with them on the television set. And this is one of the most important benefits to be derived from the use of video cassette tapes in psychotherapy.

It would be an error to conclude that all my child (and even adult) patients enthusiastically and predictably watch every tape between sessions. The same resistances that manifest themselves in other aspects of therapy are likely to occur with the videotape. Parents "forget" to bring the tape and they "forget" to remind the child to watch it between sessions. Nor is it reasonable to expect the child to remember to remind the parent to bring the tape and subsequently view it. Were the person who forgets the tape an adult in psychoanalysis, the forgetting would generally be used as a point of departure for analytic inquiry. Because children are not particularly receptive (nor even cognitively capable in most cases) of such inquiry, and because their parents (not being psychoanalytic patients) are not oriented toward such investigations either, I generally just remind the parent to bring the tape next time and emphasize the importance of doing so. However, these comments notwithstanding, most parents do remember to bring the tapes every session because of their recognition of their importance. My experience has been that just about all parents—after a few sessions of reviewing the tapes—develop deep conviction for their value in the treatment of their child.

Some children will become engrossed in the tapes after prodding or encouragement by parents. In spite of initial reluctance, they get drawn in and involved. Sometimes viewing the tape is like a homework assignment, which must be done before the child is permitted to engage in more pleasurable activities. There are children, however, who will "get hooked" into the tape of the session (even though they had to be prodded) and will gain the benefits to be derived from such viewing. And there is an occasional child who looks forward to reviewing the tapes because of the appreciation, at some level, that they are extremely useful. Often, these are children who are suffering psychological pain and have insight into the fact that they have psychological difficulties. One 4-year-old sexually abused child was in treatment for his reactions to the abuse. In the course of his play I was able to introduce a number of coping mechanisms, for example calling for assistance from a parent or teacher when a "bad man" would approach him, flight, locking the doors, and saying "No." The mother described the child as asking her to let him see the videotapes between sessions. He would then become deeply absorbed in viewing them. The mother was quite convinced (as was I) that the child improved much more rapidly because of the opportunity to repeatedly view the tapes.

It is important for the reader to appreciate that when I use the term *psychotherapeutic messages* here, I am using the term in its broadest context. I am referring to a continuum at one end of which are messages that are directly understood by the child because they are readily accepted into conscious awareness. At the other end are messages transmitted symbolically or metaphorically because the child is too anxious or guilty to consciously accept them undisguised. Messages in the former category are often transmitted via the utilization of such games as The Talking, Feeling, and Doing Game (1973a,

1983b, 1986d). Messages in the latter category are communicated by such vehicles as the mutual storytelling technique and its derivative games, especially The Storytelling Card Game (1988a).

Patients Viewing Tapes with Third Parties

One cannot discuss the issue of showing the tapes to third parties without first commenting on confidentiality. As mentioned, I generally work closely with the parents of my child patients. Because mothers are more frequently available than fathers, they are the ones who most often bring the child to therapy. However, fathers have a carte blanche invitation to come to the session whenever they are available, with or without the mother. As described in detail elsewhere (Gardner 1986a), I do not automatically include the accompanying parent throughout the whole course of every session. I do, however, involve them actively and only suggest they sit in the waiting room under very specific (and admittedly unusual) circumstances, when their presence would be therapeutically contraindicated. I believe that child therapists make too much of the confidentiality issue. I am not in agreement that one needs to be alone with the child in order to improve the psychotherapeutic relationship. A relationship is based on the nature of the human beings involved in it, their personality characteristics, and how they treat each other. Third parties in the room do not necessarily inhibit the creation of a good relationship; in fact, with children, the parent's presence can often enhance its development. The more involvement the parent has with the therapist, the greater the likelihood there will be a good relationship with him or her, and the greater the likelihood that the parent will support the child's involvement. Furthermore, what is there in the life of a very young child that is not known to the parents? When a child asks a therapist not to reveal what is said to a parent, the request is most often (but certainly not always) inappropriate and maladaptive. Usually withholding the "secret" is in the service of the child's resistance maneuvers and can compromise the parent-child relationship. Parents serve well as assistant therapists. Keeping secrets from them lessens their efficacy in this role. In short, I generally conduct therapy with children in such a way that I want "everything to be out on the table" and react with suspicion when anybody tries to keep secrets from others.

Many forms of psychopathology are related to skeletons kept in the closet and Pandora's boxes that remain locked. Therapy involves opening these closets and boxes and revealing to others (especially family members and those with whom our patients are intimately involved) things that should justifiably be discussed (within reasonable and civilized limits). The parents know the child better than the therapist, his or her special education notwithstanding. Accordingly, they can be of great value for explaining and interpreting what the child is doing or saying in the course of the treatment. They have been direct observers to what the child describes and may correct the inevitable distortions that children bring to the process. Their working with the therapist enhances their commitment to the treatment and, by extension, enhances the child's involvement as well. Parents usually feel guilty about a child's needing therapy because of their participation (overt or covert, conscious or unconscious) in the development of the child's symptoms. Such guilt can be assuaged by the parents' active involvement in the process designed to reduce the child's problems about which they feel guilty. Strict adherence to the confidentiality principle can work against these important goals of treatment. Watching videotapes at home with parents serves all of these therapeutic goals—goals that would be undermined and even made impossible by strict adherence to the confidentiality principle.

Prior to my use of videotapes in therapy I most often encouraged my patients (regardless of age) to discuss any and all aspects of their therapy with others—to the degree that they wished. I generally suggested that they err on the side of divulging too much, but did not go so far as to recommend that *everything* be revealed. Videotapes allow for an even more effective utilization of these principles. I advise my adult patients that the tape is theirs and they are free to use it in any way they wish. However, I also advise them that it would serve well the goals of their treatment if they were to show those parts of the tapes that they believed might prove useful and productive in improving difficult and even pathological relationships. Patients are free to select and delete any parts they wish, but they are also encouraged to reveal to a significant degree. With child patients I merely tell the parents that the tapes should be routinely reviewed at home by the child and any other family members who wish to participate. I present this in a matter-of-fact way with the implication that this is a normal part of the therapeutic process. If the child were to say that he or she does not wish the tape to be shown to others, I inquire into the reasons. Generally (but not always) the request is inappropriate. In fact one usually finds some psychological problem contributing to the child's reluctance for a particular person (or persons) to view the tape. If the child has a justifiable reason for not allowing a certain family member to see the tape, I will look into this issue to see what problem there is that results in such a situation. And such inquiry is generally grist for the therapeutic mill.

I want the tape to serve as a point of departure for family discussions. The videotape brings the patient's family more closely and directly into the therapy. It gives them the opportunity to benefit (admittedly in a small way) from comments the therapist makes. Again, we see here another example of "free therapy," this time for family members who are not formally designated as "patients." All therapists have had the experience of patients saying to them that a friend or relative has asked, "What did your doctor say about me?" With the videotape that question can be answered in the optimum way. In child therapy, fathers frequently ask what has gone on in the session, or wonder what the therapist has been saying lately about them. To such an inquiry the mother can now say, "If you want to know the answer to that, why don't you just look at the tape." On a number of occasions fathers have commented, "It's good to see what I'm paying for." At times, during the course of a session in which I am working with the child and mother, I may actually address myself to the father and provide him with an important message. I will advise the mother and child to tell the father that a specific communication directed toward him is on the tape. A typical message might begin: "Mr. Jones, I hope you will be viewing this tape. I hope, also, that you will see fit to come here more often. As I mentioned to you at the outset, the more involvement I have on the part of both parents, the greater the likelihood I will be able to be helpful to your daughter. I think the punishments you've been meting out to Gloria are much too punitive. The argument that that's the way your father treated you is not, in my opinion, justification for what I consider to be excessively stringent punishments. What you're doing is working against the goals of treatment, and I hope you can ease up. Again, I'll be happy to discuss this with you further, and I hope you'll come in to one of our sessions very soon. I'll be happy to rearrange the schedule if this will be helpful."

When children communicate to third parties what has gone on in the therapeutic sessions, there are often distortions, exaggerations, and misinterpretations. Third parties now have an opportunity for direct knowledge about what has gone on in the session. Such viewing may enable those who have been reluctant to become involved in the therapeutic process, either with the therapist who makes the tape or with someone else, to do so. It gives them a glimpse of what goes on and may serve to reduce initial reluctance and hesitation.

TREATMENT OF ADOLESCENTS

Although I recognize the importance of confidentiality in adolescent therapy—especially for the development of the youngster's sense of autonomy—I still encourage a significant degree of open communication between the patient, parents, and therapist (Gardner 1988a). Videotapes serve well to facilitate such free flow of communication without restricting the youngster's freedom to dub out and/or restrict others from viewing his (her) tapes or segments of them.

An adolescent boy was referred for treatment because he had sexually molested a 3-year-old girl. Specifically, he had fondled her genitals on a few occasions. In interview I learned that the boy was very repressed sexually and believed that masturbation was not only sinful but might result in a variety of diseases such as syphilis and AIDS. He also had a very puritanical attitude about pornography, pin-up pictures, and R-rated movies in which explicit sexual encounters were portrayed. Not surprisingly, he was adamantly against premarital sex and planned to be a virgin when he got married. He even believed that sexual play of any kind was sinful and inevitably resulted in various kinds of sexually transmitted diseases. I considered his sexual inhibitions to be playing a role (certainly not the only cause) in his molestation of the girl. His pent-up sexual urges could not find release with a partner who might divulge his engaging in a sinful activity. A 3-year-old child, he reasoned, would be much less likely to reveal his transgression. In my work with him I attempted to correct his distortions about sex. In addition, I tried to reduce his guilt about masturbation and encouraged his involvement with girlfriends. My hope was that changing his opinions and reducing his guilt in the sexual area would facilitate sexual release (through masturbation and sexual activities with girlfriends) and would thereby lessen the likelihood that he would turn to 3-year-olds for sexual release. This boy was an enthusiastic reviewer of his videotapes, listened to them intently, and I believe progressed more rapidly in his development of a healthier attitude toward sex than he would have without the tapes.

I treated another adolescent boy who molested a 6-year-old girl about six months prior to my initial session. His parents were divorced and he lived with his mother and stepfather. His father was remarried to a woman with two teenage daughters. Upon the disclosure of the sex abuse, his stepmother absolutely refused to allow the boy into her house because she feared that he would rape her daughters. She viewed him as an impulsive sexual psychopath with strong criminal tendencies who would, if given the opportunity, rape any woman in sight regardless of age. And, from what I could learn from his father and stepmother, the teenage daughters were living in morbid fear that he might break into the house and attack them in the middle of the night. With the patient's permission, the father showed a few of his taped sessions to the stepmother and her daughters. On the basis of what they saw, their fears of him were reduced dramatically. And it was not simply what was said that changed their opinion. I believe that his gestures, intonations, and his general personality confirmed that he was basically a nonviolent and nonthreatening person. In the course of these sessions with the patient, we discussed the likelihood of recurrence and I—as well as they—became convinced that it was extremely small. After a few such viewings, the stepmother and stepdaughters agreed to a joint session with the patient and his father. They then had further experiences with the patient that helped correct their distortions about him. We then went on to the next step of short visits, which ultimately resulted in longer visits and finally rapprochement. Although other factors were certainly operative in the stepmother's rejection of the boy, I believe that the videotapes served as an important catalyst to the family reunion; had they not been available, reconciliation might not have taken place.

IMPLICATIONS FOR THE THERAPIST'S EFFICACY

Those sessions in which the patient and I are being videotaped are more efficient and effective than those conducted without the camera lens focusing on us. Although I may find myself involved in the therapeutic interchanges and not distracted by the camera, this does not mean that I am completely oblivious to its presence. In the back of my mind I am continually aware that I am "being watched" and that others will be able to scrutinize what I am doing. I believe that this has been an important factor in enhancing my therapeutic efficiency during videotaped sessions. No therapist can claim 100 percent concentration on every one of our patients' statements, intonations, and gestures. All of us have our lapses and our distractions. When videotaping I sit up straighter in my seat and am more attentive.

Videotaping sessions has also helped me improve my technical skills. As mentioned, it generally takes many reviews of a session before I have extracted as much as possible from what has transpired. The reader should appreciate here that I do not routinely review my patients' videotapes. I only review selected ones for special purposes such as teaching. During this review process I often learn things about myself that I was not aware of. Sometimes, I will realize that I should have taken another approach to a patient's comments. Sometimes I will see and hear things I did not recognize at the time of the session. Even the most astute therapist does not appreciate the significance of every one of the patient's words and does not observe accurately every gesture. The videotape enables us to catch these errors and omissions, and it enhances our sensitivity to these subtleties. And those who, like myself, use videotapes for teaching purposes will inevitably find that students and conference participants will teach the therapist things about himself or herself that were not previously understood. In short, it can help us learn from those whom we are teaching.

THE DRAWBACKS AND RISKS OF USING VIDEO CASSETTE TAPES

Like all therapeutic instruments, video cassette tapes are not without their drawbacks and risks. As mentioned, when making a videotape recording it is often difficult to sit face to face with a patient. If one were to try to make video cassette tapes that would accurately portray face-to-face therapy, one would probably need two or three cameras, used simultaneously (with a split screen view) and/or used in alternation. If this were done in a situation in which all three cameras were mounted, there would be the technical problem of switching the cameras. Obviously, this would compromise the treatment. If one brought in a technician to switch the cameras or to move them from position to position, it would be an even greater compromise. It is unreasonable to expect any patient to provide the kinds of revelations necessary to effective therapy if a technician is in the room throughout the course of all of the sessions. I do not believe that the lack of face-to-face confrontation has significant drawbacks in my work. The patients and I still frequently look directly at each other, but our usual position is slightly sideways. On occasion, I will miss a gesture that was not in my direct view. This is especially the case when treating children. However, mothers are often in the room and will sometimes bring to my attention what I may miss.

There is always the risk that the tape may fall into the hands of those who might use it detrimentally against the patient. For example, a husband who is involved in divorce litigation might find statements made by his wife in the course of his child's treatment to be a particularly useful weapon in this conflict. Obviously, parents must take responsibility for the tapes and not place them in situations in which they might be so utilized. Parents are still free to delete material that might be so used against them. A person who forgets to take such precautions is likely to be doing so because of pathological reasons and such forgetfulness could be "grist for the psychotherapeutic mill."

Another drawback of videotapes is that they are very time consuming to review. Although a 50-minute session may take 50 minutes to watch, it can consume many hours if the therapist is going to stop and study, repeat, and discuss the session in detail. If parents do this with their children and other family members, it can be therapeutically beneficial.

ADDITIONAL USES OF VIDEOTAPES IN CHILD PSYCHIATRY

Teaching

I have found videotapes made during my sessions with patients to be useful in other ways, not directly related to therapy. They are extremely valuable teaching instruments. The students can see exactly what the teacher does. I believe that many who feel uncomfortable with making such tapes recognize, or at least think, that they don't have very much to teach and that those who could see them "in action" would be critical. In every other branch of medicine, students and residents have direct opportunity to observe their teachers at work. It is only in the specialty of psychiatry that students are generally deprived of this opportunity. Videotapes make this possible for trainees.

As mentioned, I do not routinely save every videotape. When I am making a tape that I suspect I will want to keep, I generally take a few notes during the session, at least on key points. Then, after the session, I write a quick summary of the main elements in the session. This material is kept in the patient's file and a copy is placed in the proper teaching file, for example, dream analysis, work with parents, the mutual storytelling technique, psychotherapy with adolescents, treating resistant children, and separation anxiety disorder. Obviously, I get permission from adult patients and the parents of child patients before utilizing a tape at a conference. Recently, conference organizers have requested permission to make videotapes of my presentations, including the videotaped material that I present. I grant such permission with the proviso that those videotaping the conference not point the lens on my videotape presentation but only on me. In this way I protect patients from visual reproduction of the tape and the risk of its improper utilization.

Supervision

I have also advised supervisees, who come to my office for private supervision, to videotape their sessions with me. They too have found this extremely useful. They listen to the tapes between supervisory sessions and avail themselves of the benefits to be gained from reiteration of my comments. They have repeatedly told me that this enhances the efficacy of the supervision experience. Some have shown the videotapes to their colleagues, providing them with "free" supervision. The videotape, then, enhances the efficacy of the supervisory process. Previously supervision was very much a private experience, confined solely to the two people directly involved. With the videotape, the experience and knowledge of the supervisor can reach a larger audience in a very effective way.

Sex-abuse Evaluations

I have also found videotapes extremely valuable in sex-abuse evaluations. They are especially useful when one is trying to differentiate between genuine and fabricated sex-abuse allegations. As discussed in detail elsewhere (Gardner 1987), in recent years we have witnessed a rise in bona fide sex abuse as well as fabricated allegations of sex abuse (especially in the context of custody litigation [Gardner 1986b, 1989]). The proper differentiation between these two forms of sex-abuse allegations is crucial in order to ensure that bona fide sex abusers are properly dealt with and those who have been falsely accused are exonerated. One differentiating criterion relates to the change over time of the child's rendition of the alleged sex abuse. Children who have been genuinely abused are likely to tell the same story to repeated examiners. Those who fabricate, not having actual experience to recall, are likely to change their stories with repeated tellings. Videotapes provide the best evidence for whether the story changes. And this is especially impressive in the courtroom when the series of renditions are shown on videotape. Up until recently, courts were quite hesitant to allow such tapes as evidence, with various legal reasons being given for discouraging their use. At this point the questions of legality and even constitutionality are still under consideration.

CONCLUSIONS

I consider video cassette tapes to have the potential for providing formidable contributions to the psychotherapeutic process. In fact, I consider videotaping sessions to be the most valuable psychotherapeutic modality I have used since entering the field over thirty years ago. I have described here the therapeutic benefits I have observed and derived up to this point from using video cassette tapes in child psychotherapy. I am certain that there are readers who have found other uses for videotapes in treatment, and that other therapeutic benefits of videotapes will be found in the future. It is my hope that therapists will consider utilizing videotape equipment and will come to appreciate that the pains and discomforts associated with the financial sacrifice necessary to install such equipment will be more than compensated for by the benefits to be derived for both themselves and their patients. Last, therapists do well to appreciate that video cassette tapes have the potential of providing us with our best advertisements at a time when psychotherapy (especially psychoanalytically oriented psychotherapy) is not enjoying the prestige it had in the past. Most therapists in private practice agree that their best sources of referral are patients who are pleased with the outcome of their treatment. When patients' families tell their friends and relatives about the psychiatrist who makes videotapes, this is likely to enhance his or her attractiveness to other families because of their appreciation of their value in the therapeutic process.

References

Aichorn, A. (1925). *Wayward Youth*. New York: World Publishing, 1954.

Alexander, F. (1950). Analysis of the therapeutic factors in psychoanalytic treatment. *Psychoanalytic Quarterly* 19:482–500.

Alexander, F., and French, T. (1946). The principle of corrective emotional experience. In *Psychoanalytic Therapy: Principles and Application*, pp. 66–70. New York: Ronald.

Allen, F. H. (1942). *Psychotherapy with Children*. New York: W. W. Norton.

Axline, V. M. (1947). *Play Therapy*. Boston: Houghton Mifflin.

――― (1964). *Dibs in Search of Self*. Boston: Houghton Mifflin.

Baldock, E. C. (1974). *The Therapeutic Relationship and Its Ramifications in Child Psychotherapy*. San Jose, CA: The Family Service Association of Santa Clara County Monograph.

Bender, L. (1952). *Child Psychiatric Techniques*. Springfield, IL: Charles C Thomas.

Buck, J. N. (1948). The H-T-P technique: a qualitative and quantitative scoring manual. *Journal of Clinical Psychology* 4:317–396.

Burns, R. C., and Kaufman, S. H. (1970). *Kinetic Family Drawings*. New York: Brunner/Mazel.

Conn, J. H. (1941a). The timid, dependent child. *Journal of Pediatrics* 19:1–2.

――― (1941b). The treatment of fearful children. *American Journal of Orthopsychiatry* 11:744–751.

322

—— (1948). The play-interview as an investigative and therapeutic procedure. *The Nervous Child* 7:257–286.

—— (1954). Play interview therapy of castration fears. *American Journal of Orthopsychiatry* 25:747–754.

Dickens, C. (1850). *The Personal History of David Copperfield.* New York: Dodd, Mead, 1943.

Dunn, L. M. (1965). *Peabody Picture Vocabulary Test.* Circle Pines, MN: American Guidance Service.

Dunn, L. M., and Dunn, L. M. (1981). *Peabody Picture Vocabulary Test—Revised.* Circle Pines, MN: American Guidance Service.

Elkisch, P. (1960). Free art expression. In *Projective Techniques in Children,* ed. A. I. Rabin and M. R. Haworth, pp. 273–288. New York: Grune & Stratton.

Ellis, A. (1963). *Reason and Emotion in Psychotherapy.* New York: Lyle Stuart.

Erikson, E. H. (1950). *Childhood and Society.* New York: W. W. Norton.

Freud, A. (1946). *The Psychoanalytical Treatment of Children.* London: Imago.

—— (1965). *Normality and Pathology in Childhood.* New York: International Universities Press.

Freud, S. (1900). The interpretation of dreams. In *The Basic Writings of Sigmund Freud,* ed. A. A. Brill, pp. 183–549. New York: Random House (The Modern Library), 1938.

—— (1908). The relation of the poet to daydreaming. In *Collected Papers,* vol. 4, pp. 173–183. New York: Basic Books, 1959.

—— (1909). A phobia in a five-year-old boy. In *Collected Papers,* vol. 3, pp. 149–209. New York: Basic Books, 1959.

Freud S., and Breuer, J. (1895). *Studies in Hysteria.* New York: Basic Books, 1957.

Gardner, R. A. (1968a). The mutual storytelling technique: use in alleviating childhood oedipal problems. *Contemporary Psychoanalysis* 4:161–177.

—— (1968b). Book Review, Ginnot, H. G. (1965). *Between Parent and Child.* New York: Macmillan. Reviewed in *Psychology Today* 1:15–17.

—— (1969). The game of checkers as a diagnostic and therapeutic tool in child psychotherapy. *Acta Paedopsychiatrica* 36:142–152.

—— (1970). *The Boys and Girls Book About Divorce.* New York: Jason Aronson.

—— (1971a). *Therapeutic Communication with Children: The Mutual Storytelling Technique.* Northvale, NJ: Jason Aronson.

—— (1971b). *The Boys and Girls Book About Divorce* (Paperback edi-

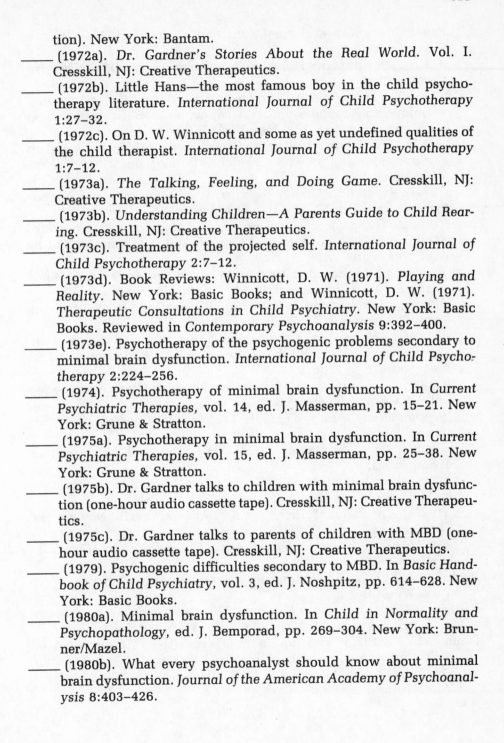

tion). New York: Bantam.

_____ (1972a). *Dr. Gardner's Stories About the Real World.* Vol. I. Cresskill, NJ: Creative Therapeutics.

_____ (1972b). Little Hans—the most famous boy in the child psychotherapy literature. *International Journal of Child Psychotherapy* 1:27–32.

_____ (1972c). On D. W. Winnicott and some as yet undefined qualities of the child therapist. *International Journal of Child Psychotherapy* 1:7–12.

_____ (1973a). *The Talking, Feeling, and Doing Game.* Cresskill, NJ: Creative Therapeutics.

_____ (1973b). *Understanding Children—A Parents Guide to Child Rearing.* Cresskill, NJ: Creative Therapeutics.

_____ (1973c). Treatment of the projected self. *International Journal of Child Psychotherapy* 2:7–12.

_____ (1973d). Book Reviews: Winnicott, D. W. (1971). *Playing and Reality.* New York: Basic Books; and Winnicott, D. W. (1971). *Therapeutic Consultations in Child Psychiatry.* New York: Basic Books. Reviewed in *Contemporary Psychoanalysis* 9:392–400.

_____ (1973e). Psychotherapy of the psychogenic problems secondary to minimal brain dysfunction. *International Journal of Child Psychotherapy* 2:224–256.

_____ (1974). Psychotherapy of minimal brain dysfunction. In *Current Psychiatric Therapies,* vol. 14, ed. J. Masserman, pp. 15–21. New York: Grune & Stratton.

_____ (1975a). Psychotherapy in minimal brain dysfunction. In *Current Psychiatric Therapies,* vol. 15, ed. J. Masserman, pp. 25–38. New York: Grune & Stratton.

_____ (1975b). Dr. Gardner talks to children with minimal brain dysfunction (one-hour audio cassette tape). Cresskill, NJ: Creative Therapeutics.

_____ (1975c). Dr. Gardner talks to parents of children with MBD (one-hour audio cassette tape). Cresskill, NJ: Creative Therapeutics.

_____ (1979). Psychogenic difficulties secondary to MBD. In *Basic Handbook of Child Psychiatry,* vol. 3, ed. J. Noshpitz, pp. 614–628. New York: Basic Books.

_____ (1980a). Minimal brain dysfunction. In *Child in Normality and Psychopathology,* ed. J. Bemporad, pp. 269–304. New York: Brunner/Mazel.

_____ (1980b). What every psychoanalyst should know about minimal brain dysfunction. *Journal of the American Academy of Psychoanalysis* 8:403–426.

—— (1980c). *Dorothy and the Lizard of Oz.* Cresskill, NJ: Creative Therapeutics.

—— (1981). *Dr. Gardner's Fables for Our Times.* Cresskill, NJ: Creative Therapeutics.

—— (1983a). Treating oedipal problems with the mutual storytelling technique. In *Handbook of Play Therapy,* ed. C. E. Schaefer and K. J. O'Connor, pp. 355–368. New York: Wiley.

—— (1983b). The talking, feeling, and doing game. In *Handbook of Play Therapy,* ed. C. E. Schaefer and K. J. O'Connor, pp. 259–273. New York: Wiley.

—— (1984). *Separation Anxiety Disorder: Psychodynamics and Psychotherapy.* Cresskill, NJ: Creative Therapeutics.

—— (1986a). The game of checkers in child therapy. In *Game Play: Therapeutic Uses of Childhood Games,* ed. C. E. Schaefer and S. Reid. New York: Wiley.

—— (1986b). *Child Custody Litigation: A Guide for Parents and Mental Health Professionals.* Cresskill, NJ: Creative Therapeutics.

—— (1986c). Child custody. In *Basic Handbook of Child Psychiatry,* vol. 5, ed. J. Noshpitz. New York: Basic Books.

—— (1986d). The talking, feeling, and doing game. In *Game Play: Therapeutic Uses of Childhood Games,* ed. C. E. Schaefer and S. Reid. New York: Wiley.

—— (1987). *Psychotherapy of Psychogenic Learning Disabilities.* Cresskill, NJ: Creative Therapeutics.

—— *Psychotherapy with Adolescents.* Cresskill, NJ: Creative Therapeutics.

—— (1988a). *The Storytelling Card Game.* Cresskill, NJ: Creative Therapeutics.

—— (1989). *Family Evaluation in Child Custody Mediation, Arbitration, and Litigation.* Cresskill, NJ: Creative Therapeutics.

—— (1992a). *The Parental Alienation Syndrome.* Cresskill, NJ: Creative Therapeutics.

—— (1992b). *True and False Accusations of Child Sex Abuse.* Cresskill, NJ: Creative Therapeutics.

Goodenough, F. (1926). *Measurement of Intelligence by Drawings.* New York: World Book.

Haley, J. (1973). *Uncommon Therapy: The Psychiatric Techniques of Milton H. Erickson, M.D.* New York: W. W. Norton.

Hammer, E. F. (1960). The House-Tree-Person (H-T-P) drawings as a projective technique with children. In *Projective Techniques in Children,* ed. A. I. Rabin and M. R. Haworth, pp. 258–272. New York: Grune & Stratton.

Hartley, R. E., Frank, L. K., and Goldenson, R. M. (1952). *Understanding Children's Play*. New York: Columbia University Press.

———— (1964). The benefits of water play. In *Child Psychotherapy*, ed. M. R. Haworth, pp. 364–368. New York: Basic Books.

Haworth, M. R., and Keller, M. J. (1964). The use of food in therapy. In *Child Psychotherapy*, ed. M. R. Haworth, pp. 330–338. New York: Basic Books.

Haworth, M. R., and Rabin, A. I. (1960). *Projective Techniques in Children*. New York: Grune & Stratton.

Heimlich, E. P. (1965). The use of music as a mode of communication in the treatment of disturbed children. *Journal of the American Academy of Child Psychiatry* 4:86–122.

———— (1972). Paraverbal techniques in the therapy of childhood communication disorders. *International Journal of Child Psychotherapy* 1:65–83.

———— (1973). Using a patient as "assistant therapist" in paraverbal therapy. *International Journal of Child Psychotherapy* 2:13–52.

Johnson, A. M. (1949). Sanctions for superego lacunae of adolescents. In *Searchlights on Delinquency*, ed. K. R. Eissler, pp. 225–245. New York: International Universities Press.

———— (1959). Juvenile delinquency. In *American Handbook of Psychiatry*, vol. 1, ed. S. Arieti, pp. 844–849. New York: Basic Books.

Kanner, L. (1940). Play investigation and playtreatment of children's behavior disorders. *Journal of Pediatrics* 17:533–546.

———— (1957). *Child Psychiatry*. Springfield, IL: Charles C Thomas.

Kellogg, R., and O'Dell, S. (1967). *The Psychology of Children's Art*. New York: CRM Random House.

Kessler, J. W. (1966). *Psychopathology of Childhood*. Englewood Cliffs, NJ: Prentice-Hall.

Khan, M. M. R. (1972). On D. W. Winnicott. *International Journal of Child Psychotherapy* 1:13–18.

Klein, M. (1932). *The Psychoanalysis of Children*. London: Hogarth.

Levy, D. M. (1939). Release therapy. *The American Journal of Orthopsychiatry* 9:713–736.

———— (1940). Psychotherapy and childhood. *The American Journal of Orthopsychiatry* 10:905–910.

Lippman, H. S. (1962). *Treatment of the Child in Emotional Conflict*. New York: McGraw-Hill.

Machover, K. (1949). *Personality Projection in the Drawing of the Human Figure*. Springfield, IL: Charles C Thomas.

———— (1951). Drawing of the human figure: a method of personality investigation. In *An Introduction to Projective Techniques*, ed. H. H.

Anderson and G. L. Anderson, pp. 341–370. Englewood Cliffs, NJ: Prentice-Hall.

—— (1960). Sex differences in the developmental pattern of children as seen in human figure drawings. In *Projective Techniques in Children*, ed. A. I. Rabin and M. R. Haworth, pp. 230–257. New York: Grune & Stratton.

Marcus, I. M. (1966). Costume play therapy. *Journal of the American Academy of Child Psychiatry* 5:441–451.

Moskowitz, J. A. (1973). The sorcerer's apprentice, or the use of magic in child psychotherapy. *International Journal of Child Psychotherapy* 2:138–162.

Napoli, P. J. (1951). Finger painting. In *An Introduction to Projective Techniques*, ed. H. H. Anderson and G. L. Anderson, pp. 386–415. Englewood Cliffs, NJ: Prentice-Hall.

Rambert, M. L. (1964). The use of drawings as a method of child psychoanalysis. In *Child Psychotherapy*, ed. M. R. Haworth, pp. 340–349. New York: Basic Books.

Rogers, C. R. (1951). *Client Centered Therapy*. Boston: Houghton-Mifflin.

—— (1967). Client-centered psychotherapy. In *Comprehensive Textbook of Psychiatry*, ed. A. M. Freedman and H. I. Kaplan, pp. 1225–1228. Baltimore: Williams & Wilkins.

Solomon, J. C. (1938). Active play therapy. *American Journal of Orthopsychiatry* 8:479–498.

—— (1940). Active play therapy: further experiences. *American Journal of Orthopsychiatry* 10:763–781.

—— (1951). Therapeutic use of play. In *An Introduction to Projective Techniques*, ed. H. H. Anderson and G. L. Anderson, pp. 639–661. Englewood Cliffs, NJ: Prentice-Hall.

—— (1955). Play technique and the integrative process. *American Journal of Orthopsychiatry* 25:591–600.

Stone, I. (1971). *The Passions of the Mind*. New York: Signet (New American Library, Inc.).

Strupp, H. H. (1975). Psychoanalysis, "focal psychotherapy," and the nature of the therapeutic influence. *Archives of General Psychiatry* 32:127–135.

Stubblefield, R. L. (1967). Sociopathic personality disorders I: antisocial and dyssocial reactions. In *Comprehensive Textbook of Psychiatry*, ed. A. M. Freedman and H. I. Kaplan, pp. 1420–1424. Baltimore: Williams & Wilkins.

Sullivan, H. S. (1953). *The Interpersonal Theory of Psychiatry*. New York: W. W. Norton.

Thomas, A., Chess, S., et al. (1963). *Behavioral Individuality in Early*

Childhood. New York: New York University Press.

Waelder, R. (1933). The psychoanalytic theory of play. *Psychoanalytic Quarterly* 2:208–224.

Winnicott, D. W. (1968). The value of the therapeutic consultation. In *Foundations of Child Psychiatry,* ed. E. Miller, pp. 593–608. London: Pergamon.

—— (1971). *Therapeutic Consultations in Child Psychiatry.* New York: Basic Books.

Woltmann, A. G. (1951). The use of puppetry as a projective method in therapy. In *An Introduction to Projective Techniques,* ed. H. H. Anderson and G. I. Anderson, pp. 606–638. Englewood Cliffs, NJ: Prentice-Hall.

—— (1964a). Mud and clay, their functions as developmental aids and as media of projection. In *Child Psychotherapy,* ed. M. R. Haworth, pp. 349–363. New York: Basic Books.

—— (1964b). Diagnostic and therapeutic considerations of nonverbal projective activities with children. In *Child Psychotherapy,* ed. M. R. Haworth, pp. 322–330. New York: Basic Books.

—— (1972). Puppetry as a tool in child psychotherapy. *International Journal of Child Psychotherapy* 1:84–96.

Index